THE FEMALE PENTECOST

THE FEMALE PENTECOST

by

Lucia Sannella

shley books inc •
Box 768 • Port Washington, N. Y. 11050

Published simultaneously in Canada by George J. McLeod,
Limited, 73 Bathurst Street, Toronto, Ontario M5V 2P8

THE FEMALE PENTECOST, © Copyright 1976 by Lucia Sannella

Library of Congress Number: 75-16565
ISBN: 0-87949-043-8

Address information to Ashley Books, Inc.,
Box 768, Port Washington, New York 11050

Published by Ashley Books, Inc.
Manufactured in the United States of America

First Edition

9 8 7 6 5 4 3 2 1

Dedicated

to

"Jungle Jim"

Part One

Chapter 1
MEMO FROM BABYLON

In the late eighteen hundreds Elizabeth Cady Stanton set out to sponsor the ambitious undertaking of writing a "female Bible." She had arrived at the conclusion that a Bible written by males, for males and to males, was not consonant with a God who had clearly declared himself to be male and female. Her ambition was never realized.

Mrs. Stanton's observation, however, has been shared by many articulate, thinking women before and after her. Today women are thrusting for their freedom from male domination. The male vision of the world is beginning to give way...to a true and long overdue reconciliation of all things.

We began this book with two objectives in mind. One; to expose the atrocious suffering of woman under the hand of her male rulers. The other was to debunk male Christendom of its biblical hall of fame wherein males occupy all the pedestals. We came up with something much more exciting. In approaching the Bible from the female point of view we struck a vein of pure gold, a "glory-hole" of scriptural proof that our Maker is and has been on woman's side in the controversy between the sexes.

Woman's break to freedom is God-ordained and God-inspired. It will go hard on women in the church especially, to stand up to the barrage of male ego that will attempt to intimidate her with spiritual penalties for her heretical effort to dethrone the male Godhead. Martyrs are certain to be made but the sufferings of "silent" martyrdom is woman's special "thing," only this time Pilate's wife will not be silenced.

The biblical story, told from the woman's viewpoint, sets the ledgers straight about the Edenic episode. Woman emerges, not as a cowed and frightened Pandora but as the glorious Woman of God who spoke the instigating words:

"Let us make man in our image...."   Gen. 1:26

Now, as then, woman is speaking her biblical first words as she initiates another new age.

It's been a long time since men have believed that God is an old man in flowing white robes with a long beard, somewhere up there; who dispenses immutable laws and moralities, stunned to immobility, like a fixed star to his own laws. We have arrived at the day when men think of God as Scripture states, a "God with us," and as Jesus said, "in us."

We've also given up the concept of a universe as inscrutable as the "up there" God. We have awakened to the realization that our universe is rational, discoverable and controllable. The prescientific view of man and the cosmos has been abandoned and the Bible has been relegated, in the lives of most Christians, to the realms of the artifact. But this is a mistake, for though the writings, musings, and spiritual meanderings of a handful of men seem to be a hopeless anachronism in a day of bio-medical genetic manipulation, astro-biology and space technology, we see that the new gods, for all their triumphs of enlightenment have not come shriven of their past debaucheries.

First of all the Bible addresses itself to man's history as an organic unity which is moving towards a goal. It has supported and today supports the universe as being a cosmos of harmony and beauty. The Bible, as man's own story, reveals the reality of the "Presence" among us that lifts us to immortality. The Bible violates nature in this respect.

Though we may believe otherwise, Scripture contains themes that are, like underground springs which flowed in ancient times and still flow today, strong undercurrents that tug and pull at our modern lives in powerful ways. These waters are not only outside of man but within him as well. One of the most treacherous undercurrents is the male doctrine of the subjection of woman.

Most people believe that the Book of Genesis was written first, preceding all the other books of the biblical library. This is not true. It was written sometime around the fifth century B.C. The physical setup of our Bible does not, therefore, represent the order of the publication of the books. Paul, for instance, wrote his letters to the churches before any of the four gospels were writen. Genesis was written as late as the fifth century B.C., which places it around the time of the prophet Amos, and gives a new slant on how the male mind had developed its theology of woman. We therefore approach the Genesis accounts as an authentic record of the enmity between male and female, as something that developed, rather than as something that was pronounced a fait accompli, in man's earliest origins. ✳The doctrine of the subjection of woman, in this light, becomes a typically male inspired theology and lends support to the challenge we make in this book to a Bible record conceived, written and interpreted by males alone for the scriptural record as a history of man's odyssey from Eden writen from the male point of view, about males, by males, for males. In short, it is the library of sixty-six books written by an all-male God. ✳

Competing with the Jewish male, at the times the earliest books were written, were many pagan religions which worshipped mythological gods and goddesses✳The most ardent struggles of the Jewish prophets and patriarchs were devoted to eradicating from the Jewish mind the traces of these polytheistic cults and supplanting them with the monotheistic, one-God concept✳The pagan god, Baal, which means "Lord, possessor or husband" was responsible for crops, flocks and fecund farm families. Worship to the male god Baal took expression in lascivious rites of self-torture and human sacrifice. The male proclivity for law and violence, and the use of woman as breeding stock of the race, as well as his drive to "own" her, is typified by Baalic worship. On the female side the sex goddess of fecundity and love was typified by such goddesses as Ishtar and Astarte. The Babylonian deity, Astoreth, another goddess with the same attributes, was Baal's partner. The prophet Samuel, as well as Jeremiah, struggled valiantly to decontaminate the Jewish men and women from the Babylonian infection in their backsliding worship of these deities. They never truly succeeded. Neither has Christendom.

It isn't hard to see why the male decided it was necessary to write the Scriptures from his own viewpoint for, to the best of what we can glean from scriptural records, males apparently decided that the easiest way to lance the pagan boil was to keep their own women, Astoreth-style, under a double standard of male semi-Baalism and monotheistic control, to themselves. Babylonian goddess, Astoreth, became the female sexual object with a change of purpose: to become the breeding stock of a nation. Jewish Baal transformed his own deistic privileges of ownership of woman to polygamous propagation, as sire of a nation. Only motives changes. The ancient dichotomy of male principles of ego, law and intellect, and female principles of submission, love and emotion are clear. Natural male and natural female energies were still in an unregenerated state in Old Testament monotheism, but a beginning had been made.

The Hebrew religion drew heavily upon Babylonian mythology of the origins of creation in its concept of creation through violence. The violence emanated from the "natural" polarity between the sexes. In the ancient Babylonian creation epic, creation is wrought by the violent death of the female at the hands of the male.

Male sun-god, Marduk, at the behest of his male peer gods slays the giant female monster, Tiamat, with his knife, slicing her great fish body from head to tail, flinging one half of her body skyward to create the heavens and the other half earthward to create the earth. Woman's body was the raw material of creation which could only be wrested from her through her violent death. Marduk is applauded for his bravery and installed as ruler King by his approving male gods.

The ancient enmity is rooted in the male psyche in his concept of the female principle as the source of chaos and darkness— a monster to be subdued. This theme is found and expressed in all religions. Several questions pose themselves to all men. Can creation be wrought by any other means than through violence by male energies against female energies? Can the male instinct to aggression and violence, that has so characterized his creative dynamic, be exorcised out of his nature? Is Marduk forever wedded to his knife and Tiamat to her tragic choice between chaos or death? Can the unregenerate kink in the psyche be straightened out delivering woman from her passive submission to the cold steel of male pride and the male from his thirst for human blood to remove his guilt? It is male pride that cannot abide guilt. It is female guilt that submits to pride. This is the tragedy of creation Babylonian-style.

It should be plain that the concept of the subjection of woman, as woman throughout Scripture and enacted by the all-male god upon his subject, woman, has been a pagan parody upon a sublime theme. Man's intellectual depravity is beginning, in increasing circles, to give way to light. The subjection of the female principle to the male in violence, has been man's baby-talk, an infantile gibberish of a pride-ridden, undisciplined male godling, who missed the point. Violence is still his only dynamic. The warrior male god is splurging in a nuclear rampage today. Woman is still subjected to greed, lust and intellectual depravity, as witnessed in the polluted, ravaged condition of earth's body. The handwriting is on the wall and it is written in Babylonian cuneiform, that the unregenerated male and female gods have been "weighed in the balance and found wanting."

Does the Bible speak today? Can it still reach out and reveal to us the Presence that would guide us to the peace we have so longed for? It can. It is the most articulate voice to be heard this day.

It tells us that the violent subduing of the creation, as typified in the stupidly asinine way that males have formerly subdued woman—the earth's symbol—must be forsaken. It tells us that, contrary to what the all male godling has thought, this creation is not an unconscious, mindless organism but a complex, living organism which will rule by edicts of plenty, or perish unless she is approached with reverence and love. It is not only earth that stands in an unregenerate condition, semi-subjected by a recent knowledge explosion. Because we believe that woman needs every support in her fight to overthrow the Babylonian towers of male confusion and violence we direct the awakening woman to the scriptural origins of her past subjection. In them she will find its primary root and the surgical procedures to cut it out and keep it out.

Like so many areas in sentimentalized Christian art, scriptural analysis suffers acutely from a stereotyped image of elevated sanctimoniousness and fiat authoritarianism. It is male instigated and hard to live down for two reasons. First off, it is very difficult to cut through our deadened sensibilities which are due to overexposure born of cliche-ridden literature, and secondly; because we have become familiar with Scripture to just the right point where everything sounds like a rehash, devoid of surprise and stimulation. Therefore we have kept Scripture down to a minimum in our attempts to wrestle with apathy born of overexposure to a hack theology.

The theme of enmity between male and female, the Edenic issue, the concept of creation through violence and the brutality of female subjection has, for the most part, escaped the average clergyman. Why not? Only the male viewpoint has been proffered to the faithful. This is all the more strange since the "church," which males profess to member, is a female organism, falling under the female principle. This should offer us the clue to the reasons why clandestine Christendom has perpetuated the doctrines of the subjection of woman. They didn't take Jesus seriously when he called them out as members of his "bride." With their usual ambivalence, the males dominating the church have instigated a ridiculous travesty upon the nature of the church itself. If they claim for themselves its female energies, and place woman under their authority, what does that make of woman?

We have reprinted (by permission) portions of the Babylonian Creation Epic by which to set the stage for Genesis. We will attempt, in part one of this book, to go from Genesis to

Revelation and show how the doctrine of the subjugation of woman weaves throughout the sixty-six books of the biblical library like the serpent who inspired it. We fight it every inch of the way, on solid theological ground. We will show how male prophets wielded it as a club to beat down the Babylonian fertility goddesses by way of its own Baalistic aberrations, and how Jesus stands in contradiction to them all. Most Bible interpreters, being males, have mined the themes of law versus love, life versus death, sin versus obedience, and the life, death, and resurrection of Jesus Christ as the main arteries of biblical anatomy. But the main artery that has pumped the infected blood of biblical tragedy and man's terrible predicament has been his intense hatred and fear of woman, which ultimately led to the crucifixion of Christ.

It is the ultimate tragedy to see, in spite of many millenia, man's preoccupation with Babylonian religion. But there are good signs on the horizon that a new Eden is in the making that can lead to love and reconciliation. To hope in the new Genesis demands that we reexplore the old one, in which the ancient enmity was born of the seed of the male.

THE BABYLONIAN CREATION ACCOUNTS

"When the heaven (-gods) above were as yet uncreated,
The earth (-gods) below not yet brought into being,
Alone there existed primordial Apsu who
    engendered them,
Only Mumnu, and Tiamat who brought all of
    them forth.

Their waters could mix together in a single stream,
Unrestricted by reed-beds, unimpeded by marsh;
For since none of the gods had at this time appeared,
These had not yet been formed, or been with
    destinies decreed.
In the depths of their waters, the Gods were created:

There appeared first Lahmu and Lahamu, they
    (first) were given name;

Having established the rules for the (astronomical) seasons,
He laid down the Crossing-line to make known their limits:
And that none should make mistake or in any way
    lose speed
He appointed, conjointly with it, the Enlil- and Ea-lines.

The great (Sun-) gates he opened in both sides of her ribs,
Made strong the lock fastening to left and right:
In the depths of her belly he laid down the elati.
He made the moon to shine forth, entrusted to him
    the night.

He placed her head in position, heaped (the mountains)
    upon it...
Made the Euphrates and Tigris to flow through her eyes,-"

The eleven monster (species-) which Tiamat had created,
Whose (weapo)ns he had broken, binding them at his feet,
That as signs (of the Zodiac) the group should ne'er
    be forgotten.
I will lay the punishment on him—be you still set
    on relief."

The great Gods, the Six-hundred, gave answer unto him,
Even to Lugal-dimmer-an-ki-a, "the King of all the gods:"
Verily it was Kingu that started the conflict,
Who made Tiamat to revolt and the battle staged.

They (formally) bound him, held him fast before Ea,
Laid the (total) crime upon him cutting into his blood:
Thereupon from his blood (he cre)ated mankind,
Imposed the service upon him, released the gods who must
    else have served."

He spoke, and at his word was the garment destroyed:
Again he commanded and the garment was remade.
And as the (great) gods, his fathers, saw the power of
    his word,
In glad acclaim they gave the blessing, crying "Marduk
    is King!"

So they came together— Tiamat, and Marduk, Sage of
    the gods:
They advanced into conflict, they joined forces in battle
He spread wide his net, the Lord, and enveloped her,
The Evil Wind, the rearmost, unleashed in her face.
As she opened her mouth, Tiamat to devour him,
He made the evil wind to enter, that she closed not
    her lips:
Her inwards became distended, she opened fully wide
    her mouth.

He shot therefore an arrow, it pierced her stomach,
Clave through her bowels, tore into her womb:
Thereat he strangled her, made her life breath ebb away,
Cast her body to the ground, standing over it (in triumph).

He rested, the Lord, examining her body:
Would divide up the monster, create a wonder
    of wonders!
He slit her in two like a fish of the drying yards,
The one half he positioned and secured as the sky....

Therein traced he lines for the mighty gods,
Stars, star group and constellations he appointed for them:
He determined the year, marked out its divisions,
For each of the twelve months appointed three rising stars.

So Marduk called in session the mighty gods,
Giving instruction in how properly to chair an Assembly:
To the conduct of his speech did the gods pay attention

While the King to the Anunnaki made formal address:

By saying, "We declare to you that the evidence is true,"
Swear now by me that you will testify to the truth.
Who is among you that started this conflict,
That urged Tiamat to revolt and the battle staged?
If he that started the conflict be surrendered to me
Marduk, thou art enrolled within the number of the
    great gods,
Thine appointment has no equal, thine authority
    is absolute.

For unspecified time shall thy word stand inviolate,
To promote and to abase lie both in thy power:
Thine utterance shall be law, thy command
    uncontrovertible,
None amongst the gods shall dispute thy decree.....
Hereby thou Marduk, art appointed our avenger,
Thus we give thee the Sceptre of Kingship,
    Kishat-kal-gimreti:
When thou sittest in this assembly thy word shall be
    paramount,
(on the battlefield) thy weapons...shall bring low
    thy foes:
Spare thou the life of the God who trustest thee,
Pour out the life of the God who conceiveth ill."

In the midst of the circle then a garment they placed,
And thus spake the gods unto Marduk, their son:
"If thy authority, O Lord, is indeed foremost
    amongst gods,
Command destruction and re-existence to come
    respectively to pass.
Speak thou again and let the garment be destroyed,
Command thou again and let the garment be whole!"

On the throne dais Rubutum which they had placed
     in position
He sat, facing his fathers, for the ceremony of
     Kingship:
Thereby thou art enrolled within the number
     of the great gods,
Thine appointment has no equal, thine authority
     is absolute.

As there saw them (the gods), so their hearts filled
     with joy,
Even Lahmu and Lahamu and all of his fathers:
Ansgar turned to him and hailed him with the
     royal address,
Anu, Enlil and Ea presented him with gifts.

As Marduk acknowledged this appeal of the gods,
He decided to create another wonder of wonders:
Opening his mouth he spake forth to Ea,
Invited him to comment on the theory he proposed.

Blood will I compose, bring a skeleton into being,
Produce a lowly, primitive creature, "man" shall
     be his name:
I will create Lullu-amelu—an earthly, "puppet" man.

To him be charged the service that the gods may
     then have rest.

Ea gave answer, spake forth a word to him,
Relating to him a counter plan for the relief
     of the gods:
Nay, let one of their own number be surrendered
     to me,
Let him be put to death and peoples cast upon
     the mould;

And if the guilty one be surrendered in a great gods'
   Assembly,
The rebels can be legally re-established (as gods).

Chapter 2
GENESIS

Sigmund Freud, father of modern day psychiatry, was reported to have asked Marie Bonaparte "What does woman
want? By God, what does she want?" Coming from the man
who had built one of the world's most impressive edifices dedicated to the definition of woman's soul and mind, that is a
strange question indeed! Freud, like Adam, pontificated puzzled
hypotheses about the nature of this bewildering creature which
comprises half the human race, but with small results. Woman
is she whom "he cannot live with and cannot live without"—
ever enigmatic, ever mystifying him. Woman and mystery have
become to him, synonymous.

Gertrude Stein lay dying. Her faithful life-time friend, Alice
Toklas, sat at her bedside watching in anguish, as Miss Stein
struggled for those last few hours of breath. In her agony Alice
cried out, "Oh! What's the answer?" The dying woman smiled
and replied, "Not what's the answer, my friend, but what's the
question?" With swift female insight, she posed the right
question, which was exactly what Eve did. Eve was not looking
for answers until she had found the source of the right
questions.

Male inability to fathom the nature of woman is the same
inability which has driven him in his past primitive state to the
worship of pagan gods and goddesses. He has somehow sensed
that woman and creation were equated in their mystery to him.
When nature lavished him with her bounties and astounded him

with her beauties, he built an altar to her. When she whipped him in the fury of her winds on land and sea, or withheld from him her fruits, he did the same thing. He built an altar to her, and in fear, worshipped in appeasement. Fear and love.

Having consigned her to the sublime, or to the pits of hell, or to the realms of mystery, he has in his theology and psychology, feared and distrusted her because he has feared he could not control her. Until the last fifty years or so, with the great explosion of scientific knowledge, he has seen himself as her unwilling prisoner. Had he asked her the question, "Why?", he might have begun to free himself of his fear long ago. Males have not asked the right question. Man has always asked, "What is woman?" It would have been better to ask, "*Who* is woman?"

The Bible is a volume of impressive size. It is not one book but actually a library of sixty-six books of both Old and New Testaments. The first three chapters of the book of Genesis are perhaps its three most important chapters. Within the first three pages of chapter one, the portentous events of Eden are stated in stark, terse language, framed in imagery which is deceptive in its utter economy and simplicity.

Yet in spite of the gigantic implications for man contained within the simple account of the physical creation and of man, subsequent to his "fall" from innocence, the average Christian is generally content to leave it all to his pastor to freeze and otherwise pre-package his spiritual food, after receiving it from theologians who mass produce it on large corporate farms. We are all familiar with the popular conception of Adam and Eve in the garden. Adam was alone in the garden and everything was fine until God made Eve. Before Eve, Adam had been a perfect, full-grown son of God, in every respect mature and sinless. Eve was perfect too, until she fell into temptation led by the serpent, and ate the forbidden fruit, traditionally held to be an apple. She coaxes Adam to join her and instantly, God curses *her* and gives them their eviction notice.

Because of misconceptions theologians have implanted about the perfect manhood of Adam before Eve and the "Fall," most people have accepted without question the false doctrine of their fall as a fall from "grace," which is totally fallacious. Grace is only possible where there is a possible choice between good and evil. Everything in Scripture indicates that before the so-called "Fall" the man and the woman knew neither! The fall from grace is the male theologians' pipedream, rooted deeply in the male psyche. It is a tragedy of the first order that theology has been left to males alone these long millenia. We could have used woman's insights into Eden to read between the lines which unlock the deeper truths of the deceptively simple Genesis account of the Creation and Fall. We state that we hold the Genesis accounts to be true. We hold that they offer reliable data concerning the nature of man as well. We further hold them to be accurate historical narratives. Therefore, we allow for theories of creation which hold to the possibility of direct creation rather than those of evolutionary ascendancy. There has been much confusion about Genesis due to the fact that there are two creation accounts: one in the first chapter and another in chapters two and three. The differences between them are grist for mills of contradiction as we shall later see. Both accounts give us data on the conditions of that life from which our first parents came, and the consequent effects upon them at their expulsion, which are integral to some facets of this book. Scientific discovery on the nature and origins of man are shattering the former easy postures of those who long ago pronounced the study of the scriptures as an impossible anachronism of stunted mentalities. Creation and science have become handmaidens to each other, and the Bible speaks to both.

We referred to two creation accounts in Genesis. The first one gives us that setting of the divine drama in which the Creator plots, in sweeping concept, the whole of His plan. We compare this to an "immaculate conception" by God. He sees in one sweep all as it ought to be, and ultimately will be, when the Creation is finished. The words are spoken and the hammers of the heavens and earth swing against the anvils of darkness and formlessness in majestic and orderly rhythm:

"And God said, Let there be light: and there was light."

Gen. 1:3

Like a grand and solemn liturgy, God moves in each creative day, earth and sea, vegetation, the lights in the firmament of the heavens, the living creatures of the sea and air and the living land creatures, and then, on the sixth day, man!

The next few lines of Scripture are the cornerstone of the premise of this book. The premise is that the true God is a male *and* female God, that is, He was, until males took it upon themselves to usurp the female half of His nature. With the keen edge of a sharply honed axe, male pride split the Godhead in two, felling the female half to near oblivion. The male half punched his quivering roots back into the reverberating earth in hopes that it would root. It rooted, but grew into a phantasm; half-alive, half-branched and half-leafed—prey to every wind of pride and passivity that presses it off center, its inner core exposed to every parasite and destroyer in the garden. Centuries of male inspired theology would now declare God to be MALE despite what is clearly stated in chapter one:

> "And God said, Let US make man in OUR image, after OUR likeness: and let THEM have dominion over the fish of the sea and over the fowl of the air, and over the cattle, and over all the earth, and over every creeping thing that creepeth upon the earth.
> "So God created man in his OWN IMAGE, in the image of God created he him, MALE and FEMALE created he THEM."[1]   Gen. 1:26, 27

It is clearly stated that God is male and female. Woman's equal co-regency is denoted in the term "them" in regards to what amounts to a title deed to the earth. Their dominion was to be over everything. They were to be lords of the earth. The account continues:

---

[1] Author's capitalization.

"And God blessed them, and God said unto them, be fruitful, and multiply, and replenish the earth, and subdue it: and have dominion over the fish of the sea, and over the fowl of the air, and over every living thing that moveth upon the earth. And God said, Behold, I have given you every herb bearing seed which is upon the face of all the earth, and every tree, in the which is the fruit of a tree yielding seed; to you it shall be for meat. And to every beast of the earth, and to every fowl of the air, and to everything that creepeth upon the earth, wherein there is life, I have given every green herb for meat: and it was so."

Gen. 1:28-30

And God rested from His work on the seventh day.

This ends the first creation account of Genesis. There is no mention of a forbidden tree. The couple had complete freedom to eat what they would, and their dominion was complete. The chasm between this first creation account and the second is a terse symbol of the chasm between men and their God, for they have never truly known Him in His nature as Creator. Only a creator is capable of knowing the great gulf fixed between an idea, or conception, of a thing and the processes involved in its realization. The failure to understand what appear to be contradictions between the two Genesis accounts is a failure to recognize that God as Creator is continually in process.

This first creation account, therefore, is how the Creator conceived his "idea" of this Creation and the kingship of man over it. This first account is the concept. The second creation account is the initial stage of the process of bringing the original concept to reality. It is the creative process swung into motion. We are still trying to bridge that gap.

With His sleeves rolled up and His paint pots filled, the Creator begins to apply the first brush strokes upon the massive canvas of man and heaven and earth in a new Genesis.

Adam was formed before Eve, of the "dust of the ground." He was created somewhere outside of Eden, according to the account. God "planted a garden eastward in Eden and there he put the man...." Here, we see the first mention of the trees of the "knowledge of good and evil" and the "tree of life." Strangely, they both seemed to occupy the middle of the garden:

> "And the Lord God took the man and put him into the garden of Eden to dress it and to keep it. And the Lord God commanded the man saying, Of every tree of the garden thou mayest freely eat; but of the tree of the knowledge of good and evil, thou shall not eat of it: for in the day thou eatest thereof, thou shalt surely die...."   Gen. 2:15-17

Let us not assume at this point that Adam was a male as we know the male to be. Before Eve's arrival, her femaleness was somehow still incorporated within Adam. It is very possible that Adam was some sort of hybrid, radically different from the Adam we know. So, the man was placed in the sanctuary of Eden to "dress and keep it." But didn't we just read in the first account that man (mankind) was given sovereignty over the Creation? Now, he is placed in what can best be described as a "custodial capacity." Besides, something else has been introduced to this man. He is given a command to refrain from eating from a certain tree, at the threat of death. How can a lord be commanded to the most difficult of all disciplines, blind obedience, and at the same time bear threats against his life if he disobeys? Was Adam just a "pretender to a throne?" Could "dressing and keeping" the garden have allowed for any creativity? Let's say his custodial capacity of the garden was rewarding and did allow for some minor decisions for minor changes, but it would have had to be mainly repetitious, unimaginative work. There were no animate creatures to communicate with; Adam probably threw himself into the work and was satisfied for a time.

How often did his thoughts turn to that forbidden tree? After the glow had worn off the challenge of "dressing and keeping," did that tree become more and more an object of conjecture, perhaps even temptation? Apparently, Adam suffered no curiosity about the tree. Maybe, he was afraid to die. Fear is a good impetus to obedience, but what did it truly mean, to die? Had Adam brushed with death? How could he? Death hung luscious and untasted upon the tree.

After who knows how many thousands of years Adam probably began to slip in his work. His situation was certainly far from our concepts of paradise much less of lordship. Was he lonely? Probably, yet he certainly couldn't have known what ailed him. With his morale low and his work slipping, Jehovah decides:

> "It is not good that the man should be alone:
> I will make him a helpmeet for him."   Gen. 2:18

God concludes it is not good for man to be alone. On what did he base this conclusion? Loneliness? I do not think so. There was a much more portentous reason behind his assessment of Adam's solo condition, but we get to that a little later.

Enter animals!

> "And out of the ground, (not the dust of the ground out of which Adam was formed) the Lord God formed every beast of the field and every fowl of the air; and brought them unto Adam to see what he would call them and whatsoever Adam called every living creature, that was the name thereof. And Adam gave names to all cattle, and to the fowl of the air, and to every beast of the field; but for Adam there was not found a helpmeet for him."
> Gen. 2:19, 20

This must have taken quite a time span, creating and naming of the animals. But what's more interesting is that Adam has graduated from menial custodial work to something higher on the scale of endeavor. One would almost suspect Jehovah was priming Adam's mental pumps, or, at least attempting to.

What is involved in naming that wasn't involved in "dressing and keeping?" For one thing, intellect. So in naming the animals, Adam is to awaken to his intellectual faculties. While this is a considerable step for him, it does not lift his stature to that of a creator. The exercise of the intellect, unless fertilized by the intuition or imagination, remains sterile, and while capable of imitation, it cannot create. But how could imagination, or intuition, fertilize his intellect, not yet knowing good and evil? Without the knowledge of good and evil, Adam was doomed to remain an imitator. Sad to say, Adam was not curious about the forbidden tree. Now, besides his awakening intellect, the man has acquired some animate companionship. Also, the animal creation could afford many object lessons to a man who knew neither good nor evil. Did Adam learn about reproduction from observing the animals? If they reproduced, he would have had to. Perhaps he was introduced to death by this means as well. Still, hadn't God said he would make a "helpmeet" for the man? Why did he not do so immediately? We contend that the Creator was indeed, "priming Adam's mental pumps" to lead him gradually towards some as yet unrevealed goal in the mind of the Creator. We can now discern an orderly process in the development of Adam. After the last animal had been brought for naming to the man, God kept faith with His original intent of creating a companion for him:

> "And the Lord God caused a deep sleep to fall upon Adam and he slept; and He took one of his ribs and closed up the flesh instead thereof. And the rib which the Lord God had taken from the man; made He into a woman and brought her unto the man."   Gen. 2:21, 22

Aside from the secretiveness of the creation of woman, in that God does not permit Adam to be party to the woman's creation, this passage arouses many curiosities. Eve was not made of the "dust of the ground" as Adam was, nor of the "ground" alone, as the animals were. Eve came from a substance higher in the hierarchy of raw materials. Is it possible that Eve, scheduled as she was on the creation timetable as last and made of superior material to the others, might be possessed of a more advanced nature than Adam? It does seem, if one has a choice, that it is far better to be made of a rib than a scoop of dust. And what about the "deep sleep" of Adam? No sooner has the woman been brought to the man than more questions than orthodox or popular theology can answer start exploding all over the place. Read carefully:

> "And Adam said, This is at last bone of my bones, and flesh of my flesh! She shall be called Woman because she was taken out of man. Therefore shall a man leave his father and his mother, and cleave unto his wife and the two shall become one flesh...." Gen. 2:23, 24

How did Adam become suddenly so knowledgeable? Adam, according to everything the Bible has thus far recorded, could not possibly have acquired the wisdom that pours from his lips. Everything he says is ultimately based on some knowledge of good and evil. How did he come to know these things? The question is how could he have helped not knowing? Jehovah had told him. Not in words but in exposing him a step at a time, to some of the realities of life which sprang from his observation of the life that teemed around him. Adam had developed powers of observation and had begun to not only define that which he saw, but to order it. Still Adam was not yet possessed of the means to become a creator. The die is cast. Adam is no longer alone in the Garden and "the days of wine and roses" are numbered.

ADAM AND EVE IN THE GARDEN

The work must have picked up considerably. Adam probably experienced a fresh burst of energy and enthusiasm for the work of "dressing and keeping" his charge. While the tree apparently caused no immediate influence over Adam, we know that the same cannot be said for the woman, who had not, as yet, acquired a name. We have to assume that Adam had instructed his partner in the ordinances against the fruit of the tree, of the knowledge of good and evil. Yet the woman must have pondered over and over in her mind the words she had heard uttered by the man upon her arrival:

> This one shall be called woman, for out of man was she taken. This is now bone of my bone and flesh of my flesh, therefore shall a man leave his father and his mother and shall cleave unto his wife....

What's a mother? What's a father? What's a wife? What does it mean, to "cleave"? Taken out of man?

There was one question that rose like a mountain above the others. What was death? It is possible that Adam and the woman had witnessed death among the animal and plant life of the Garden, but like a three-year-old child, they assumed that the deaths were not what they appeared to be. Fantasies mixed with violent bewilderment must have swarmed over these events which, if they did occur, must have marred the benevolence of the place.

Adam seemed content to settle for the "what" of things, but the woman hungered for the "whys." Amid all the extravagant and lush landscape of the place, one tree burgeoned in her brain larger than the rest, until it took over the horizons of the Garden by day and the diamond studded sky by night.

The serpent enters, but not really for the first time. The seeds of discontent and curiosity had been broadcast upon the teeming soil of the woman's mind with the first words that baptised her ears.

Before we explore the woman's temptation according to Scripture, let us take an imaginary trip into the walled-off sanctuary of Eden. There was so much beauty to astound the senses. The earth was overwhelmingly benevolent, providing fruits and nuts, succulent and profuse. The animals were a delight and the bird life a constant riot of surprise.

Knowing neither good nor evil, the human couple was absolved from the experience of either blame or praise. There could be no failure in Eden. Neither could there be achievement. Sorrow had been quarantined outside the sanctuary, but so had joy! Yet, the woman pondered and pondered the questions that arose in her heart.

THE TEMPTATION OF THE WOMAN

"Now the serpent was more subtle than any beast of the field which the Lord God had made. And he said unto the woman, Yea, hath God said, Ye shall not eat of every tree of the garden? And the woman said unto the serpent, We may eat of the fruit of the trees of the garden: but of the fruit of the tree which is in the midst of the garden, God hath said, Ye shall not eat of it, neither shall ye touch it, lest ye die...."   Gen. 3:1-3

Observe that the serpent approaches the woman with a question, "Is it really true that you can't eat from this tree?" Why did the woman say they couldn't "touch it?" That had not been forbidden in Jehovah's command to them. Did this betray a misreading of the command? Did Adam, perhaps, relay the command in this way to her? Would simply a "touch" have produced death? How could it? They had already experienced a Jehovah-induced "touch:" a touch which was to have tremendous consequences. Another important point is that the woman refers to the forbidden tree here as, "of the tree that is in the midst of the garden," yet back in Gen. 2:9 two trees are said to occupy this "midst," or middle, of the garden: the tree of life and the tree of knowledge of good and evil. Which is it? Are they the same tree?

The next passage contains issues of great importance concerning the character and veracity of the serpent, and the plan and purpose of the Creator, as revealed in the first chapter of Genesis:

"And the serpent said unto the woman, Ye shall not surely die: for God doth know that in the day ye eat thereof, then your eyes shall be opened, and ye shall be as gods, knowing good and evil. And when the woman saw that the tree was good for food, and that it was pleasant to the eyes, and a tree to be desired to make one wise, she took of the

> fruit thereof, and did eat, and gave also unto her husband
> with her; and he did eat...."   Gen. 3:4-6

"Ye shall be as gods, knowing good and evil." Quite a
statement! Let's tally up the serpent's score for veracity: That
they would not die if they ate, that their eyes would be opened,
and that they would become as "gods," knowing good and evil.
So far, he has told the truth about two things: that their eyes
would be opened and that they would know good and evil. Let's
see what happens:

> "And the eyes of both of them were opened, and they knew
> that they were naked; and they sewed fig leaves together
> and made themselves aprons...."   Gen. 3:7

Enter death? No. Enter CONSCIOUSNESS.

Consciousness is to know. The leap which our first parents
had to make from the level they had existed upon, of innocence,
to the higher level that "knowing" would demand, would be a
traumatic one.

Before we dig into the immediate results of the fateful act,
let's be sure we understand the quality of the existence they
have just forfeited. It is sad but true that most theologians have
idealized the life of Eden before the advent of the woman and
the expulsion. It is difficult to imagine a life knowing neither
good nor evil, so used have we become to the daily necessity of
exercising judgmental faculties in making the hundreds of
decisions we make each day in regulating our actions and
making our choices. Perhaps mankind has needed more today
than at any time in his history, a fantasy within which he can
escape the relentless choices between good and evil this life
demands, and escape to a place where he can be temporarily
absolved of it. Thus, do we all dream of a life lost and yet to be
regained. This concept of a return to Eden is a tragic reality in
Christendom today. Millions of frightened Christians still yearn
for the unaccountability of a totally carefree Edenic existence.
Some who are naive enough, eagerly anticipate this restoration
but for most it is semi-conscious, self-deception wherein they

realize they are carrying over into Eden whole carloads of goodies from this world, which they mixed into a neatly balanced, "best of two worlds" existence which seems to liberate them from the necessity of choosing between the goods and evils of this world. Included within these goodies are their personal perversities or ennoblements, which have either heightened or diminished the enjoyment or displeasure of their pursuits, while denying knowledge of good and evil that makes this possible. It is mainly in the orthodox church that we still hear the old theologies of the spiritual "Peter Pan" among us, clinging to a worn out hope of a return to innocence which is truly a flight from reality. The hardships of this life, lightened by the burning lenses of conscience, help us to understand what confusion faced our first parents so freshly out of Eden.

What is consciousness? Consciousness is a state where one voluntarily remains aware of the integrating mechanism of the mind (will and emotions included in the definition of the mind) of that data input, fed through the senses from the physical or invisible world around us. This mechanism is in a constant process of organizing related or unrelated ideas of things into what we call concepts. It is a logical process. If there is a base of absolutes from which we operate in evaluating the conclusions that this conceptualizing process comes to in any matter, we call that base a moral or ethical system. It is upon this moral system that we make final judgments which in turn regulate what action to take, regarding the situation under consideration. We can control this process, or ignore it. If we ignore it and become unconscious of the process, we will make mistaken identifications, form faulty concepts and ultimately make faulty judgments which can affect our actions unfavorably. The reverse is also true. The most important aspect of the exercise of judgmental faculties lies in having a base or foundation, upon which a system of morals or ethics can be built. Without this base, we have no solid foundation from which to make final judgments.

How well equipped were Adam and the woman to exercise judgments? They weren't equipped at all. What systems of morals or ethics could they have based judgments upon, since their only morality had been blind obedience in a state where they knew neither good nor evil? They were truly starting from scratch, but something happened here which gives hope for the future; and it has to do with the woman.

The couple had sinned and experienced shame at their nakedness, followed by guilt and finally fear, when apprehended by Jehovah. Adam says in his defense:

> "And they heard the voice of the Lord God walking in the garden in the cool of the day: and Adam and his wife hid themselves from the presence of the Lord God, among the trees of the garden. And the Lord God called unto Adam, and said unto him, Where art thou?" Gen. 3:8, 9

Adam answers:

> "I heard thy voice in the garden, and I was afraid, because I was naked; and I hid myself." Gen. 3:10

Being fully conscious, with a thorough knowledge of good and evil, Jehovah deduces correctly that the man had eaten of the forbidden tree:

> "Who had told thee that thou wast naked? Hast thou eaten of the tree whereof I commanded thee that thou shouldest not eat?" Gen. 3:11

Observe Adam's inadequate reply. It is truthful, but it is the reply of a child who does not yet fully understand what has happened:

> "And the man said, The woman whom thou gavest to be with me, she gave me of the tree and I did eat...." Gen. 3:12

That is only a small part of the truth. Adam skipped a lot in

between the woman's temptation and fall, and his eating. But it is a typical male answer: short and leaping over the "why" of it.
Watch what happens when Jehovah deals with the woman:

> "And the Lord God said unto the woman, What is this thou hast done? And the woman said, The serpent beguiled me, and I did eat."   Gen. 3:13

That tells it all. Notice, she could have said, "I ate because I wanted my eyes opened as the serpent said they would be," which would have been true. But she simply says, "the serpent beguiled me and I did eat." In that one statement, she makes the same leap of consciousness Jehovah made. The woman has taken the first step along the road to full human consciousness, to her everlasting glory.

The next three passages are probably the most misunderstood of the whole Bible. They are the three curses pronounced upon the serpent, the woman and the man. We will set them down in their entirety for those who are not familiar with them, but we will not touch upon all the theology locked within them, except that which pertains to our subject. It is the curse upon the serpent which is most crucial to our premise, and the curse pronounced upon the woman.

The Three Pronouncements

> "And the Lord God said unto the serpent:
> Because thou hast done this, thou art cursed above all cattle, and above every beast of the field: upon thy belly shall thou go, and dust shalt thou eat all the days of thy life:
> AND I SHALL PUT ENMITY BETWEEN THEE AND THE WOMAN, AND BETWEEN THY SEED AND HER SEED:[2]
> It shall bruise thy head,
> and thou shalt bruise his heel.

---

[2]Author's capitalization.

"And unto the woman He said:
   I will greatly multiply thy sorrow and thy conception; in
   sorrow shalt thou bring forth children; and thy desire shall
   be to thy husband,
   AND HE SHALL RULE OVER THEE.

"And unto Adam He said:
   Because thou has harkened unto the voice of thy wife, and
   hast eaten of the tree of which I commanded thee, saying,
   Thou shalt not eat of it: cursed is in the ground for thy
   sake; in sorrow shalt thou eat of it all the days of thy life;
   thorns and thistles shall it bring forth to thee; and thou
   shalt eat the herb of the field; in the sweat of thy face shall
   thou eat bread; till thou return unto the ground;
   FOR OUT OF IT WAST THOU TAKEN: FOR DUST
   THOU ART, AND UNTO DUST SHALT THOU
   RETURN."[4]   Gen. 3:14-19

Male theologians have concentrated on the so-called curse
upon Eve, to the utter neglect of the pronouncement upon the
serpent, where the woman is clearly blessed and pardoned by
God when He chooses her, not Adam, to be the serpent's
adversary in the millenia ahead. To the serpent, He said:
   "...and I shall put enmity between thee and the woman, and
   between thy seed and her seed."
This speaks of a two-way enmity, not a one-sided one. In
taking an obviously male viewpoint of this pronouncement,
males have taken this to mean that woman, from that point on
was up for grabs, in a no-holds-barred kind of one-sided persecution as punishment for her instigation of the fall from innocence. Hadn't she, after all, unleashed death, and sin, and all
the demon powers of hell upon mankind, and induced the
perfect "son of God," Adam, to sin? This is so much
poppycock! Adam was far from being the perfect "son of God."
Caretakers are not gods and neither are those commanded to

---

[3] Author's capitalization.

blind obedience! This is a male theological fantasy, just as is their mistaken cliche about the fall being a "fall from grace."

God deliberately chose the woman to be Satan's adversary—an incomparable honor. One does not choose an inferior soldier to do battle with a seasoned warrior, unless one has confidence in that soldier. Now the question we ask, and the one Adam must have asked: "Why the woman. Why not me?"

The answer is simple. The woman was being rewarded for her courage and faith in taking the portentous step for them both, disobedient or not. Also, she apparently was able to sort things out and find the "why" of her act. Adam seemed to be a slower learner in this area. Is it hard to suppose the male reaction to this transaction between God and the woman? The male ego was punctured. Adam's ego was probably not then what the male ego is now; but whatever the mustard seed of pride was at that time, Eve's commission was the yeast to leaven it and at that moment the serpent entered Adam! From this moment on, both sacred and profane history has been written in the indelible ink of male persecution of woman. Like the very serpent who inspired it, it has coiled and slithered in and out the history of every culture upon the face of the earth.

It is obvious from the sequentially ordered pattern of development Jehovah laid out for the man, that his curiosity threshold was amazingly high. How long had he been in the garden without so much as a nod in the direction of the forbidden tree, and yet every inducement had been offered to turn his attention to it? Yet, curiosity cannot be instilled where one is satisfied with the status quo of a hum-drum existence. Recall the first chapter accounts of Genesis, and the original conception by the Creator of man as master of all he surveys, and there can be no doubt that Adam lacked the initiative to step out and up. The woman did exactly what God had hoped she would do. If God had commanded one of them to eat from the tree, who would have been the culprit? Man had to desire more life: a life of more meaning and purpose, life fitting for a lord of a planet, and he had to will it for himself. Gently and gradually, he nudged the man along the road of mental development, yet man failed to disobey for lack of imagination. Eve literally, saved the day, and took the plunge.

It is not really so difficult to understand the Creator's motives in first forbidding the tree to them, while hoping they would eat from it anyway. Is not our every counsel directed towards producing the mature child able to cope, able and willing to put away the playthings of the nursery where he has been shielded from the harsh realities of the world, and step out to do battle with things as they are or of things as they ought to be? It could be no different for a God whose prime attribute is that of Creator. Eve thrust Adam from the spiritual womb of Eden to unwilling glory and he's been kicking her around ever since.

How have we dared to miss the fact that the tree bore two kinds of fruit: good *and* evil? Our male theologians have eaten only half an apple in building the theology of hatred towards woman. The first bite brought the evil of death. But why have they ignored the simple fact that the same first bite had to bring something as cataclysmically good, such as eternal life, at the same moment? Because male pride could not allow it, and for one very imposing reason: Adam refused to accept his share of the blame. Once having heaped it all upon the shoulders of Eve, as Adam put it:

> "The woman whom thou gavest to be with me, she gave me of the tree and I did eat."   Gen. 3:12

Adam absolved himself of his doltish acquiescence to eat. Eve, on the other hand, lost her faith, took the blame, and she's been paying ever since.

Next in the account is the most perplexing passage in all the Bible, for on this decision of God has hung all the last 6,000 years of recorded human sin and suffering and blessing and glory! After making the pronouncements on the three, Jehovah calls a top level conference:

> "And the Lord God said, Behold THE MAN HAS BECOME LIKE ONE OF US, TO KNOW GOOD AND EVIL: Now,

lest he put forth his hand, and take ALSO OF THE TREE OF LIFE, AND EAT, AND LIVE FOREVER…"[4] Gen. 3:22

This is one of the only two sentences in the Bible that are broken off. Now something unforeseen by the serpent happens:

"Therefore, the Lord God sent him forth from the Garden of Eden, to till the ground from whence he was taken. So he drove out the man and he placed at the east of the Garden of Eden cherubim, and a flaming sword which turned every which way, to keep the way of the tree of life…."
Gen. 3:23-24

So, it is decided that the man will not remain in the Garden and he will be denied access to the tree of life. Right here, we can drive the last nail in the coffin of the "return to paradise" fantasy. There is nothing to be found anywhere in the Bible to support the male theology of a way back to the tree of life. Jehovah places angels and a flaming sword to guard the "way to the tree of life," not the way back to it! This tree, we contend, is the same tree of the knowledge of good and evil. But now the forbidden fruit of knowledge has become the forbidden fruit of life; and why? Why had the Creator blocked their way to eternal life? Because there was much learning to be done before these two spiritual infants could handle immortality.

Here's another relevant point: the serpent's score sheet for truthfulness. My figures give him 100%. Male theologians flunked him. Let's review. He promised they would begin to know good and evil. He further promised they would become as gods in so doing. The only test he appears to have flunked was his promise that they would not die. Yet, did he really fail in this one? According to what Jehovah said:

"now, lest he put forth his hand, and take also of the tree of life, and eat, and live forever…."   Gen. 3:22

---

[4] Author's capitalization.

It was apparently possible at that moment to do just that! The only reason they couldn't was because God took unforeseen methods of intervention. They could have immediately eaten from the tree of life and lived forever. Eating from the tree was not instant death. This puts the serpent in a new light! He told the truth, but it also reveals another: he was not privy to all God's plans. In either case, the unexpected happened.

Immediately after the fall, a curious thing occurs. This female, who until the "curses" are pronounced, had been called only by the title "woman," now after she sins in disobedience, suddenly acquires a personal name:

> "And Adam called his wife's name Eve; because she was the mother of all living."   Gen. 3:20

Dare I conclude that sin is the qualification for identity before God?

There seems to be no limit to the Pandora's boxes Eve has opened. I have left out one last, loose string in the vindication of the serpent's promises to Eve, because it involves a skip and a jump into the New Testament which we'll do now.

"Ye shall be as gods...."

We go to the Gospel of John. Jesus was teaching on Solomon's porch. The Jews had been challenging Jesus to openly admit He was the Messiah. At first He refuses. He refers them to His works which He says plainly testify of Him, and accuses them of unbelief, comparing them unfavorably to His "sheep" who He says, "hear His voice." He caps the whole reply by stating that He and His father "are the one:"

> "Then the Jews took up stones again to stone Him. Jesus answered them, Many good works have I showed you from my Father; for which of those works do ye stone me? The Jews answered him, saying, For a good work we stone thee not; but for blasphemy; and because that thou, being a man, makest thyself God.
>
> Jesus answered them, *It is not written in your law, I said,*

Ye are as gods? If He called them gods, unto whom the word of God came, and the Scripture cannot be broken;[5] say ye of Him, whom the Father hath sanctified, and sent into the world, Thou blasphemeth; because I said, I am the Son of God?...they sought again to take Him; but He escaped out of their hand...."   John 10:31-36, 39

Out of Jesus' own mouth comes the confirmation that the serpent had not lied when he told Eve, "ye shall be as gods...." To make sure that there's no mistake about what He means, He makes the ultimate appeal to these Jews by showing them that He bases His remark on the authority of their own Scriptures, which are also His Scriptures.

The serpent, it seems, has a perfect score. We get to this again in a later chapter. For now, there is one vital observation to be made about Lucifer, or the serpent, which is that Scriptures record his fall from grace through pride—pride which was pricked to rebellion when it was discovered that he was not perfect: that he could make mistakes because he was not omniscient. The Scriptures tell us he was astonishingly beautiful and the most perfect of all God's creations:

"Thou sealest up the sum, full of wisdom, and perfect in beauty. Thou hast been in Eden the Garden of God; every precious stone was thy covering, the sardius, topaz, and the diamond...thou wast upon the Holy Mountain of God; thou hast walked up and down in the midst of the stones of fire. Thou wast perfect in thy ways from the day that thou was created, till iniquity was found in thee."
          Ezek. 28:12-15

What exquisite poetry! Amid all his grandeur and knowledge, he developed a pride which would not allow for the imperfection of sin in himself. This was the pride which slithered

---

[5] Author's italics.

into Adam's soul when he could not accept his proper share of the Edenic disobedience. It is the pride which first absolved, then turned inward in self-adulation and outward in persecution of the woman upon whom his lust and anger were projected. Eve, on the other hand, was humble enough to admit openly that she had sinned; and at that moment, the battle lines were drawn. Yet Eve, in mistakenly accepting all responsibility for "half a fall," betrayed herself. Guilt would render her passive to Adam's pride. The Creator prophesied this in the pronouncement upon her:

> "...and thy desire will be to thy husband, AND HE SHALL RULE OVER THEE...."[6]   Gen. 3:16

To put it as simply as possible, Adam blamed Eve and absolved himself, and she let him get away with it. Where do we go from her? To a new Genesis.

Once again, a new chaos erupts and a new darkness descends. Like a crack of lightning, a new creative day must begin and the violent rupture of the old order splits into new polarities; new opposites which must be reconciled.

The Creator's spirit must spread its great wings over a new cosmic egg to brood over the waters of a formless void fixed between the man and the woman at war with each other; the axes of their souls tilted to earthquake and upheaval; lopsided and trembling to near universal collapse. The harmony and balance of the old order is a spade in the memory of an old grave. The male principle has taken to rampage and the huge female dragon, Tiamat, again quivers under the disemboweling knife of the male, Marduk, who must slit her great fish body into a new heaven and a new earth.

Ahead lies the murder of Abel by his brother Cain. Ahead lies the embryo of civilization and the establishment of the lines of Seth and Enosh: the twin umbilicals which pump the sin-in-

---

[6] Author's capitalization.

fected blood of Eden to Noah, the righteous, whom God saves after He is forced to "scrap the whole thing," seing that in man, "...every imagination of the thoughts of his heart was only evil continually...and it grieved him at his heart." Gen. 6:5-6. Ahead lay the destruction of man by the flood and the rainbow covenant of God with Noah, where God promises never again to destroy the earth by water. From Noah, the family of nations is born which narrows down to one man: Abraham, who begins the "people of God." Now the fresh white canvas is etched in and the composition plotted, and God's new canvas is ready for the first brush strokes of recognizable shapes and hazy details.

For woman, the road would be long and tortuous and her shapes would be pressed and grooved under the cold steel of the palette knife of male pride and serpent-inspired persecution, rooted in the ancient hysterical fear of her who would not rest in things as they were: of her who would be eternally obsessed with things as they ought to be.

Chapter 3

WOMAN IN THE PATRIARCHAL SOCIETY
OF THE OLD TESTAMENT

From the earliest scribblings of recorded history, woman has known that this is a man's world and to all appearances God has been a male God. Confining myself within the context of the Bible alone, I have found more evidence than it was possible to present here for the case of male persecution of woman as offered in my presentation of the Genesis Creation accounts. Out of the roots sunk deep into the minds and emotions of all men, the Old Testament tree, gnarled and primeval, towers like a despairing ghost against the strange new light of a modern sky, some 6000 years later. Someone once said that even the light in certain ages of man seems to change with the age. The difference seems to be in the aura of the air. With this same melancholy the ancient oak of the Old Testament age lingers in the memory of man today; identifiable yet bathed in a new light which renders it grotesque. In the light of Jesus' gospel of love and spirit it is grotesque and pathetic. While its crown is of stone, its roots are very much alive and probing below the surface of our every hope and expression of life. The main artery of its root system is the ancient Edenic issue of the serpent enmity born of pride against his enemy: woman. This artery was once a tiny sprig that grew into the sturdy young sapling of Genesis and Exodus; Leviticus and Deuteronomy, wherein the laws of the male God stood strong against the winds of Baal and Astoreth, but it is a male tree which has despised the soil which bore and nurtured it, believing itself to be master of her from whom it had sprung.

In the patriarchal religion of the Jews, woman was conceived as something akin to a clean animal, sometimes giving pleasure to the sight for symmetry of line and beauty of conformation; at times giving satisfaction in the field as a beast of burden; sturdy for plowing the fertile fields of race perpetuation, with ornaments on her collar jingling as she pulled her heavy weight across the long, weather-beaten wanderings of her master's world. Obedient and satisfied by a stroke of the neck or a word of approval, she asked and expected little but the privilege of serving her male owners. Woman had no authority outside the nursery which was subject ultimately to the rule of her husbandly purchaser. Religiously she was in total subjection, bearing fully the same responsibilities of obedience to the religious laws but enjoying none of the privileges which flowed from the religious ordinances into areas of politics or education. She was semi-human. Although she was oriented from birth to conceive of herself as primarily a womb, she accepted as natural the omission of her name from the geneological records that charted the fruits of that womb. The teeming soil of her inmost parts yearned only for the sacred and miraculous seed of her male owners and within the precious fruits of her soil only male seed was counted for new harvests. To be barren was to be unfit for sowing and consigned only to ritual plowing, but fallow and ashamed. Concubinage decreed that she must suffer to lie adjacent to or surrounded by her master's additional acreage which blazoned with wheat and corn, grape and flax; proud in the wind and humble in the sun. If there was any meaning in her existence it lay only within her body, but at times her thoughts struck her with more terror than the reality of a "barren" womb, for it too teemed with seed, but of her own making; seed which had no soil but secret to take root in, no field to furrow in but the silence of submission and a pain of wisdom that grew within her, like a tree of forbidden fruit in her memory. Bound like the god Leokum by a living chain of taboos against her body and her mind, the patriarchal woman learned to live below her emotions.

The biblical record of the women who turn up like casual stones along the paths of biblical male biography are more mineral than plant life. The universe of sentient living organisms is primarily male in which the neurological storms of passion and the great catastrophes of the heart, hopes, dreams, and fears feed off a hothouse environment of controlled temperatures and ideal conditions; legitimate organisms in a legitimate world. Only woman is the inanimate mineral kingdom; unobtrusive spectator to the authentic life teeming about her.

The myth of the God-ordained subjection of the female principle to the male principle rationalized its violence against her by imputing to woman a nature inherently docile and passive.

When she rebelled (as in later ages), the myth was appended with the imperative to force her into subjection. The human psyche demanded that conscience be appeased as to this act of violence against her, and so it must needs follow that woman be conceived by the offending males as "unclean" that male hands might be washed in her dirt. Thus the rituals of body bathing after menstruation and ceremonies of "purification" after childbirth—being unclean seven days after the birth of a male child but 14 days after a female. Male seed was washed clean of contamination by woman's pollution.

The fear conditioning of males after the Edenic experience was heightened to a great degree by the early creation myths of Babylonian and Sumerian accounts. The male hysteria prevailed that should the female principle regain its former sovereignty, a universe brought back into order from her primal chaos by the male principle, would plunge back into the dark watery anarchy of wild disorder and death. Woman had been chained in the male mind long before Moses appeared on the scene, when the victory of the male God over the female dragon, Tiamat, had been wrought. Yet one must ask who created the great female dragon who laid the gigantic cosmic egg?

Like a small child whose plate has been heaped too high with food, most people thumb through the Old Testament "begets," battles, intrigues and tongue-twisting names, and lose their appetites. They wonder how the few characters and stories they learned about in Sunday school ever found their way to light in popular knowledge. Moses, Samson, Abraham, Jacob, David and others seem too much effort to find tucked as they are between great sweeps of historical migrations and frequent changes of kings, judges and prophets. Actually, most of the "romanticized and popularized figures" are found in the first five books commonly attributed to Moses. Beyond these lie the Psalms of David, Job, Esther and the major and minor prophets who devote themselves to current history of the time, mingled with exhortation to the nation to remain faithful to her God. The laws or moral code and the men who laid their foundations lie in the distant past of the earliest books.

In attempting to explore the uncontestable evidence of male instrumentality in the serpent's persecution of the woman, we have found one pattern to be consistent immediately after the Edenic expulsion. That is the pattern of woman in the lives of the prime movers of Hebrew history who become either victim or pawn or both, between two male warring factors.

In selecting "popular figures;" David and Bathsheba, Samson and his wife, Abraham and Isaac, etc., we are touching typical cases which prove to be typical in others elsewhere in the Old Testament cast of characters. The *laws* we explore are also typical, since they remained in force till the end of the age.

We have approached these figures and incidents from a female viewpoint to validate our premise of Genesis that *Adam* became the serpent's instrumentality of persecution of the woman.

If we seem to be employing a "witch-hunting" technique or if it seems that we are harping, we can only agree that we are, for the evidence of female persecution and heartless sub-human existence consigned to woman revolves like a broken record through the lives and deaths of the males under scrutiny and the women who fell under their influence.

From the grand epochs of the Sumerian and Babylonian creation acounts to the Creation hymn of Genesis, we come down to earth to deal with men of flesh and blood who created their God in their own image; male.

ABRAHAM, SARAH AND HAGAR

Abraham was called of God and it was promised that he would be the founder of the nations and a blessing to all the families of the earth:

> "And I will bless you and make your name great...."
>
> Gen. 12:2

But how can that be: Abraham and his wife Sarah are childless. How could these promises be fulfilled unless there be a "seed," a son to carry that seed and that name?

According to ancient Near East custom, where a wife is hopelessly disgraced unless she produces a son, a barren woman may amend her sentence of childlessness by adopting the child of her personal slave girl if her husband is the father. All this is legal so long as the child is literally delivered on the knees of her mistress. Abraham agrees to take matters into his own hands, to obtain that son God promised them, and Hagar, Sarah's slave, conceives a child.

What about Hagar? The Scriptures refer to her as a "slave girl." Could a slave girl refuse to have sexual relations with her master? Probably not. It is very possible that to Hagar the thought of having sexual relations with this old man was repulsive and perhaps she didn't wish to become pregnant. What were her feelings when Sarah ordered this of her? Only later events can give us some insights into the apprehensions she may have had. At any rate Hagar is a slave and obeys her mistress's command to bear her and Abraham a son. Trouble rears in Sarah's natural jealousy, and perhaps Hagar's contempt. To conceive and bear a child was woman's only lease on existence, allowed her by the male God, and so while the Scripture states that Hagar "despised Sarah" because she had conceived, we can feel Sarah's humiliation and understand her reaction:

> "And when Sarah dealt harshly with her [Hagar], she fled...."
>
> Gen. 16:6

Hagar is driven out into the desert apparently pregnant and homeless, but an angel of the Lord comforts her, telling her that her son would become a "great nation," and to return to her owners. She returns and the child is born; a son called Ishmael.

The tensions between Hagar and Sarah come to the breaking point and Abraham probably had his hands full with the rivalry between them. While it is obvious that woman suffered intensely in this age from the concept of her as a purely sexual object, males paid a price also in the devastation of the peace of their homes in the polygamous situation.

Still Sarah longed for a son of her own and yet the promise is unfulfilled. One day three mysterious strangers appear to Abraham informing him that his wife Sarah will become pregnant and deliver him the long awaited son of the "covenant." Sarah, probably hiding in the tents, overhears their prediction and laughs. And why not? She had stopped menstruating and was very old. This single line:

> "Therefore Sarah laughed within herself, saying, After I am waxed old shall I have pleasure, my Lord being old also?"
> Gen. 18:12

is a theme repeated in the Old Testament. We see it repeated in the book of Job where his wife says: "curse God and die...." It is necessary to depict woman not only as incapable of much beyond childbearing but also as a creature without spirit which is accorded exclusively to males. Abraham reproves Sarah for her laughter which she denies out of fear, as the passage says, proving woman's faithlessness.

While Sarah is awaiting the conception of her son, there is an interlude where Abraham gets involved with his relatives who live in sin-ridden cities of Sodom and Gomorrah which the angels inform him are about to be destroyed because of the widespread practice of the sin of sodomy. We have here an expansion of the theme of sexuality which runs through the Old Testament.

Abraham's nephew Lot and his family become his prime concern as he intercedes with God to spare the city. He goes to Sodom to persuade his nephew to leave before the coming destruction. While staying the night at his nephew's home, a mob of male homosexuals surround the house and demand that the three men (angels) be surrendered to them for a sexual orgy. As was the custom, Lot offers them his virgin daughters instead, upon which to spend their lust. This is the first time we are exposed to the cowardice and vile female theology of the age which demanded that in such cases women were to be thrown to the animal pack to save the lives of males. This time God intervenes and the angels blind the mob. Males and females are spared. However, there is a later incident where the young girl is thrown to the pack and is killed by lust.

Abraham convinces Lot to flee with his family. The angel had warned that they were not to look back, else they die. In order to reinforce the lesson of the need for obedience it stands to reason someone must look back to suffer the consequences and drive home the point. Naturally it is a woman. We all know that somewhere near the old sites of Sodom and Gomorrah stands a "pillar of salt" in the shape of a female; Lot's wife who looked back. It remains necessary to use woman as symbol of frailty, in contrast to male strength. The sex theme permeates the entire incident in that Lot's daughters had apparently been virgins, and since Lot cannot select for them husbands from among the males of the Moabites and Ammonites where he is forced to settle, these daughters have sexual relations with their own father in order to continue his line. Incest is also the lot of woman; the sexual "tool."

Let's not forget Sarah who is pregnant, and Hagar who is probably still fending off the barbs of her hostile mistress, as Abraham's household moves from his main camp at Hebron, southward into Gerar, the community of King Abimelech. The Scriptures say that Abraham called Sarah his sister while in this country. King Abimelech was attracted to Sarah:

"And Abimelech...sent and took Sarah...."   Gen. 20:2

This is history repeating itself. One other time Abraham, while in Egypt, had called his wife his sister, out of fear of Pharaoh who also sent for her. Abraham, in his cowardice, did nothing to prevent Pharaoh's lust for Sarah who, when he finds out that she is Abraham's wife becomes angry with him for lying. King Abimelech is more noble than Abraham, in refraining from what would have been adultery, when he learns the truth for which he upbraids Abraham as Pharaoh also did. Woman; victim of male cowardice and male lust yet continued in her assigned role as "frail" in the patriarchal fantasy of male superiority. At last Sarah conceives of Abraham, and bears the "miracle son" who is called Isaac. The fruit of the polygamous tree bears bitter fruit, and it is not long before Hagar and Sarah are at each other's throats in earnest. Ishmael was probably about three or four years old, a difficult age to handle. Whatever the case, Sarah demands that Hagar and her son be thrown out. Abraham should have been upset and probably was, since records of the customs or law of the times indicate that such action against an adopted slave son would be illegal. But being weak and touched with a little cowardice, the omnipotent male takes the path of least resistance and with no hint of genuine love for either the mother or the son, expels them with a great dowry for their trouble:

> "And Abraham rose up early in the morning and took bread and a bottle of water, and gave it unto Hagar, putting it on her shoulder, and the child, and sent her away: and she departed and wandered in the wilderness of Beersheba."
>
> Gen. 21:14

Abraham must have realized that they could not survive for long in the desert with one bottle of water and a little bread. The Bible account says as much:

> "And the water was spent in the bottle, and she cast the child under one of the shrubs. And she went and sat her down over against him a good way off...for she said, let

me not see the death of the child. And she sat over against him, and lifted up her voice and wept...."   Gen. 21:15, 16

God intervenes for Hagar and the boy; quenches her thirst by leading her to a well and they depart into oblivion as far as Bible record is concerned.

Abraham and Sarah, alone at last and rid of the tensions of the harem jealousy between Sarah and her slave girl, settle down to what must have been sheer bliss. Isaac grows into a beautiful young boy, and Sarah's heart must have overflowed with gratitude at having been at last granted her reason for existence. But the male God has other plans for all three. Jehovah, Abraham's God, demands that Abraham sacrifice his beloved son to Him as an act of faith:

"...take now thy son, thine only son Isaac, whom thou lovest, and get thee into the land of Moriah, and offer him there for a burnt offering, upon one of the mountains which I shall tell you of.

And Abraham rose up early in the morning, and saddled his ass, and took two of his young men with him, and Isaac his son, and clave the wood for the burnt offering, and rose up and went unto the place of which God had told him. Then...Abraham...saw the place afar off. And Abraham said unto his young men, Abide ye here with the ass; and I and the lad will go yonder and worship, and come again to you. And Abraham took the wood of the burnt offering, and laid it upon Isaac his son; and he took the fire in his hand, and a knife; and they went both of them together. And Isaac spoke unto Abraham his father, and said, My Father: and he said, Here am I, my son. And he said, behold the fire and the wood: but where is the lamb for the burnt offering? And Abraham said, My son, God will provide himself a lamb for a burnt offering: so they went both of them together.

And they came to the place which God had told him of; and Abraham built an altar there, and laid the wood in order, and bound Isaac his son, and laid him on the altar upon the wood. And Abraham...took forth the knife to slay his son."   Gen. 22:2-10

Abraham's suffering in this incident must have been intense because he dearly loved this son. But Abraham aside, we turn our attention to the two other persons involved in this terrible transaction of "child sacrifice" which was later strictly forbidden under the laws of Moses.

Imagine Isaac's terror as he sees the knife poised over his own breast as in an instant he realizes that he himself, is the offering to his father's God. And, Sarah! The devastation of her whole life was to come upon her and she is powerless to influence in any way this greatest of decisions in her life. Woman had no say as to the transactions of males with the all-male God. Impotent; inconsequential and irrelevant Sarah: woman has no validity before the God of her husbandly owner...for indeed, her husband is her God! The echoes of Eden wash around Sarah and Hagar like waves from an endless sea:

"...and thy desire shall be to thy husband, and he shall rule over thee..."   Gen. 3:16

God spares Isaac, and Abraham's faith has withstood the test, yet we cannot but wince at the criminality involved in the near-murder of a son by his father and the betrayal of his wife. The incident of Isaac and Abraham on Mount Moriah sets the theme of the Old Testament concept of male ego as a run-away machine, grinding under its wheels the heart and humanity of woman by the chatteling of her body and the overriding supremacy of the male ego before the male God. It is the theme which demands the sacrifice of all others, if need be, to ONE MAN, if his god demands that as his expression of faith.

The story of Abraham and Sarah and Hagar ends with the saddest note of all to prove our contention for the tragic lot of woman when the male God rules. It has to do with the death of Sarah:

"And Sarah died in Kirjath-arba...and Abraham came to mourn for Sarah and to weep for her."   Gen. 23:2

SAMSON AND HIS WIFE AND DELILAH

Samson was one of the judges of Israel whose birth was announced to his mother by an angel who also told her the child would deliver the Hebrew nation from the hands of the Philistines. The preternatural strength attributed to Samson was supposed to have emanated from God, and in the use of it Samson showed a consistent stupidity governed by self-righteous pride and slavish passions.

He insisted, against the advice of his parents, on marrying a woman of Timnath; a Philistine. The Philistines were the enemies of the Israelites. His parents were naturally upset since they expected their son to select a wife from among his own people but Samson insists that he wants this woman.

Even among peoples who were not Hebrews, women were given and taken with the same abandon as in trading horses. The fate of the Timnath woman, who is so inconsequential to the biblical record as to be accorded no name, is sealed in the ambitions and passions of Samson, who had an ulterior motive for wanting her.

Samson's head is teeming with ideas as to how he will free his people. On the way to Timnath with his parents, Samson is separated from them and meets up with a young lion who roars at him. In true heroic style, he tears the young strong lion apart with his bare hands, and leaves the carcass where it fell. The Scripture at this point makes certain that we are informed that none, not even Samson's parents, know about this episode. He finally meets up with the Timnath woman and after looking her over once more decides that he wants her for his wife. The fact that he had selected her because of his political ambitions has nothing to do with admitting to himself that if he must select a wife as a political pawn she might as well be attractive. The account says:

"And he went down and talked with the woman, and she
pleased him well...."   Judg. 14:7

He returns home. Later he goes back to fetch her, and on the
way he passes the carcass of the young lion he had slain and
there within the carcass is a swarm of bees! He reaches in and
eats of the honey. Still he tells no one of the lion or the bees.

It is time to take the woman as wife, so Samson and his father
go down to Timnath to prepare a feast. Thirty young men join
the celebration and Samson, seeing this as his opportune moment, starts his plot to usurp the Philistine grip on his people.
He poses a riddle to the thirty young men. Samson promises
that if they can solve the riddle within seven days of the feast he
will give them:

"...thirty sheets and thirty change of garments: But if ye
cannot declare it me, then shall ye give me thirty sheets and
thirty change of garments...."   Judg. 14:13

They agree and Samson puts forth the following riddle:

"...Out of the eater came forth meat, and out of the strong
came forth sweetness."   Judg. 14:14

Three days later they were still trying to break the riddle. The
intensity with which this challenge spurred the men to rivalry
was truly in dead earnest. After all, Samson was a male from an
"enemy" camp. But on the last day they were still unable to
figure it out so they approached his wife and threatened her and
her father with death by fire if she did not tell them the answer.
Driven with tears for herself and her father the Timnath woman
begged Samson, now her husband, to tell her the secret. He remains heroically adamant until her begging convinces him that
he can share the answer with her. Again, the graphic picture of
woman trapped between two male warring factions driven to
actions the male God considers "frail and faithless." The answer
Samson confides to her is the following:

> "What is sweeter than honey? And what is stronger than a
> lion?" Judg. 14:18

The woman shares the riddle with the males whose egos are
restored at winning the wager, but storm clouds appear on the
horizon when Samson retaliates with this classic gem about his
wife?

> "If ye had not plowed with my heifer, ye had not found out
> my riddle...." Judg. 14:18

Now Samson, enraged but bound to pay off his debt on the
wager, goes to Askelon and slays thirty of their own men; takes
their goods and pays off the thirty sheets and garments to the
riddle solvers. He promptly skulks home to his parents. Her
father, assuming that Samson no longer wants the woman,
gives her to a man Samson had "used as a friend" while there.

After cooling off, Samson returns to her expecting to resume
where he had left off, but to his amazement finds that his
deserted wife now belongs to another man. Her father remains
adamant in his refusal to let him resume the relationship,
explaining that he had understood Samson's desertion to mean
he did not desire her any longer. There is a verbal scuffle but the
father wins out; yet he tries to make amends by offering
Samson her younger sister.

But Samson's mind is not on the younger sister. He is
weighing on the scales of the law his righteousness against that
of the Philistines! The loss of his wife is the legal door he needs
to wreak more havoc on the already offended enemy. In
revenge he catches 300 foxes, ties their tails together with
burning firebrands and sets them loose in the fields of the
Philistines, burning their standing corn and their vineyards.
The enraged Philistines promptly take revenge on the woman,
naturally! She and her father are burned to death, along with
their home. Samson retaliates:

> "And he smote them hip and thigh with a great slaughter:

and he went down and dwelt in the top of the rock
Etam."   Judg. 15:8

He allows them to take him, but at the propitious moment
seizes the jawbone of an ass and slays 1,000 of them.

The next woman on the agenda is a harlot in a place called
Gaze. Followed by the Philistines, he outwits their trap and
tears the gates of the city and two posts and carries them away
to a mountain top. Needless to say, the Philistines are determined to take him at all costs...and so: ENTER DELILAH.

DELILAH

This has been the woman popular wisdom would present as a
warning to males who waste their substance on a woman. After
all, could the male God allow Samson to fall from grace by any
other instrument than woman?

Delilah has been depicted as a "she-wolf;" a female cannibal
of males, yet this scriptural account says that Samson loved
Delilah. It does not say Delilah professed love for Samson. I am
reasonably certain that nowhere in the Old Testament can it be
found to say that any woman "loved" any man. Women, as a
whole, were simply given or traded to owners or husbands
whether they loved the male or not. So how can it be attributed
to Delilah's lack of character that she betrayed him? She
perhaps did betray his love for her, but in no way did she betray
her love for him. It should be obvious that love was not allowed
in the life of woman. Smart women like Delilah had no doubt
learned how to make the best of the situation and had mastered
the techniques of sexual submission to males, devoid of emotion
or pleasure. How long could a woman last in such a society,
who dared to allow herself the luxury of loving a man? At first
glance it appears to be justice at the hand of a mere woman, but
not so. The ancient theme of woman, victim and pawn, while
not so obvious in this case, is nevertheless recurring in that the
male God selects a woman to play culprit.

The Philistine leaders, bribing Delilah with money, have

secured a willing accomplice in discovering the secret of this man's strength so as to avenge the sweeping destruction he had single-handedly brought upon them. Delilah, well-trained by the male-dominated society in plying her trade—the "use of her body" for utilitarian purposes (in this case as informer)—after a couple of unsuccessful attempts finally gets Samson to reveal the secret of his strength, which lies in his hair.

It has been generally accepted by popular fiction that Delilah was a deceiver in the most notorious fashion, yet if we examine the account it is obvious that Samson lacks brain power. After each episode wherein Samson gives Delilah false information, she applies the false formula and armed guards swarm from behind walls and curtains to seize him. This seems more a comment on Samson's stupidity than his heroic shrewdness. When he finally tells her the true source of his strength, he must know he is deliberately handing himself over.

Now blinded by his enemies, Samson sinks to the depths of degradation. He becomes a buffoon in the court of the Philistines, but as his hair grows back he begins to regain his lost strength. In one last effort to regain his male pride, he asks a young boy who was assigned to attend him at the feast of the god Dagon, to set him to rest between the pillars of the building. He takes hold, after praying to God to help him once more, and with a mighty effort moves the pillars from their sockets and the building collapses. The Scripture records that he killed more people than he had killed in all his previous adventures. Samson was buried with full honors for this last endeavor.

It is really difficult to believe that Sunday school teachers still select stories about the greatness of Samson to present to young and impressionable children. Samson is a hero of God? What God? Certainly not the true God. Perhaps it is long past time that "Bible thumpers" give up presenting men such as Samson as "great servants of God" or as moral examples to young and old. Taken in the context of our theme of the Edenic issue and woman, Samson's downfall was intricately woven with the downfall of an innocent woman. He triggered a series of self-inflicted circumstances that led ultimately to his own demise.

Yet woman goes down with him; one in death, the other in infamy.

Job's Wife

We speak of the "patience of Job; the sufferings of Job; of Job comforters." The Scriptures inform us that Job was a very wealthy man who owned seven sons, ten daughters, seven thousand sheep, three thousand camels, five hundred yoke of oxen, five hundred she-asses and a great household of employees. Job feared God. He was a righteous man obsessed with retaining an upright standing before his male God. So law-ridden was he that he continually attempted to cover the sins of his children by his own righteousness with burnt offerings. Job was a very proud man; proud of his ability to keep the law and apparently God was as proud of Job as Job was of himself. Lost somewhere in the battle between a proud man and a proud God is Mrs. Job, who the male God, as is customary, elicits as a sample of frailty and faithlessness. Woman is useful for almost every unpalatable purpose the male God can employ.

Job wears a white hat and rides a white horse and Mrs. Job naturally wears the black hat and rides the black horse! Yet, if one questions why it all came about, one will see something very different about Mrs. Job. Her anguished "curse God and die!" stemmed from much more than the frailty of faithlessness male Bible interpreters have accorded her. It arose from the agony of a woman trapped between male factions at war with one another which ultimately destroyed everyone caught in the path. One of the victims was Mrs. Job.

How many Christians are aware that there was a transaction in heaven between the male God and Satan which instigated the death of ten men and women, (servants) and countless innocent animals? The scene is heaven:

"Now there was a day when the sons of God came to present themselves before the Lord, and Satan came also among them. And the Lord said unto Satan, Whence comest thou? Then Satan answered the Lord and said, From going to and

> fro in the earth, and from walking up and down in it. And the Lord said unto Satan, Hast thou considered my servant Job, that there is nothing like him in the earth, a perfect and an upright man, one that feareth God and escheweth evil?"   Job 1:6-8

This sounds very much like a challenge from the male God to Satan. It is a kind of boast knowing the contention that is supposed to have existed between God and his adversary. It is a show of pride.

> "Then Satan answered the Lord, and said, Doth Job fear God for nought? Hast not thou made a hedge about him, and about his house, and about all that he hath on every side? thou hast blessed the work of his hands, and his substance is increased in the land."   Job 1:9, 10

The rivalry has begun and Satan throws some unavoidable truths at the male God.

> "But put forth thine hand now, and touch all that he hath, and he will curse thee to thy face."   Job 1:11

The battle is on.

> "And the Lord said unto Satan, Behold, all that he hath is in thy power; only upon himself put not forth thy hand."
>   Job 1:12

There it is. This was not so much a test of Job's faith but a contest, a wager between two powers who were not equal, since God can call the shots and set the limits. With no irreverence for the Word, we contend that this is and could only be the action of a male God, made in the image of males, for males. It smacks of the sophomorism of Samson's self-concept of omnipotence and even shrewdness. It is the sin of pride.

We know that twice Satan enters heaven with a report of the

calamities he has brought upon the head and home of the proud Job and Jehovah and Satan lock horns again:

> "...Hast thou considered my servant Job, that there is none like him...and still he holdeth fast his integrity, although thou movest me against him, to destroy him, without cause."   Job 2:3

Who moved who first? And cannot the male God control His own pride? Could He not have simply walked away from the whole thing? He could have, if He had been the true God who is possessed of attributes of mercy and justice, but the male God was prone to ego. Thus, would He be unable to resist such a wager.

> "And Satan answered the Lord and said, Skin for skin, yea, all that a man hath will he give for his life. But put forth thy hand now, and touch his bone and his flesh, and he will curse thee to thy face. And the Lord said unto Satan, Behold he is in thy hand, but save his life."   Job 2:4-6

The rest is history. Trouble and tragedy pile in on the heels of one another so speedily that there is no time to breathe between them.

> "And there was a day when his sons and his daughters were eating and drinking wine in their eldest brother's house: And there came a messenger unto Job and said, The oxen were plowing, and the asses feeding beside them: And the Sabeans fell upon them, and took them away; yea, they have slain the servants with the edge of the sword; and I only am escaped alone to tell thee. While he was yet speaking, there came also another, and said, The fire of God is fallen from heaven and hath burned up the sheep, and the servants, and consumed them; and I only, am escaped alone to tell thee. And while he was yet speaking, there came also another and said, The Chaldeans made out three

bands, and fell upon the camels, and have carried them away, yea, and slain the servants with the edge of the sword; and I only am escaped alone to tell thee. While he was yet speaking, there came also another, and said, Thy sons and thy daughters were eating and drinking wine in their eldest brother's house: and, behold there came a great wind from the wilderness, and smote the four corners of the house, and it fell upon the young men, and they are dead; and I only am escaped alone to tell thee." Job 1:13-19

It is when the second wager between the two heavenly parties is sealed and Job is smitten in his body, that Job's wife loses her control:

"So went Satan forth from the presence of the Lord, and smote Job with sore boils from the sole of his foot unto his crown.... Then said his wife unto him Dost thou still retain thy integrity? Curse God, and die." Job 2:6, 9

Mrs. Job has paid for that remark for 6000 years, and modern Bible preachers have had a grand time with it. Yet if we read the Book of Job from the female point of view, we get a picture of a woman so utterly desolated that it would be hard to find her equal. In the first place, woman at that time believed that God's actions depended upon males' actions. It was believed that God dealt with His males according to their worthiness. Woman was utterly dependent upon God's graces as flowing from the hands of the males who owned her. Did Mrs. Job suspect that Job was himself in some way responsible for the calamities that had befallen them? Secondly, a woman's whole reason for being rested in her wealth of children and Mrs. Job had borne ten. To her, camels and she-asses were insignificant; her children were her very breath of life.

Yet the biblical account takes no notice of Mrs. Job except to mention her only in her understandable weakness brought on by incomprehensible anguish.

Job, on the other hand, has almost forty chapters of space allotted him to bemoan his fate poetically. That he closely parallels her remark several times is craftily avoided by the male God. He goes so far as to wish he had never been born. While his wife suffers alone and unmentioned, the male God provides for Job a bevy of three "comforters" who say all the wrong things.

Finally the Lord turns back His hand from Job after being satisfied that he has learned that he is indeed a proud man. Job calls himself a "worm" and the ordeal is over-stated thus:

> "And the Lord turned the captivity of Job, when he prayed for his friends: also the Lord gave Job twice as much as he had before...So the Lord blessed the latter end of Job more than his beginning: for he had fourteen thousand sheep, and six thousand camels, and a thousand yoke of oxen and a thousand she-asses. He had also seven sons and three daughters." Job 42:10, 12-13

The restoration of another ten children is remarkable. Can ten children be replaced as easily as one replaces she-asses and camels? The future occupation of Mrs. Job had become the agony of ten more childbirths.

Forgotten perhaps, to the male mind, are the lives of ten young men and women whose misfortune it was to get in the way of a challenged male God and His wager. Most of all, is the total absence in this account of the value of love for the lost children as irreplaceable in the hearts of their parents. Again last but least, in the mind of the male God, such tragedy continues without one word of comfort by Job to his stricken wife who had had no say in either the heavenly or earthly transactions that shattered her life.

The upshot of the whole thing is the folly of law without love; the male principle of might and power unrestrained by spirit and love, the disaster of a male God made in male image alone.

Jacob, Leah and Rachel

If there ever was a man who even the male God could be ashamed of, it would have to be Jacob. From the day he was born Jacob cheated his way through life by playing upon people's weaknesses which he was able to sniff out with unfailing accuracy. Esau, his twin and legally the firstborn, was successfully cheated out of his inherited blessing reserved for the "firstborn" through his mother, Rebecca, with the complicity of Jacob, her pet. Jacob managed in one sweep of his greed to disinherit his brother and engineer Esau's exile from the family. In order to escape the resentment of his defrauded brother, Jacob runs like a "scared rabbit" to his mother's relatives, who live in an area called Paddan-aram.

The story of Jacob's illicit conniving with his uncle Laban is a classic study of two men evenly matched for shrewdness. That other people are caught in their webs is a tragic fact of Jacob's self-love, and Laban's reactions to it. Alone in this far-away country, Jacob happens upon a well which belongs to his uncle Laban. There it's love at first sight when he spies his beautiful cousin, Rachel. His uncle Laban is hospitable to his nephew, and Jacob decides that Rachel will be his wife. Laban insists on the traditional custom of placing a penniless man in servitude for seven years to earn a bride. Jacob agrees and works for his lovely Rachel the allotted time. Laban decides that he will secretly pass Leah, Rachel's older and "weak-eyed" sister, off on Jacob in Rachel's place. This was easily done since a Hebrew bride comes to the wedding ceremony so heavily veiled that even the bridegroom cannot recognize her until the marriage is consummated in the dark of the night.

The agony has now started for both women. The Edenic issue has preened its feathers and is ready to soar from the highest pinnacles of the hopes and dreams of both these women. It is obvious that Laban did not feel at all unjustified in dealing with Jacob whose natural craft and cunning had more than asserted themselves in the seven years he was in Laban's employ. So Leah is smuggled in marriage to Jacob:

"And it came to pass, that in the morning, behold, it was Leah: and he said to Laban, What is this thou hast done unto me? did not I serve with thee for Rachel? wherefore then hast thou beguiled me? And Laban said, It must not be so done in our country, to give the younger before the firstborn."   Gen. 29:25, 26

Laban assures Jacob that he will make good in a week's time:

"Fulfill her week, and we will give thee this also for the service which thou shalt serve with me yet seven other years."
                                                                        Gen. 29:27

After another torturous seven days, Jacob consummates his love for Rachel. But this signals the beginning of a struggle between the two sisters, symbolic of the struggle in Rebecca's womb between Jacob and Esau as firstborn.   Gen. 29:31

"And when the Lord saw that Leah was hated, he opened her womb: but Rachel was barren."

It would seem that the male God forbids love within marriage as a penalty to a woman who might find sexual expression of love anything other than animal. Love raises the sexual act to a place higher than the morality of the Mosaic code permitted. It must therefore be punishable by barrenness. On the other hand, a woman who is "hated" (unloved) is rewarded by bearing children. Hate is the morality of sex in the patriarchal age:

"And Leah conceived, and bare a son; and she called his name Ruben: for she said, Surely the Lord hath looked upon my affliction; now therefore my husband will love me."   Gen. 29:32

Poor Leah; now...will my husband love me." It was a futile hope. She bears Jacob six sons and one daughter named Dinah who seems to have all the importance of a postscript. Finally, Rachel bears a son who is named Joseph. The rivalry becomes heartbreakingly intense between the sisters as Rachel, wishing to win her husband's approval, strives against Leah who hopes to win his love. There is a touching little vignette within this story about some mandrakes. Mandrake root was from a plum-like plant which was thought to increase fertility and increase sexual appetite. It seems that Ruben, Leah's son, had gathered some of these prized roots. Rachel asks Leah for some:

> "...Give me, I pray thee, of thy son's mandrakes. And she said unto her, Is it a small matter that thou hast taken my husband? and wouldst thou take away my son's mandrakes also?" Gen. 30:14, 15

Is this typical harem conflict? Rachel is driven in her desperation to compete with the fecund Leah, to promise to talk Jacob into sleeping with her that night if she will give her some of the prized roots. Leah agrees, and Rachel tells Jacob she has hired him to sleep with Leah for the roots. He complies, and Leah conceives and bears her sixth son, Zebbulin.

The daughter named Dinah is raped and becomes the central figure in an intertribal war that breaks out over the incident between the Israelites and the Canaanites. It is the same old story of bloodshed and violence triggered by the so-called "violation" of the male God's purchased possession: woman.

JOSEPH AND POTIPHAR'S WIFE

After David, perhaps no male has so inspired other males as Joseph, the youngest son of the crafty Jacob. Every ingredient for heroism has been mixed in him in equal proportions. But it was not always so. Joseph grew into a man of God through a series of personal catastrophes that would have broken the spirit of any man.

His transformation to the gentle, trustworthy, forgiving man of his later years is a remarkable contrast to the arrogant, conceited and insufferable pomp of the younger Joseph, the "favorite" of his father. Was it any wonder that this blatant favoritism produced a cocky youth and a group of dangerously jealous brothers? At the first opportunity his siblings carry out their plan to get rid of him by selling him into slavery in Egypt. With God on his side, he rises from slave to overseer of the entire nation, under the tutelage of Pharaoh.

Two elements of Joseph's life history have been harped upon by male interpreters, in their eagerness to play up Joseph's undeniable excellence of character. One is the nobility with which he endured the severe suffering that his brothers' conspiracy led to, and the magnanimity with which he strove to rise above it, and ultimately forgive it. With this we have no quarrel. Our quarrel is with the male scholars who conveniently overlooked a very pertinent fact concerning the unfortunate woman with whom Joseph came to grief. Potiphar's wife is the second element seized upon in Joseph's life, to play up superb male virtue while down-grading female virtue.

The story of Joseph and Potiphar's wife tells how this woman, failing to seduce Joseph, turns her rejection to hatred and falsely accuses him of attempted rape, resulting in Joseph's imprisonment.

> "And it came to pass...that his master's wife cast her eyes upon Joseph; and she said, Lie with me. But he refused, and said unto his master's wife, Behold, my master...hath committed all that he hath to my hand...how then can I do this great wickedness, and sin against God?"   Gen. 39:7-9

Over a period of time she continues her advances. A day comes when fate conspires. The servants are all out and Joseph is alone with Potiphar's wife. She propositions him again. As Joseph turns and flees, his garment comes off in her hand. Crushed by the rebuff, her humiliation turns to hatred and using his garment as evidence, she accuses him of attempted rape to her husband. Joseph lands in prison without a trial which he doesn't demand. His reasons for this are obviously chivalrous for he could have done so.

Joseph's stamina and high sense of loyalty to his employer are extremely commendable but the woman has fared badly in history's assessment of her behavior at the hands of male interpreters. There were grievous extenuating circumstances of her life that should have figured in future analyses. They are revealed in the first 11 words of this chapter. They read as follows:

> "And Joseph was brought down to Egypt: and Potiphar, *an officer*[7] of Pharaoh...."   Gen. 39:1

The Hebrew meaning of the word, "officer" is translated literally to be *"eunuch."* This explains the tragic circumstances of Potiphar's wife. Why this aspect of her desperation has been ignored by male theologians can only be explained by assuming they either failed to see it, or felt it would detract from Joseph's legend of supreme nobility and woman's inexcusable "faithlessness."

Eunuching was a male-instituted practice, as apparently was the practice of giving wives to eunuched males. A woman placed in a marital situation like this, hardly needs to be defended. This was Joseph's seeming appraisal, as well, for at a later trial, he remained silent, refusing to accuse her, in spite of his unjust imprisonment.

In view of his chivalry and forgiving spirit we can see why he is considered a foreshadow of the coming Christ. It is also a shocking commentary upon the patriarchal religion that this Jewish male should find honor, justice, position and power among those whom his fathers considered the worst among heathens. How does that address itself to the Old Testament morality and concept of God?

---

[7] Author's italics.

Potiphar's wife addresses herself to the eagerness with which males of all ages have been quick to seize upon the myth of woman's "weakness," plays of male strength of character. She was a woman caught within an impossible male-instigated institution and should be seen more as hostage and victim than infamous temptress.

David

David was Israel's greatest and most beloved king. A biblical Horatio Alger, he rose from a humble shepherd to the greatest honor before man and God. His career as "Jehovah's anointed" was never eclipsed by any other male in the history of patriarchal rule. He was colorful, brilliant, apparently very attractive to women. Though there were many women whom he took as wife, to all appearances he never truly loved any of them. David is an enigma. At times he was capable of great sensitivity which comes through in the beautiful poetry of his Psalms. His emotion of grief at the deaths of his sons, Amnon and Absalom, is deep and intense. His daring with Bathsheba is astonishing, yet he never held an abiding love for any of his women. At least the Bible record declares as much.

David's exploit of slaying the giant Goliath, his courage and honor in his difficult situation with Saul, his defeat of the Jebusites, recovery of the Ark, the expansion of the kingdom and his plans for the temple, only skim the surface of his political and religious conquests. But in the realm of his personal life, like Samson, David had a knack for bringing tragedy into the lives of the women closest to him.

In every case, David's wives, like other women who figured in the lives of male biblical heroes, found themselves caught between male-instigated political forays which left their lives shattered. Like other biblical tales, the story of David and Bathsheba has been mistakenly thought to be the highlight of David's love life. David had lived the sexual life of ten men, intimate legal "affairs" with many women. Bathsheba was by no means the climax of his love life. The climax she brought to David's life was not one of shattering love, but one of astounding spiritual repercussions that were to affect the rest of his life.

The Bathsheba affair ironically brought a self-directed Goliath stone into his own life in which the unbridled lust of the patriarch male caught up with him. If we trace David's conjugal history leading up to Bathsheba, we realize that he could have ended up no other way than he eventually did.

In David we see the degenerating effects of polygamous marriage and the hideously tragic results not only for the males that used women devoid of love, but for their women. David's first wife set the stage for Bathsheba. She came to David as a political pawn of her father.

DAVID AND MICHAL

When David was an apprentice in the court of King Saul, he was a young man fresh off the farm, yet he managed to charm his way into the hearts of everyone in the court. Saul himself had sought David out as advisor and comforter. But the day came when Saul's affection turned to jealousy.

Saul had offered Merab, his eldest daughter, to David as wife. An espousal, in those days was as good as a ceremony, but Saul changes his mind, withdraws the offer and gives Merab to another man. Insanely jealous of David, and wishing to kill him, Saul plans David's death. When he learns that his youngest daughter, Michal, loves David, he hits upon a plan to engineer his demise in battle with the Philistines. Willing to use his daughter as a political pawn, Saul offers her to David for the price of one hundred foreskins of Philistine men. To obtain the foreskins of one hundred Philistines would be a risky business, to say the least, and in Saul's mind there was an excellent chance David would not survive the exploit. David returns not with one hundred but two hundred foreskins. Saul is defeated and David and Michal are married.

This may sound like the beginning of a happy ending for a

woman. In Michal's case, things take their predictable turn for the worse a little later.

Saul's hatred for David in the meantime has grown. He decides to murder David in his bed. Jonathan, Saul's son, warns David as does the faithful Michal, and the night before his intended slaying she lowers him through a window and he makes his escape. Michal improvises a figure of his body by rolling pillows and sheets together, and when Saul's henchmen burst into the bed-chamber they discover they are tilting with bedclothes. Saul is furious with Michal and promptly pimps the daughter he had previously betrayed as political pawn, by giving her as wife to another man. We may be sure he paid Saul as considerable a dowry as David had for her sexual services. Michal joins the long list of women whose lives were shattered when caught between two males at each other's throats.

David, meanwhile, is on the run from Saul. While hiding out in a wilderness, David and his men are forced to turn to near thievery in order to get food and supplies. Camping near the property of a wealthy man named Nabal, known to be churlish, David sends a few of his men to ask for assistance. Nabal refuses. David decides that he will take what he needs by force. A woman of "fair countenance," named Abigail, Nabal's wife, intercedes with David to scrap his plans and accept the generous provisions she offers him and his men. She convinces him that bloodshed would make both him and her husband losers.

David relents. Abigail then returns home and tells Nabal what she has done. He is so stunned that he literally dies of shock ten days later, leaving the beautiful Abigail a widow. David loses no time in acquiring Abigail as a wife:

> "And David sent and communed with Abigail to take her to him to wife. And when the servants of David were come to Abigail to Carmel, they spake unto her, saying, David sent us unto thee, to take thee to him to wife. And she arose, and bowed herself on her face to the earth, and said, Behold, let thine handmaid be a servant to wash the feet of the servants of my Lord." I Sam. 25:39-41

So Abigail gets a small percentage of David and David gets all of Abigail. While he's at it he takes a couple more females to add to Michal and Abigail:

> "David also took Anhinoam of Jezreel...But Saul had given Michal his daughter, David's wife, to Phaltiel, the son of Laish..." I Sam. 25:43-44

Apparently mourning the loss of Michal, David embarks on a matrimonial and paternal spree in Hebron. Here's the record:

> "And unto David were sons born in Hebron: and his first born was Amnon, of Ahinoam the Jezreelitess; And his second, Chileab, of Abigail the wife of Nabal the Carmelite; and the third, Absalom the son of Maacah, Daughter of Talmai, king of Geshur; and the fourth, Adonijah the son of Haggith; and the fifth, Shephatiah the son of Abital; and the sixth, Ithream, by Eglah, David's wife...."
> II Sam. 3:2-5

In the meantime, with Michal ceremoniously cast into the bed of another man, David, suffering the pangs of loneliness and celibacy, is approached by Abner, a politician, to make a pact which would install David upon the throne of the nation. David agrees, but one of his terms is that Michal be returned to him who, as he puts it:

> "...I espoused to me for a hundred foreskins of the Philistines." II Sam. 3:14

It's time for Michal to play leap-bed again so Abner fetches her and brings her to her purchaser:

> "...and took her from her husband, even from Phaltiel the son of Laish. And her husband went with her along weeping behind her to Bahurim. Then said Abner unto him, Go, return. And he returned." II Sam. 3: 15, 16

Passed over lightly, it is not only Michal's trauma, but Phal-tiel's. Still, a deal is a deal, and Michal is returned to her husband's aching arms and, incidentally, to a bevy of numerous wives and a host of sons. Michal, who "loved David," hadn't seen anything yet, for at Jerusalem, David:

> "...took him more concubines and wives out of Jerusalem, after he was come from Hebron: and there were yet sons and daughters born to David:
> "And these be the names of those that were born unto him at Jerusalem; Shammuah, and Shobab, and Nathan, and Solomon, Ibhar also, and Elishua, and Nepheg, and Japhia, and Elishama and Eliada, and Eliphalet."   II Sam. 5:13-16

Shortly afterwards, David is made King of Israel. He orders the sacred Ark of the Covenant to be installed at Jerusalem. This event triggers one of the strangest stories of the Bible. David dances semi-naked before the sacred Ark:

> "And David danced before the Lord with all his might; and David was girded with a linen ephod."   II Sam. 6:14

The ephod was a ceremonial dress of the Jewish high priests. It was a sacred vestment made of "gold, blue, purple, scarlet and fine twined linen, with cunning work." Ex. 28:44. The ephod itself was only part of the vestment and can best be compared to a type of bolero that came down as far as the lower hip. Beneath the ephod was worn the "blue robe of the ephod," having a hole for the head and extending to the feet. Samuel was said to have worn an ephod also as a "child," to which his mother added a "coat," for decency. At any rate, David, clad in ephod alone, celebrates his victory as king and mighty warrior by dancing wildly before the Ark.

After the party, David returns home and Michal goes out to meet him. She scolds him:

> "...How glorious was the king of Israel today, who

> uncovered himself today in the eyes of the handmaidens of his servants, as one of the vain fellows shamelessly uncovereth himself!"
>
> II Sam. 6:20

David replies:

> "...It was before the Lord, which chose me before thy father, and before all his house, to appoint me ruler over the people of the Lord, over Israel: therefore will I play before the Lord. And I will yet be more vile than thus, and will be base in mine own sight: and of the maidservants which thou hast spoken of, of them shall I be had in honor. Therefore Michal the daughter of Saul had no child until the day of her death."
>
> II Sam. 6:20-23

David probably literally "put her away" sexually from then on. Whatever the case, Jehovah, the all-male God, has struck the undeserving woman again.

Michal, first of David's multitudinous wives, used as a political pawn by her father, shunted about sexually between two males, who risked her life to save David's and who "loved" the man, chides him for bad taste, is dealt the most deadly blow a female can be dealt; she is unmothered by barrenness.

Soon, another woman would be flung across the sacrificial altar of the male godling. Her name was Bathsheba. She would be called David's queen of tragedy, for her anguish would surpass Michal's in its multiplicity and persistence.

David and Bathsheba

Like all popularized Bible stories, David's encounter with Bathsheba has become mythologized in the minds of Christians. Movies have been made and books written about this incident which generally romanticize the entire affair, placing emphasis upon the seductive qualities of Bathsheba which mythmakers find necessary to transform a tragic woman into a romantic

heroine. Bathsheba, once endowed with the sex symbol pre-
requisites, can then safely neutralize the predatory instincts of
David and minimize the infamy of his actions. Myth would
have it that Bathsheba was seductively beautiful and David irre-
sistably handsome and at his summons Bathsheba instantly
swoons in his arms, throwing all caution to the winds, and despite the losses involved for her, lives happily ever after as his
queen. If interpreted from the male point of view, we can accept
this portrait of woman devoid of morality which is convenient
to the doctrine of the male domination of the female principle in
God-given authority. Should we see this crime from the female
point of view, we see something entirely different.

David was the "anointed servant of Jehovah the God of Israel" and in that capacity was spiritual leader of his people with
every connotation of a Pope to Catholics. When David summons Bathsheba, she could only obey. He was her spiritual as
well as political ruler. If we keep this in mind, then we realize
that Bathsheba, as woman, in other situations, had no say in
what was to transpire. There can be no question as to whether
she could have resisted his advances. The matter was settled before she even set foot upon the palace property. How did it all
start? David was apparently having trouble sleeping and decided to go for a stroll on the palace roof:

> "And it came to pass in an eventide, that David arose from
> off his bed, and walked upon the roof of the King's house:
> and from the roof he saw a woman washing herself; and
> the woman was very beautiful to look upon." II Sam. 11:2

He looked upon her long enough to examine her beauty and
to lust after her. So excited at her beauty was he that the next
day he begins inquiring about her:

> "And David sent and inquired after the woman. And one
> said, Is not this Bathsheba, the daughter of Eliam, the wife
> of Uriah the Hittite?" II Sam. 11:3

So she was married to one of David's own soldiers.

> "And David sent messengers, and took her; and she came in
> unto him, and he lay with her; for she was purified from
> her uncleanness: and she returned unto her house."
>
> II Sam. 11:4

This is not only deliberate pursuit of a woman, it amounts to seduction. What could this woman do against her king, her spiritual head and her husband's commander-in-chief? It is at this point that male interpreters freeze, hence the fantasy of Bathsheba's swooning surrender to David's sexual appetite; but the truth is probably that Bathsheba was terrified. There is more proof that Bathsheba loved and preferred Uriah, her husband, over David. Later Scriptures bear this out. The complications of David's lust begin with a message from Bathsheba to him:

> "And the woman conceived, and sent and told David, and
> said, I am with child...."
>
> II Sam. 11:5

What follows is a masterpiece of treachery and cunning as David attempts to hide his sin. He realizes that he must cover the paternity of this child, so he engineers what he hopes will be sexual relations between Bathsheba and Uriah, to prove Uriah is father of the child. To do this he calls Uriah home from the war on leave. But he is confounded by Uriah's noble concern for his fellow warriors battling for their people and their lives, when the honorable Uriah says:

> "...the servants of my lord, are encamped in the open fields;
> shall I then go into my house, to eat and to drink, and to lie
> with my wife? as thou livest, and as thy soul livest, I will
> not do this thing."
>
> II Sam. 11:11

Uriah sleeps at the door of the king's house. Thwarted in his attempts to cover the paternity of the child, David decides that

Uriah must die, so he orders him to an area where the fighting is thickest and as planned, Uriah meets his death.

> "And when the wife of Uriah heard that Uriah her husband was dead, she mourned for her husband."   II Sam. 11:26

Let's analyze this from Bathsheba's side. Did she know that David had engineered Uriah's death? Nothing in Scripture says that she did. Another interesting question is, did David confess as much to her? One thing we can be sure of; it would be difficult for Bathsheba to have anything but resentment and perhaps hatred in her heart for David. If read, as it is written, from the male point of view, Bathsheba is an inconsequential postscript to the story with no feelings and no comment one way or another about the shredding of her life thus far, but then that is the way of the all-male God. Bathsheba's troubles are far from over since someone must pay for these crimes. But who? Of course, the woman.

> "And the Lord sent Nathan unto David...and said unto him, There were two men in one city; the one rich, and the other poor. The rich man had exceeding many flocks and herds: but the poor man had nothing, save one little ewe lamb, which he had bought and nourished up:...it grew up together with him, and with his children; it did eat of his own meat, and drank of his own cup, and lay in his bosom, and was unto him as a daughter. And there came a traveller unto the rich man, and he spared to take of his own flock and of his own herd, to dress for the wayfaring man that was come unto him; but took the poor man's lamb, and dressed it for the man that was come to him."
> II Sam. 12:1-4

David is swelled with indignation over the injustice done the poor man and pronounces sentence upon the rich man:

> "...And as the Lord liveth, the man that hath done this thing

shall surely die: And he shall restore the lamb fourfold, because he did this thing, and because he had no pity."

II Sam. 12:5, 6

"And Nathan said to David, "Thou art the man!"

But David doesn't die. The innocent child in Bathsheba's womb must die. And thus is our theme repeated: woman caught as victim and pawn between two males at war. This time it is the male God at war with David. And what about the child? David's punishment is the death of an innocent child. Bathsheba? Tragedy has come full circle for her since this man entered her life. Male Bible expositors would have us believe that after the death of her child, Bathsheba bounced back like a butterfly to take up her queenly duties. At this point one can only be sure that Bathsheba's heart had turned to stone for David. Thus the Scripture:

"Now therefore the sword shall never depart from thy house...."

II Sam. 12:10

That sword would be the cleavage of resentment and suffering borne by the tragic Bathsheba. It would lie below the surface of their lives. Later events with children bear out the fact of that "sword" which Bathsheba would suffer from and innocently.

Bathsheba: seductress, courtesan, adoring queen—or Bathsheba: tragic victim of the male God?

ABSALOM OH, ABSALOM

When Nathan, the prophet, predicted that the sword would never depart from David's house because of his betrayal of Uriah and Bathsheba, David did not know that it would fall again through one of his sons, Absalom.

David had a beautiful daughter named Tamar. One of his sons by another concubine named Amnon fell in love with her. So smitten with love was Amnon that he fell to love sickness.

His cousin Jonadab, a very "subtle man," suggests to Amnon that he play sick, so that Tamar could be maneuvered into nursing him back to health. Amnon feigns sickness and persuades his father, the king, to send her to minister to him. David sends the beautiful Tamar to Amnon's house and as she is preparing food for him he calls her into his bedroom and proposes she "lay with him." Tamar at first refuses, then pleads with him to release her, saying that if he really desires her, the king will give her to him in marriage. The text goes on:

"Howbeit he would not hearken unto her voice: but, being stronger than she, forced her and lay with her."

II Sam. 13:14

After her rape, Amnon's love turns to hate:

"...so that the hatred wherewith he hated her was greater than the love wherewith he had loved her...." II Sam. 13:15

He simply dismisses her. She pleads with his honor saying:

"...There is no cause: this evil in sending me away is greater than the other that thou didst unto me. But he would not hearken to her. Then he called his servant that ministered unto him, and said, Put now this woman out from me, and bolt the door after her." II Sam. 13:16, 17

Tamar weeps and rends her clothing.

The familiar theme of male indifference and the double standard surfaces in David's anger but failure to apply the law of death by stoning, for Amnon. Tamar tells her brother Absalom, who tells her to remain silent about it. To all appearances he has chosen to overlook it. He takes the desolate Tamar into his house, saying nothing to his brother Amnon.

Two years later, Absalom engineers an occasion where he and Amnon will be together in an area where Absalom had a large flock of sheep tended by sheepshearers in his employ. He orders them to kill Amnon. They obey, and Tamar is revenged. Absalom flees to Geshur and remains there three years. After his grief for his slain son Amnon, David begins to long for the return of Absalom, but pride deters him. Joab arranges with a woman to fake a similar situation with her own son and under the pretense of seeking his advice as to how to deal with it, persuades David to relent and forgive Absalom. The king sends a message to his son in Geshur and Absalom returns home, but David will not see him. For another two years, Absalom is denied an audience with his father. Finally, after another intercession by Joab, David consents to a face-to-face reconciliation. The breach is apparently healed and all forgiven. But the estrangement is never really overcome, for Absalom rebels against David and attempts to dethrone him later and is killed.

Why did David fail to deal with Amnon? Was it guilt over his own betrayal of Bathsheba that stayed his hand? Why did he think his own sons were above the law of Moses? Isn't it strange that one of the few males who undertook for a woman's honor is not only exiled, but killed, as a consequence of defending her?

David's tearful prayer, after Absalom's death, that he would have died in his place, is all the more sad when we know that had David dealt with Amnon as he should have, perhaps Absalom would have been appeased and his death avoided.

What has happened to Tamar all this time? We don't know, except to say that the crime against her was, like so many other biblical incidents, triggered by the same old mechanisms that place a woman as victim and pawn, between two male factions at odds with each other. Though the blood flowed, Tamar remained the pathetic, violated woman who not only suffered rape but lived to see her beloved defender slain because he cared when no one else did.

THE BOOK OF ESTHER

There are only two books in the whole of Scripture written by or about women. The Book of Ruth, which is a rehash of the

Hebrew woman seeking a husband to give her children, reads more like a Hebrew Cinderella story. The Book of Esther is something else because it is deadly serious about one issue: female subjection.

The authenticity of the Book of Esther had been challenged by the church fathers and others when decisions were made as to what books would be included in the Word. Bible scholars have since considered this book peculiar in that there is no mention in it of God's name, or of prayer. To our mind, the inclusion of the Book only serves to further support our contention that the main issue of both dispensations has been the ancient Edenic one, for this book deals mainly with the subjection of woman in obedience to the all-male God.

It is the story of a Jewish orphan girl raised by her cousin Mordecai, a minor official in the palace of the Persian King Ahasuerus. It is interwoven with palace and political intrigue with Esther as Queen interceding successfully with the king to save her people from destruction. Her tools? Her beauty and her body, but mostly her obedience to the male rule of her lord, the king.

The Book opens with a lavish feast as King Ahasuerus greets the princes and diplomats of his far-flung kingdom. His queen, Vashti, throws a similar week-long party for the women of the king's appointees. After a week's binge, the king sends his chamberlain to fetch Queen Vashti to show her off to his cohorts. She refuses to come. His rage is to be expected and is probably multiplied by his drunkenness. Nevertheless this refusal of a mere woman to come at his bidding is an acute embarrassment to him. He summons his "wise men" and court counselors for advice. Here is their analysis:

> "...the queen hath not done wrong to the king only, but also to all the princes, and to all the people that are in all the provinces of King Ahasuerus. FOR THIS DEED OF THE QUEEN SHALL COME ABROAD UNTO ALL WOMEN, SO THAT THEY SHALL DESPISE THEIR HUSBANDS

IN THEIR EYES, WHEN IT SHALL BE REPORTED,[2] the king, Ahasuerus commanded Vashti the queen to be brought in before him, but she came not. Likewise shall the ladies of Persia and Media say this day unto all the King's princes, which have heard of the deed of the queen. Thus shall there arise too much contempt...."   Esther 1:16-18

There we have it! The male establishment is threatened with rebellion if this insult to the male God is allowed to pass unpunished. An edict goes forth:

"...let there go a royal commandment from him, and let it be written among the laws of the Persians and the Medes, that it be not altered, That Vashti come no more before king Ahasuerus; and let the king give her royal estate unto another that is better than she. And when the king's decree that he shall make shall be published throughout his empire, (for it is great), all the wives shall give to their husbands honor, both to great and small....For he sent letters into all the king's provinces...and to every people after their language, that every man should bear rule in his own house...."   Esther 1:19-22

The affronted male God throws his thunderbolt at the heart of rebellious woman and order is restored by force. Esther steps into Vashti's shoes and the king's bed, appropriating to herself through her model submission to male authority favor, and ultimately the redemption of her people from certain destruction. The marvel of her accomplishment is not laid directly to her intelligence or her wisdom. It is laid to the accident of her beauty and the favors of her body. Obedience and submission were her "anointing" of the all-male God.

---

[2] Author's capitalization.

MOSES AND ZIPPORAH

Cecil B. DeMille's *Ten Commandments* blazoned the silver screen with a cast of thousands and the majesty of Charlton Heston striding in patriarchal grandeur as Moses, through smoke and fire to free his people from Pharaoh and deliver to them and to the world the Ten Commandments. The glamorous start of his life in the palace of Pharaoh and his calling of God to free his people, and his marriage to Zipporah, are all standard treatment of Moses' life according to Hollywood, and according to male theologians.

Moses was not all that both of these portrayed. There are two incidents, conveniently avoided by Bible preachers and movie directors, which would somewhat tarnish his image as a faultless servant of the most high God. Moses in these two incidents appears as a man who goes by the old adage, "Don't do as I do; just do as I say."

He had commanded that the Jews give to their wives a bill of divorcement, if they wished to "put them away." A male enjoyed the prerogative of summarily dismissing a wife if she did not please him. (Jesus was questioned about this practice in his own ministry by Jews attempting to trap him in legalistic discussions about adultery and the law.) Although Moses had commanded this to be done, Scriptures indicate that he did not practice what he preached.

Moses married a Midian woman named Zipporah, who bore him two sons. The union was good for a time but he apparently tired of her. The Bible records his going to Africa where he marries an Ethiopian woman and sends Zipporah and their two children home. Nowhere does the Bible record that Moses gave Zipporah the mandatory bill of divorcement. Everything points to the conclusion that he didn't, since after a few years Jethro, Zipporah's father, takes her and the two boys back to Africa to talk to Moses. The two men fall upon each other's necks, embrace and kiss. Yet see what happens:

"And Moses went out to meet his father-in-law and did

obeisance, and kissed him; and they asked each other of their welfare; and they came into the tent. And Moses told his father-in-law all that the Lord had done unto Pharaoh...and Moses let his father-in-law depart; and he went his way into his own land."   Exod. 18:7-8;27

This doesn't sound like a warm welcome for the family, especially for the wife and children. They seem hardly worth mentioning. It's the same old story of the males engaged in the super important work of the male world to the exclusion of the woman. Moses did not obey his own command. He violated the rights of Zipporah and his children. Miriam, a prophetess of God, and Aaron, Moses' mouthpiece, are not a little upset by the marriage of Moses to the black woman, and they discuss it between themselves and later confront Moses with it. God through Moses reasserts the fact of Moses' primacy among them and proceeds to show his displeasure at the unholy duo by striking the woman with the most dreaded disease of any time, leprosy. And Aaron? Well, Aaron gets off with a tongue lashing. Echoes of old Eden?

MOSES AND THE CIRCUMCISION

Moses apparently was never circumcised of his own free will. This Moses who strode down the mountain with the two stone tablets, sneaked off and spared himself the ritual of circumcision until Jehovah met him head on, ready to kill him for it. The Lord had commanded Moses to go to Egypt. So mounted on an ass, he and his wife, Zipporah, and their sons began the journey. Then something strange occurs at an inn on the way:

"And it came to pass by the way in the inn, that the Lord met him, and sought to kill him. Then Zipporah took a sharp stone, and cut off the foreskin of her son, and cast it at his feet, and said, Surely a bloody husband art thou to me. So he, [Jehovah], let him go: then she said, A bloody

husband thou art because of the circumcision."
Exod. 4:24-26

Zipporah saves his life at the hands of his angered God, Whom he had disobeyed. Infallible servant of God? Not so! We would imagine that the male ego was not a little punctured by the swiftness of Zipporah's spiritual discernment and the decisiveness of her action in saving Moses' life.

How could a mere woman seize male authority in so grave a spiritual matter as this? By all precedents Zipporah should have been struck a leper, like the hapless Miriam. Paul's, "let the woman keep silent in the church...I do not allow a woman to teach...to usurp authority over the man," would be destined to embarrassment by this episode. The issue of the circumcision was to trouble not only Moses, but Jesus and the disciples as well. Moses, hero and hypocrite. Zipporah, woman and victim.

ELISHA AND THE BEARS

A decade ago the world was shocked by an incident in which a woman who, within sight and sound of more than a dozen witnesses, was stabbed repeatedly by an assailant without one of them coming to her rescue. We have since come to see this incident as a sign and portent of a world, sick in mind and heart, becoming progressively more and more dehumanized by the impersonal forces bred of materialism and non-involvement.

There is a curious little passage in the Old Testament which, like other passages in the Good Book, have been too acutely embarrassing in the cult of hero worship material generally assigned to Sunday school curriculae. It is the incident of the egomanical Elisha and the forty-two children.

"and as he was going up by the way, there came forth little children out of the city, and mocked him, and said unto him, Go up, thou bald head; go up, thou bald head.

And he turned back, and looked on them, and cursed them in the name of the Lord. And there came forth two she-bears out of the wood, and tare forty and two children of them."   II Kings 2:23,24

Is this the stuff that heroes are made of? The all-male God says so. Paranoic delusions of grandeur would be more like it. Elisha is still touted as a great example of a servant of God even by modern preachers. Why don't we hear more sermons on the slaughter of forty-two children who, as kids will, teased the pompous Elisha?

After reading this account one does not have to use great gifts of imagination to understand why they teased the man. This passage is an acute embarrassment to the church and why not? It is much safer to the preservation of the mythological male passion for hero images to preach of Elisha's battle with the wicked Queen Jezebel who truly so thoroughly routed the nasty Elisha that he scampered off to the hills, begging God to let him die because he was afraid of her. And why wouldn't a male wish to die in that age after he had been beaten and scared to death by a mere woman? But the male God finally gets his revenge, and Jezebel is killed and cut and eaten by the jackals with only the palms of her hands left.

THE LAWS OF MOSES

Moses, after receiving the Ten Commandments, naturally proceeded to interpret and expand upon them. In the Books of Exodus, Numbers, Deuteronomy and Leviticus we find some of these laws. A good number of them dealt with the Edenic issue of the subjection of female to male, out of which sprang most of the violence of the age. In our enlightened times we wince at these laws, but keep in mind that Moses would implement according to his partial light, and through the traditions of his time. Perhaps in this section, as in no other, the last holdouts against our contention that the serpent entered Adam, thereby using males as his instrumentality of persecution against woman, will run up the white flag of surrender.

For the sake of those readers who are not familiar with the Bible per se, I will set down the whole Scripture for the sake of clarity and comparisons they may wish to make.

"When thou goest forth to war against thine enemies...and thou hast taken them captive, And seest among the captives a beautiful woman, and hast a desire unto her, that thou wouldst have her to thy wife; Then thou shalt bring her home to thine house; and she shall shave her head and pare her nails; And she shall put the raiment of her captivity from off her, and shall remain in thine house, and bewail her father and her mother, a full month: and after that thou shalt go in unto her, and be her husband, and she shall be thy wife. And it shall be, if thou have no delight in her, then thou shalt let her go whither she will; but thou shalt not seest her at all for money, thou shalt not make merchandise of her, because thou hast humbled her."

Deut. 21:10-14

This is legalized rape as we know it and Moses was its founder. The shaving of her head was the trumpet sound that echoed in the Apostle Paul's ears when he used the same figure in regards to women who will not submit to male domination. Observe the puerile implications in the ceremony of forcing her to shave her head and pare her nails; puerile in that it is to symbolize the willing surrender of her beauty so that her male captor can pretend that he rapes her in full control of his mind and body rather cold-bloodly, than in the heat of any passion at her beauty. Augustine drew from this absurd male fantasy, symptom of the underlying male hysteria produced by the sexual appetite he cannot control. Her vanquished condition and the childish charade of surrendered beauty is also indicative of the male obsession of "humbling women" so that males may be proud. This law degraded not only woman, but men also, in that it encouraged the very lust it was designed to regulate.

There is a pathetic play for honor in forbidding him to sell her for money. In what males knew to be a thoroughly dishonorable act, there had to be some chivalry extended, hence the refusal to sell her for money. Could she have been sold for cattle or goods? Perhaps. With this self-deception, the male God retains his honor and the serpent has been served. Where males are told if they have no "delight in her" she is to be "let go" smacks more of the releasing of a captive animal than it does of freeing a human being. Women were not human beings.

> "If a man have two wives, one beloved and another hated, and they have borne him children; both the beloved and the hated; and if the first-born son be hers that was hated: Then it shall be, when he maketh his sons to inherit that which he hath, that he may not make the son of the beloved firstborn before the son of the hated, which is indeed the firstborn: But he shall acknowledge the son of the hated for the firstborn, by giving him a double portion of all that he hath: for he is the beginning of his strength; the right of the firstborn is his."   Deut. 21:15-17

The theme of desperation for honor where there is no honor recurs here. Again we see the dishonorable deed masked in a puritanical escapade of hypocrisy. Here as elsewhere we see that justice is for males only. The concern in this law is not for she "who was hated" but for the male child who might be disinherited because she was hated. We come full circle when given the reason why this son will not be disinherited with the words: "for he is the beginning of thy strength." Back to male supremacy!

> "If any man take a wife, and go in unto her and hate her...and say, I took this woman, and when I came to her, I found her not a maid: Then shall the father of the damsel, and her mother, take and bring forth the tokens of the damsel's virginity unto the elders of the city in the gate: And the damsel's father shall say unto the elders, I gave my

daughter unto this man to wife, and he hateth her; And, lo, he hath given occasions of speech against her, saying, I found not thy daughter a maid; and yet these are the tokens of my daughter's virginity. And they shall spread the cloth before the elders of the city. And the elders of that city shall take that man and chastise him; and they shall amerce him in a hundred shekels of silver, and give them unto the father of the damsel, because he hath brought up an evil name upon a virgin of Israel: and she shall be his wife; he may not put her away his days. But if this thing be true, and the tokens of virginity be not found for the damsel: Then they shall bring out the damsel to the door of her father's house, and the men of her city shall stone her with stones that she die: because she hath wrought folly in Israel, to play the whore in her father's house; so shalt thou put evil away from among you."   Deut. 22:13-21

A woman's life is at stake, either by death by stoning, or a living death with this man who clearly hates her enough to even gamble, if he is lying, on her execution if the "tokens cannot be produced." If she is proved innocent, which means he lied against her, then his punishment is a money payment of 100 shekels and to whom? To another male of course; her father! Woman, victim between two males at odds with each other.. And what sort of justice is it that subjects a human being to such humiliation and then, when found innocent, is rewarded with having to live out the remainder of her life with a lecher who lied enough and hated enough to risk her very life to get rid of her. What did the male risk? Only 100 shekels of silver and oh, yes, he must take her as wife all the rest of his days. What did that matter to males who could pluck women off the male vine as often as they wished? Thus does the all-male God dispense justice and thus does the serpent coil and uncoil and coil again....

"When a man hath taken a wife, and married her, and it comes to pass that she find no favor in his eyes, because he

hath found some uncleanness in her: then let him write her
a bill of divorcement, and give it in her hand, and send her
out of his house. And when she is departed out of his
house, she may go and be another man's wife. And if the
latter husband hate her...and sendeth her out of his house;
or if the latter husband die, which took her to be his
wife...after that she is defiled; for that is abomination
before the Lord: and thou shalt not cause the land to sin,
which the Lord thy God giveth thee for an inheritance."

Deut. 24:1-4

Moses doesn't make it too clear what is the "uncleanness"
about a woman who is twice wed and once widowed. Paul had
the same idea; that of a woman who is widowed being "damned
if she marries again."

The preoccupation with the virginity of woman is primarily
and almost exclusively a male one. What is there about the virginity of a woman which so excites males except the prideful
sense of being he who has "humbled her" first. The "virgin
purity" of woman is a male fixation of aggression against other
males, and has nothing to do with woman. This law defiles
woman and passes her from defilement to defilement in the
name of the all-male God.

"There shall be no whore of the daughters of Israel; nor a
sodomite of the sons of Israel. Thou shalt not bring the hire
of a whore, or the price of a dog, into the house of the Lord
thy God for any vow: for even both these are abomination
unto the Lord thy God." Deut. 23:17-18

Whoring is a sexual sin for women and sodomy a sexual sin
for males. What about the whore's partner who is male? This
amounts to putting all the blame upon women in the sexual sins
possible between man and woman.

"If brethren dwell together, and one of them die, and have
no child, the wife of the dead shall not marry without unto

a stranger; her husband's brother shall go in unto her, and take her to him to wife, and perform the duty of a husband's brother unto her. And it shall be, that the firstborn which she beareth shall succeed in the name of his brother which is dead, that his name be not put out of Israel. And if a man like not to take his brother's wife, then let his brother's wife go up...the gate unto the elders.... Then shall his brother's wife come unto him in the presence of the elders, and loose his shoe from off his foot, and spit in his face, and shall answer and say, So shall it be done unto that man that will not build up his brother's house."

Deut. 25:5-9

This complicates matters for male sexuality, since he gets stuck with his brother's wives, should he pass away. Again woman has no say. Should there be a man so honest who will not submit his own body to be "used" as a tool, then he is spat upon for his honesty and discrimination. The loosing of the shoe crops up in other places in the Bible and has the connotation of integrity about it. The sexual morality of the male God did not make room for sincerity on the part of either male or female, and in this case was caught in its own trap.

The next two Scriptures take some sort of prize for stupidity or naivete, and one wonders how many innocent men and women met their deaths by stoning because of them:

"If a damsel that is a virgin be betrothed unto a husband, and a man find her in the city, and lie with her; Then ye shall bring them both out unto the gate of that city, and ye shall stone them with stones that they die; the damsel, because she cried not, being in the city; and the man, because he hath humbled his neighbor's wife: so thou shalt put away evil from among you."   Deut. 22:23-24

What does "being in the city" have to do with whether you are heard or not, when crying out? Women are raped everyday in cities, and are kept from crying out by their assailants.

> "But if a man find a bethrothed damsel in the field, and the
> man force her and lie with her: then the man only that lay
> with her shall die: But unto the damsel thou shalt do
> nothing.... For he found her in the field, and the betrothed
> damsel cried, and there was none to save her."
>
> Deut. 22:25-27

Just as today, rape in those days must have been difficult to
prove.

> "And whosoever lieth carnal with woman, that is a bond-
> maid, betrothed to a husband, and not at all redeemed, nor
> freedom given her; she shall be scourged; they shall not be
> put to death, because she was not free. And he shall bring
> his trespass offering...the priest shall make an atonement
> for him...for his sin which he hath done: and the sin which
> he hath done shall be forgiven him."   Lev. 19:20-22

In other words, a woman sold into slavery but married,
would be scourged by males for lying sexually with a man other
than her husband. The male involved would not be scourged
but could take the life of an innocent animal or bird as a sin
atonement for himself. Where is the justice? And why is the
male freed so easily? Only the fact that she is slave saves her
from death. If it saves her from death why does it not save her
from scourging? Moses, like the dishonest butcher, always slips
his thumb onto the scales of Justice to short-change the female.

> "Now these are the judgments which thou shalt set before
> them. If thou buy a Hebrew servant, six years shall he
> serve: and in the seventh he shall go out free for nothing. If
> he came in by himself, he shall go out by himself: if he were
> married, then his wife shall go out with him. If his master
> have given him a wife, and she have borne him sons or

daughters; *the wife and her children shall be her master's,*[3] and he shall go out by himself."   Exod. 21:1-4

Slavery! The selling of human flesh by man to man, legalized pimping by a master to male slaves of female slaves; the temporary "use" of a woman while in servitude! How can we continue to accept Moses as the church has presented him to us? We have passed through a Civil War over just such an issue. It appears that the woman may not earn her freedom after seven years. Was that the prerogative of males only?

> "And if a man sell his daughter to be a maidservant, she shall not go out as the men servants do. If she please not her master, who hath betrothed her to himself, then shall he let her be redeemed: to sell her unto a strange nation he shall have no power, seeing he hath dealt deceitfully with her. And if he have betrothed her unto his son, he shall deal with her after the manner of daughters. If he take him another wife; her food, her raiment, and her duty of marriage shall not he not diminish. And if he do not these three unto her, then shall she go out free without money."
> Exod. 21:7-11

So, if a woman is sold into slavery to a man, she cannot serve her time as males could, and go free. She still had before her an obstacle course in lust before she might breathe the air of freedom.

The following two are classic when put end to end in the exposition of justice male style.

> "If men strive, and hurt a woman with child, so that her fruit depart from her, and yet no mischief follow: he shall be surely punished, according as the woman's husband will

---

[3] Author's italics.

lay upon him; and he shall pay as the judges determine. And if any mischief follow, then thou shalt give life for life, Eye for eye, tooth for tooth, hand for hand, foot for foot, Burning for burning, wound for wound, stripe for stripe."

Exod. 21:22-25

In other words, if the woman loses the baby, the man is punished but not by death. Only if the woman dies, will he die. The child's life is less valuable than the offending male's. But look at the next Scripture:

"When men strive together one with another, and the wife of the one draweth near for to deliver her husband out of the hand of him that smiteth him, and putteth forth her hand, and take him by the secrets: Then thou shalt cut off her hand, thine eye shall not pity her."   Deut. 25:11,12

"And if a man entice a maid that is not betrothed, and lie with her, he shall surely endow her to be his wife. If her father utterly refuse to give her unto him, he shall pay money according to the dowry of virgins."   Exod. 22:16-17

So he pays full price for damaged goods to get her. This is a twist on the selling of woman's body for money with a slight variation, but it amounts to prostitution in the long run.

These laws need no further comment nor does the age itself. I have, therefore left until last the passages from Judges which collect into one story almost all the evils of the age which sprang directly from the doctrine born of Eden. What better commentary to close this chapter than the story of the Levite and his concubine which, if read carefully, speaks on and between the lines of lust, murder, injustice, pride and woman; pitiful victim and pawn.

First, from the Book of Numbers.

VOWS ACCORDING TO MOSES

This passage from the Book of Numbers could have been a great influence upon the Apostle Paul, for in it one hears the faint echoes of his theology of headship over woman. This group or ordinances definitely cut woman off from direct relationship to her God, if her husband interfered, making her father or husband or both her God or her arbitrator, between her and Himself. Woman, as depicted in this passage, is not only disenfranchised spiritually but physically, mentally and emotionally. Moses took in these ordinances woman's very soul:

> "If a man vow a vow unto the Lord, or swear an oath to bind his soul with a bond; he shall not break his word, he shall do according to all that proceedeth out of his mouth."
> Num. 30:2

The male is a free agent before his God. Observe what the all-male God proscribes for woman:

> "If a woman also vow a vow unto the Lord, and bond herself by a bond, being in her father's house in her youth; And her father hear her vow, and her bond wherewith she hath bound her soul, and her father shall hold his peace at her: then all her vows shall stand.... But if her father disallow her in the day that he heareth; not any of her vows...shall stand: and the Lord shall forgive her, because her father disallowed her. And if she had at all a husband, when she vowed, or uttered aught out of her lips, wherewith she bound her soul; And her husband heard it, and held his peace at her in the day...then shall her vows stand.... But if her husband disallowed her on the day that he heard it; then he shall make her vow...of none effect...."
> Num. 30:3-8

The text goes on to say that these same laws apply to both

widows and divorced women (put away by their husbands since women could not divorce), yet in the case of these two situations the almighty male hand reaches beyond the grave to allow or disallow for the living women:

> "And if she vowed in her husband's house, or bound her soul with a bond by an oath; And her husband heard it and held his peace...then all her vows shall stand.... But if her husband hath utterly made them void on the day he heard them...the bond of her soul shall not stand: her husband hath made them void.... Every vow, and every binding oath to afflict the soul, her husband may establish it, or her husband may make it void. These are the statutes, which the Lord commanded Moses, between a man and his wife, between the father and his daughter, being yet in her youth in her father's house."   Num. 30:10-13; 16

Women had no standing with the true God in matters of oath or covenants unless her husband or father permitted it. A male could even enforce this from beyond the grave, or after he had put his wife away via divorce.

Notice the coy condition of "hearing her vows." One can only imagine the craft women and men resorted to in the handling of this ridiculous law based on insufferable injustice to women due to male pride. Considering the pimping, selling and slavery of women instigated by the male God, one wonders why Scripture is so lacking in commensurate responsibility for women; commensurate that is, with the privileges.

In view of the practice of selling daughters to slave masters, and the tradition of selling daughters in marriage, one wonders if these laws were to make sure the women didn't bind themselves to physical virginity thereby squelching the male ambition to make money in her purchase.

BIG BROTHER IS WATCHING...YOU!

George Orwell's *1984* is the story of a world controlled by the desire for a perfect rule of obedience and tranquility through the annihilation of the individual in the society through a rule of fear and betrayal. The climate of the same idea was enacted in Nazi Germany, where children betrayed parents in the name of the "good of the state." The patriarchal society had its Orwellian seasons as well. We all have been touched, directly or indirectly, by the rebellion of our youth against the hypocrisies of our religion and our society. Imagine the agony of parents in the age of Moses' iron fist laws, who had the misfortune to have a child who did not see quite eye to eye with Moses' "tooth for tooth:"

"If a man have a stubborn and rebellious son, which will not obey the voice of his father, or the voice of his mother, and that, when they have chastened him, will not harken unto them: Then shall his father and his mother lay hold on him and bring him out unto the elders of his city, and unto the gate of his place; And they shall say unto the elders of his city, This our son is stubborn and rebellious, he will not obey our voice; he is a glutton and a drunkard. And all the men of his city shall stone him with stones, that he die: so shalt thou put evil away from among you; and all Israel shall hear, and fear...."   Deut. 21:18-21

We are proud of America and the religious freedom we enjoy. Our modern soul winces at the adolescent gyrations of the Crusades of the dark ages:

"If thy brother, the son of thy mother, or thy son, or thy daughter or the wife of thy bosom, or thy friend, which is as thine own soul, entice thee secretly, saying, Let us go and serve other gods, which thou hast not known, thou, nor thy fathers; Namely, of the gods of the people which are round about you, nigh unto thee, or far off from thee, from the one end of the earth even unto the other end of the earth; Thou shalt not consent with him; nor hearken unto him; neither shall thine eye pity him, neither shalt thou spare, neither shalt thou conceal him; But thou shalt surely kill him; thine hand shall be first upon him to put him to death, and afterward the hand of all the people. And thou shalt stone him with stones, that he die; because he hath sought to thrust thee away from the Lord thy God...."

Deut. 13:6-10

Did you notice that all the people had to have a hand in the execution? That was so that all would share any guilt that might result. I wonder what happened to genius in such a society. Probably what happens to genius in every society stuck in the muck of mediocrity and tradition. I suppose any who were gifted or sensitive enough to see past the idiocy of such a society went the way of all stones. Then, no doubt there were those who just in self-righteous indignation, as in our own society, simply slip through the cracks of the establishment to certain annihilation.

But this facet of the patriarchal society was the least of it for there was far better yet to come.

The Levite and His Concubine

Only an Edgar Allen Poe, with his peculiar knack of horror, could write a sequel to this bizarre tale of depraved injustice and male insanity. Taken from the Book of Judges, it is a frighteningly lucid potpourri of the consequences of the male principle unleashed in vicious rampage against not only women, but males, and one is confounded to explain how such madness could possibly be attributed to any God worthy of the name, so vile are the fruits of the moral code upon which this incident in the Jewish history is anchored. Like most Jewish epochs this has a cast of thousands, and when brought to its final scenes the blood runs ankle deep as it gushes from the severed artery of

Eden: the subjection of the female principle to the male:

> "And it came to pass in those days, when there was no king
> in Israel, that there was a certain Levite [of the priestly
> caste] sojourning on the side of Mount Ephraim, who took
> to him a concubine out of Bethlehem Judah. And his con-
> bine played the whore against him, and went away from
> him unto her father's house to Bethlehem Judah, and was
> there four whole months. And her husband arose, and
> went after her, to speak friendly unto her, and to bring her
> again, having his servant with him, and a couple of asses:
> and she brought him into her father's house: and when the
> father of the damsel saw him, he rejoiced to meet him.
> And his father-in-law, the damsel's father, retained him;
> and he abode with him three days; so they did eat and
> drink, and lodge there."   Judg. 19:1-4

Finally on the fifth day the father tries to restrain him again:

> "...Comfort thine heart, I pray thee. And they tarried until
> afternoon, and they did eat both of them. And when the
> man rose up to depart...the damsel's father, said unto him,
> Behold, now the day draweth towards evening, I pray you
> tarry all night...and tomorrow get you early on your way,
> that thou mayest go home."   Judg. 19:8, 9

Apparently the father had a deep affection for his daughter
which was returned. But the account states that the Levite
remained firm in his intent to leave, so they do, on the fifth day;
the Levite, his concubine, his servant and his animals, journey
until dusk. His servant, tired and hungry, suggests they find
lodgings for the night. The Levite, member of the priestly caste
and bound by certain laws, refuses to go into a "city of
strangers," which was called Jebus or Jerusalem, insisting they
continue on 'til they come into Gilbeah, an area where one of
the twelve tribes, the tribe of Benjamin resided. Once in Gilbeah
they sit, as custom was, in the street, awaiting an invitation

from one of his relatives to spend the night at one of their homes. No invitation is forthcoming except from an old man, a stranger, who offers them his hospitality which they accept. No sooner had they sat down to eat then there is a knock at the door:

> "...behold, the men of the city, certain sons of Belial, beset the house round about, and beat at the door, and spake to the master of the house, the old man, saying, Bring forth the man that came into thine house, that we may know him. And the man, the master of the house, went out unto them, and said unto them, Nay, my bretheren, nay, I pray you, do not so wickedly; seeing that this man is come into mine house, do not this folly. Behold, here is my daughter a maiden, and his concubine; them I will bring out now, and humble ye them, and do with them what seemeth good unto you: but unto this man do not so vile a thing."
>
> Judg. 19:22-24

Sex was equated with a kind of humbling process; but don't do "so vile a thing" to a male. There is a reappearance also of the unspoken male code of the preservation of honor between males from which woman was excluded. The pre-Eve Adamic paradise must be rescued from itself. The woman is expendable.

> "But the men would not hearken to him: so the man took his concubine, and brought her forth unto them; and they knew her, and abused her all the night until the morning: and when the day began to spring, they let her go. Then came the woman in the dawning of the day, and fell down at the door of the man's house where her lord was, till it was light."
>
> Judg. 19:25, 26

Notice the unconcern of the Levite. Why is he not concerned that he finds this young girl lying in the door in the early dawn light? Because women were of as much value as a stray dog come home from a night of wandering, perhaps. The command to get up is short and to the point:

> "And her lord rose up in the morning, and opened the doors
> of the house, and went out to go his way: and, behold, the
> woman, his concubine was fallen down at the door of the
> house, and her hands were upon the threshold. And he said
> unto her, Up, and let us be going. But none answered.
> Then the man took her up upon an ass, and the man rose
> up, and gat him unto his place. AND WHEN HE WAS
> COME INTO HIS HOUSE, HE TOOK A KNIFE, AND
> LAID HOLD ON HIS CONCUBINE, AND DIVIDED
> HER, TOGETHER WITH HER BONES, INTO TWELVE
> PIECES,[4] and sent her into all the coasts of Israel."
>
> Judg. 19: 27-29

There is no hint of concern about her death. So vile is the hatred
of woman's physical body by the all-male God that this final
depraved act of desecration damns any who will not admit it for
what it symbolizes: the poisonous inedible fruit of the tree of
male persecution of the human body in its symbol, woman.
With the same detachment the old man had thrown this hapless
girl to the beasts, this man carves her body and dispatches it to
the nation as a report of "lewdness and folly" in Israel. It was
the male obsession with the preservation of the people as a
nation that motivated his act, not vengeance for the woman
personally. How is he reprimanded for this violation of humanity? He is shunned by the other members of the community.
"We will not any of us go to his tent; neither will we any of us
turn into his house." Judg. 20:8. The Scripture account continues: "The people arose as one man," mustering an army of
400,000 men and confront the tribe of Benjamin with a demand
for those men who had committed the crime. They refuse and
war breaks out. It is mass slaughter with the Benjaminites losing
18,000 men before they retreat to the wilderness of Rimmon
where an additional 5,000 are killed, then to Gidon where 2,000
more are slain, to total a casualty list of 25,000 killed.

---

[4] Author's capitalization.

> "But six hundred men turned and fled to the wilderness unto the rock Rimmon, and abode in the rock Rimmon four months." Judg. 20:47

Meanwhile, the Israelites turn against those left in the cities of the tribe and slay all men, women and children and even animals. They finish with the flourish of burning everything to the ground.

At the Israelite camp, the males decide that no daughters of Israel will ever again be given as wives to a Benjaminite. This is a sworn vow to God. However, now bound by their oath they are faced with a dilemma. Since most of the female population of the Benjaminites has been decimated by their hand, the sole remaining males, 600 turncoats hiding out in the rock of Rimmon will have no wives to repopulate the tribe. The tragedy of civil war and schism within the nation is a great sorrow but the possibility of the tribe of Benjamin dying off is even greater because it constitutes a threat to their very own "inheritance" from God. What can they do but make peace with the remaining males and hope to somehow restore the solvency of the whole nation. In true patriarchal fashion they hit upon an inspiration: they will find a scapegoat in order to justify the "stealing of woman," to provide wives for the 600 males:

> "And they said, What one is there of the tribes of Israel that came not up to Mizpeh to the Lord? And, behold, there came none to the camp from Jabesh-gil-e-ad to the assembly. For the people were numbered, and, behold, there were none of the inhabitants of Jabesh-gil-e-ad there.
> And the congregation sent thither twelve thousand men of the valiantest, and commanded them, saying: Go and smite the inhabitants of Jabesh-gil-e-ad with the edge of the sword, with the women and the children. And this is the thing that ye shall do, Ye shall utterly destroy every male, and every woman that hath lain by man. And they found among the inhabitants of Jabesh-gil-e-ad four hundred young virgins, that had known no man by lying with any

male: and they brought them unto the camp at Shiloh, which is in the land of Canaan." Judg. 21:8-12

The scapegoat had been found. It was the innocent pawn; woman. But now they have an arithmetic problem to cope with: 600 men and only 400 virgins.

"...How shall we do for wives for them that remain, seeing the women are destroyed out of Benjamin? And they said, there must be an inheritance for them that be escaped of Benjamin, that a tribe be not destroyed out of Israel." Judg. 21:16, 17

Someone remembers that the people of Shiloh would soon be celebrating a yearly festival to the Lord. The male rustlers make ready:

"Therefore they commanded the children of Benjamin, saying, Go and lie and wait in the vineyards; And see, and, behold, if the daughters of Shiloh come out to dance in dances, then come ye out of the vineyards, and CATCH you every man his wife of the daughters of Shiloh, and go to the land of Benjamin."[5] Judg. 21:20, 21

How does a pornographic movie end? Strangely enough with an appeal to mercy and compassion which interestingly enough is where the whole thing could have ended or been avoided at the very beginning, if mercy and compassion had been extended to the unfortunate concubine thrown like a cat among a pack of dogs. But it is males who collect the mercy for themselves. Woman is excluded from any pacts of mercy and compassion between the all -male God and his "blood buddies." This is what they are told to say to the offended fathers and brothers of the hustled women:

---

[5] Author's capitalization.

"And it shall be, when their fathers or brethren come unto us to complain, that we will say unto them, Be favorable unto them for our sakes: because we reserved not to each man his wife in the war: for ye did not give unto them at this time, that ye should be guilty."   Judg. 21:22

"And the children...did so, and took them wives, according to their number, of them that danced, whom they caught: and they went and returned unto their inheritance, and repaired the cities, and dwelt in them."   Judg. 21:23

Has the woman been avenged, or have males been avenged of their own folly? Woman is again the pitiful pawn between males at war with males. Her blood flowed like water; woman the "livestock" on the breeding farm of a nation. Woman's spiritual blood oozes from every word of their account of the doctrine of the subjection of woman to the male God.

Woman: this Eve of the old dispensation had for over 2000 years reaped violence in the use of her body and unutterable loneliness in the rape of her soul, which in her guilt and shame she allowed. Thus was her desire for her husband and thus did he rule over her with an iron fist. The prophecy of Eden seemed to be fulfilled as a split Godhead drags his female foot limping into the age of the Messiah.

Chapter 4

"FRAILTY, THY NAME IS WOMAN"

Logically we would go to Jesus and the New Testament, but I would like to leap from Moses over the heads of both Paul and Jesus, into the third and fourth century church. Through the binoculars of time, the reader will get a broader sweep of the impact of the Apostle Paul's theology of woman, down to the present day.

We must remember as we read this section that having leaped Jesus and Paul, we have at the same time bridged the advent of the Virgin Mary who was the embodiment of that virgin purity which alone would have satisfied the tortured yearnings of Augustine and Tertullian for that woman who had been scoured clean of the sewage they had attributed to her nature and body.

Was the beast appeased? Apparently not, for nowhere in all of Christian literature has the hysteria of male fear of the female principle been equaled or surpassed as in these males. These are the writings of men around whose souls the serpent coiled in so deadly a fashion as to squeeze the breath of all "flesh" from their bodies in self-hatred for appetites they could not control. This self-hatred was projected upon woman as the embodiment of all their tortured sexuality.

St. Bernard—"...her face is as burning wind and her voice: the hissing of serpents."

Tertullian—"Woman! you are the Devil's doorway. You have led astray one who the Devil would not dare attack directly. It is your fault that the Son of God had to die; you should always go in mourning and in rags."

St. Ambrose—"Adam was led to sin by Eve and not Eve by Adam. It is just and right that woman accept as Lord and Master him who she led to sin."

St. John Crysotom—"Among all savage beasts none is found so harmful as woman."

St. Jerome—"Let us take axe in hand and cut off at its roots the fruitless tree of marriage."

St. Thomas—"Woman is an occasional and incomplete being... It is unchangeable that woman is destined to live under man's influence and has no authority from her Lord."

The uneasy conscience of males due to uncontrollable sexual drive is again equated with woman.

St. Augustine—"Concupiscence is a vice...human flesh born through it is a sinful flesh...."

St. Thomas—"The union of the sexes transmits original sin to the child, being accompanied through the Fall, by concupiscence...."

Tertullian—"Woman is a Temple built over a sewer...."

St. Augustine—"We are born between feces and urine...."

One stands in amazement at the lack of simple Christian charity towards the women who bore these ingrates. There is a strange ring to words like these and the echoes are not those of Christ.

Through the intervention of the church, fathers' laws were passed which denied women the right to male occupations. They were also denied power to bring suit in court or offer valid testimony. Both in civil and canon law, the evil of woman's nature was upheld and legislated against.

Saint Paul's teachings about the subjection of woman to the man in marriage are echoed in the words of St. Methodius:

"Now consider my dear virgins, how Paul in his desire to have all the faithful practice chastity as far as possible, endeavors to emphasize the dignity of chastity by many arguments. So, for example, when he says: 'concerning the things whereof you write me, it is good for a man not to touch a woman,' in proposing and proscribing it without qualifications he already shows that it is good not to touch a woman!"

St. Jerome inferred that if it was good not to touch a woman then it must be bad to touch her. This, in spite of the Genesis command to multiply.

God thought it "good" that man touch woman in his mandate to them to "be fruitful and multiply and replenish the earth."

St. Jerome—"woman is...the scorpion's dart...a dangerous species...."

St. John Damascene—"woman is a sick she-ass...a hideous tape worm...The advance post of hell...."

Woman was the irrational half of mankind. Having successfully relegated woman to the confines of a totally sexual existence, it is now necessary to vindicate the duplicity of his motivation by declaring that woman is, by her very nature, mentally and spiritually inferior to the male.

St. Gregory declares that woman is slow in understanding. Her unstable and naive mind renders her by way of natural weakness to the necessity of a strong hand in her husband. Her "use," he says, is two-fold; animal sex and motherhood.

Further rationalization drives Tertullian as a defense against her possible rebellion and advises woman that she should render herself ugly since "her beauty is a danger to those who look upon it...."He takes it a step further by demanding woman's assistance in protecting male lust from itself!

St. John Chrysotom warns husbands to mold their wives when they are young and warned woman not to think of herself as equal to her husband.

Having declared woman mentally inferior, St. Clement of Alexandria cleverly hits upon the idea of insuring that woman does not test such definition of herself by warning her that, "it is shameful for her to ponder her nature, since through her nature, sin entered the world."

In the Middle Ages, the anti-feminist spirit persisted, somewhat dulled from the church fathers but as savage in its suspicion and disdain. Their hysterical imperatives to chastity and domination threw them into the final negation; a hatred for all life as evil, as we see from the Manicheans.

St. Thomas—"Woman is misbegotten and defective for the active force in the male seed tendst to the production of a perfect likeness in the masculine sex; while the production of woman comes from defect in the active force or from some material indisposition, or even from some external influence, such as that of a south wind, which is moist."

Now we come to a deadlock of a sorts in the preference for male births. The Manicheans advised avoiding all procreation by means of contraception, so as to avoid the evils of earthly life.

St. Augustine, ever tortured between the evils of pleasure and the propagation of the human race, gave it a new twist by opting for procreation without pleasure.

"Holy married people...have used them [sex organs] solely for the sake of generation so that this exercise of them was in no way filthy because it was not subjected to lust but to reason."

Here is Augustine's idea of the "ideal union" of man and woman in paradise:

"Those members [sex organs], like the rest, would be moved by command of the will, and the husband would be mingled with the loins of his wife without the seductive stimulus of passions, with calmness of mind and with no corruption of the innocent body...because the wild heat of passion would not activate those parts of the body, but as would be proper, a voluntary control would use them...."

Pope Gregory agreed with Augustine that all married sexual pleasure was sinful, even if performed for generative purposes. Finding themselves in a corner, St. Thomas attempts a rescue thusly:

"On the other hand, woman is not misbegotten, as regards human nature in general. Woman is included in nature's intention as directed to the work of generation.

"The misadventure of woman is only a comparative one, with man as our standard; in herself, she is valuable as a mother. Her deficiency is God's will and God has given her man to think for her...in man the power of reason predominates...justice compels man to stay with his wife after she grows old....

"It was necessary for woman to be made as Scripture says, as a helpmeet for man, not indeed, as help in other work, as some maintain, for in any other work a man can be more suitably helped by another man than by a woman,— but precisely for generation."

Round and round we go and always back where we started from. Woman: harlot or mother....

A Jesuit theologian once said, "It will be a long time before the Genesis ideal [of love and companionship between male and female] reveals itself to the heart of man, who is prone to sin, unfortunately, to adopt an attitude of domination of the female sex."

So far it has been six thousand years and the battle still rages.

While it is probably true that St. Paul would recoil in disgust at the contortions bred of hatred and suspicion of woman by these males, one can only admit that he must share the guilt of their debasement of woman. It was from his doctrines on woman that these men drew their sanctions of repression and sublime chastity as the ideal. There are, in their hysterical theology, echoes of Paul and Moses, both of whom suffered from the identical afflictions of male pride born of fear. Had the serpent any need to exercise himself in the persecution of the woman with men such as these? Hardly! My contention is that the serpent entered Adam; the male upon the pronouncements of Eden stands on solid uncontestable biblical and secular historical ground.

Let's pluck some more of Paul's theological fruit to see if it is edible.

Aristotle—"Woman is to man as slave to master; the manual to the worker, the barbarian to the Greek. It conduces to temperance not to marry too early as women who marry early are apt to be wanton; and in men too, the bodily frame is apt to be stunted if they marry while growing...."

Nietzsche—"Equality between the man and woman is impossible because war between them is eternal; there is no peace without victory...peace comes only when one or the other is acknowledged master. It is dangerous to try equality with a woman. She will not be content with that; she will rather be content with subordination if the man is a man.... Above all, her perfection and happiness lie in motherhood. Everything in woman is riddle and everything in woman has one answer: its name is childbearing."

Spengler—"Woman are more liable to waver from true religion, have weak memories, and it is natural in them not to be disciplined but to follow their natural impulses without any sense of what is due."

Hegel—"Woman can of course be educated, but their minds are not adapted to the higher sciences, philosophy or certain of the arts."

Freud—"Woman is hostile to the demands of civilization."

Schopenhauer—"In the last resort woman exists solely for the propagation of the race."

Gladstone—"That by trying to share male rights...."

Rousseau—"For to make woman our superiors in all qualities proper to her sex and make her our equal in all the rest, what is it but to transfer to woman the superiority which nature has given to her husband?"

Byron—"Man's love is of man's life a thing apart, 'Tis woman's whole existence."

Freud—"It is really a stillborn thought to send woman into the struggle for existence exactly as a man. If, for instance, I imagined my sweet girl as a competitor it would only end as it did seventeen months ago, that I am fond of her and that I implore her to withdraw from the strife into the calm uncompetitiveness of my home."

A little honey mixed with the venom!

Ibsen—Torvald, in *The Dolls House*:
"Before all else you are a wife and mother...your most sacred duties are to your husband and children...."

Freud's remark, which drips with honey and venom, is laughable when one scans the history of women in primitive tribes and even among many eastern countries and cultures today where women, far from being sheltered, in some... "calm uncompetitiveness of my home" have been made beasts of burden, digging, planting, harvesting, cooking, sewing, carrying, etc. besides bearing and nurturing the children.

In many cultures women were and are still bought like animals and slaves. In the Fiji Islands, India, and New Guinea a widow was killed and buried with her husband so that she could continue to serve the male in her next life.

In the Islamic world a man can collect wives like some males collect guns or antique autos. Women could be divorced by their husbands without being informed, since the great decision to sever the bonds should be left to the sounder judgement of the male.

In China a woman's feet were cruelly bound in childhood in order to physiologically condition her for the confines of marriage under the all-pervading eye of her master and husband. Female children were abandoned to cold, wild animals, and starvation in the fields.

In many primitive tribes, cruel and disfiguring surgery was performed upon the female sex organs to keep women so marked free from male tampering other than her owner. Young girls were made to submit to sexual intercourse with several or all of the males in a tribe as signal of her coming of age.

The savagery which placed traditions of suicide upon women at the deaths of their husbands is too well-known and documented to be denied. Paul, indeed, would have cringed at suicide for females at widowhood, but he did the next best thing and rejected them if they were married twice, and damned their souls if they married again "out of the Lord." Some might have opted for suicide.

Our reason for projecting into the first few hundred years of the church's early theology has been to expose the inheritance bequeathed by the Apostle Paul to mankind in his theology of woman. In no way can we possible reconcile such obvious hatred with the true God. It is a theology of hate, inspired of evil. Jesus once said:

"Wherefore by their fruits ye shall know them."   Matt. 7:20

Paul's tree bore good and evil fruit, the evil being his doctrine of the subjection of woman. For male Christendom to blind their eyes to this rotted and inedible fruit is to deliberately choose to give Paul, a perfection, a sinlessness, which were not his to claim.

The sickening theology of the inferiority and animality of woman, as recorded in these few quotes is the venom which flows from Paul, whose Gospel is preached over and above the Gospel of Christ, for it is rooted in the Gospel of Moses. Our initial leap from the third and fourth century theology doesn't seem like a leap at all for it has been but a step away, on a well-beaten path marked by familiar signposts. We take one pace backwards now, to examine the theology of woman according to Paul.

Chapter 5

A GOOD WOMAN'S HARD TO FIND

Few women and a fewer men have read the Apostle Paul's teachings on the place of women in the church without wincing at the acrid and biting tones of his Epistles to the Corinthians in which they are introduced. Most women have read them with something akin to sorrow, some with anger. Paul was a complex personality as was Moses. His religious and cultural heritage was the heritage of Moses, which before his conversion to the Christian religion drove him to the murder of Christians with an incomparable zeal. Paul has strong Pharisaical leanings. Much as he protested to the contrary, he could be cutting and sarcastic when he deemed it necessary, and his clever dialectics in defense of himself before the irritated Corinthian congregation do not absolve him from being the boastful man he protests so vehemently he is not. Paul could be jealous and possessive in a way which we are sure he would never have permitted an underling to be. This possessive jealousy led him unto alienations which he was hard put to understand.

The issue of woman's place in the church was brought to a head by the congregation at Corinth. Corinth was one of the most cosmopolitan cities of the ancient world; every language was spoken there and its streets teemed with all races and nationalities. Artists, philosophers, and teachers of a Hellenistic bent flourished there, along with the basest and noblest of religious worships. The Corinthian congregation was one of the largest of the Christian communities founded thus far. The majority of its coverts were pagans from all strata of society. They were a brilliant congregation and there is every reason to believe that this brilliance was not confined to the men alone. It was probably inevitable that Paul would lock horns with both men and women in this community.

These Corinthians had not been as isolated from cultural, religious and intellectual influences in their society as were the Jews, or women of other congregations. With the quickness natural to women in matters of spirit, they took the emancipation Jesus held out to them in its fullness. They did not misread the doctrine of the Christ. Their lives had been of unrelieved tyranny of body and soul, bound monogamously to polygamous husbands who retained for themselves all autonomy before man and God, of spirit and soul, while the women languished, dependent in all ways upon arrogant males who demanded worship and, by way of law, received it. Jesus salved the old, old wound that woman had handed down mother to daughter, for thousands of years, and their sighs of relief echoed around the world. But the anodyne was fated to be short-lived for the canker worm of male pride was already boring at the new release of man's oldest captive. Paul, with the swiftness of an eagle, swooped upon them to bring them up short from their joy of new freedom, to drop them back into the old, old nest of subjection to their husbands and to himself.

Paul had a tiger by the tail and he swung it hard. His measures were harsh and arbitrary as he took up the cudgel of Moses and summarily relegated the woman back to the bed and stove. The women of the Corinthian congregation fought back, so Paul played his trump card. Smitten as he was with the ancient hysteria, he came down hard upon the rebellious female threat by retaliating against her in the context of sex. He dealt with her as Moses had—as an institutionalized incompetent. The chosen institution was marriage; the incompetence was woman's inherent "weakness" due to the so-called Edenic deception. Paul, in dealing with what he considered a spiritual issue, resorted to the law, within whose edifice he envisioned the only safe shelter from woman's natural debasement of the human body due to her biological function of child-bearing. Marriage, to Paul, was a necessary evil to be shunned, or conceded to strictly for the purposes of racial propagation, and a container of lust.

He proceeds like a good criminal lawyer to draw up the marriage contract wherein the exchange of body use between husband and wife is set down in legal terms with the ultimate appeal to "fraud," should either withhold the other's goods. He placed males over the woman in "spiritual headship," thereby encompassing her whole being. In this chapter we challenge Paul's teachings in the context of Christian doctrine which he violates on every count— these teachings which are a travesty against half the human race.

Creator Paul swings his hammers of creation and opens his Genesis epoch with the statement:

"It is good for man not to touch a woman...."

His premise is therefore that human sexuality is not good, and what is not good is lust. Love he relegates to the backrooms of nebulous spirituality of which the male is "head." His antidote to lust is marriage; loveless to be sure, but, as he puts it:

"But if they cannot contain [remain celibate], let them marry: for it is better to marry than to burn."   I Cor. 7:9

With marriage safely defined as a framework within which to contain the burning of those who "lust," he proceeds to bring order out of primal chaos by delivering the bodies of married couples to each other in legal exchange, warning them of "fraud," should one deny the other his legally acquired goods:

"The wife hath not power of her own body, but the husband: and likewise also the husband hath not power of his own body, but the wife. DEFRAUD YE NOT[1] one the other, except it be with consent for a time, that ye may give yourselves to fastings and prayer, and come together again, that Satan tempt ye not for your incontinency."

I Cor. 7:4-5

The Pauline Genesis creation account therefore reads thus:

Therefore shall a man not leave his lustful mother and father and cling to his wife and the two shall not become one flesh for all that is of the flesh is lust....

What a pity that Paul's concept of profound love between a man and a woman is undergirded not by admiration and pure pleasure, but by the hideous tape worm of lust who "disguises himself as an angel of love," fit only to be constrained behind the institutional walls of legal marriage. Thus did the ravenous beasts of lust roam the primeval mists of Paul's creation and thus did he sever man's body from his soul and his spirit in a new Edenic expulsion; but this time it was man's body alone that was exiled outside the paradise—Adam, a two-headed gorgon carrying his own and Eve's head and Eve; a headless monstrosity feeling her way behind and under him. This is the cornerstone of Paul's theology: the two-headed man and the headless woman.

PAUL AND VIRGINITY

Paul, like his heirs to follow, held virginity to be the ideal towards which all men should strive. He placed males in positions of control over the virginity of women where such authority existed which echoes the Old Testament ownership by the father of his daughters and his wives. He says:

---

[1] Author's capitalization.

> "...It is good for a man not to touch a woman. Nevertheless, to avoid fornication, let every man have his own wife, and let every woman have her own husband."   I Cor. 7:2

Why is it good for a man not to touch a woman? Is Paul of the same mind as those who were to follow him that life on this earth is evil and the greatest good would be that it cease? Where does this put the original mandate of Eden to "increase and multiply and fill the earth?" Where does that put Jesus' remark "Suffer the little children to come unto me,...for of such is the kingdom of God"? If God is both male and female, as we have proven him to be in Genesis, then is God in some kind of conflict within himself? Did not God touch a woman when he impregnated the Virgin Mary with the sperm of the Holy Spirit? Can a virgin bear child without being touched by either man or God? What does Paul mean, it is good not to touch a women? Would not all creation cease by both man and God if such were so? Strange! He enlarges upon his reasoning:

> "But I would have you without carefulness. He that is unmarried careth for the things that belong to the Lord, how he may please the Lord: But he that is married careth for the things that are of the world, how he may please his wife."   I Cor. 7:32-33

He recommends virginity as the ideal for women also:

> "There is a difference also between a wife and a virgin. The unmarried woman careth for the things of the Lord, that she may be holy both in body and spirit: but she that is married careth for the things of the world, how she may please her husband."   I Cor. 7:34

Looking at these two passages, it appears that Paul is thoroughly democratic in his ideal of virginity for both male and female, yet there is a strange contradiction inherent in his teachings which command that women place themselves in willing subjection to their husbands as their "heads." First Paul extols the freedom of the female virgin to serve her Lord alone as the reason for her virginity; then he commands married women to abdicate such freedom within the institution of marriage by acceding to their husbands as lord and master. This leaves a woman in marriage bound to her husband's pleasure whether she desires it or not. In short, Paul's theological reasoning as to the motivations for the virgin life for woman is not based on reality and is indeed punitive towards the married woman, but not toward the married male. And who says that a married woman or man for that matter, automatically "careth for the things of the world" over the things of the Lord? If such happens to be the case with a woman or a man, Paul slams the door on any possibility for woman to be free of the bond of marriage when he says:

"The wife is bound by the law as long as her husband liveth; but if her husband be dead, she is at liberty to be married to whom she will; only in the Lord." I Cor. 7:39

What about the husband? Is he not bound as long as his wife lives? Paul doesn't deem it necessary to utter the reverse of this situation. Why? Is it because he feels that it need not be said that a man would choose to marry again if his wife dies? There is not one word from Paul on the widower, to be found anywhere. Why? By its very omission the Scriptures expose Paul's bias on the subject of remarriage as punitive to the female.

Paul's bias also shows up in his other remarks about virginity which are a little hazy in some respects but continue the theme of woman in subjection to the decisions of males, whether married or unmarried.

"But if any man think he behaveth himself uncomely towards his virgin, if she pass the flower of her age, and need so require, let him do what he will, he sinneth not: let them marry." I Cor. 7:36

No one has ever agreed as to what Paul meant by, "his virgin" which denotes a connotation of ownership reminiscent of Old Testament chattelism; but whatever the case, we see again the fate of woman utterly dependent upon the decision of the male. Concessions are made for males however, if things get a little sticky for him in this ideal of virginity. Paul makes a gracious way out for an unfortunate male with a problem virgin on his hands who has perhaps succeeded in making him feel guilty about not marrying her. Notice it is the male who decides that "he behaves uncomely towards his virgin." The male always has an out: the woman is always the aggressor:

"Nevertheless he that standeth steadfast in his heart, having no necessity, but hath power over his own will, and hath so decreed in his heart that he will keep his virgin, doeth well." I Cor. 7:37

Keep her for what? Only to prove that he had the will-power to say "no" to a woman? And why is it assumed that a woman need not have to say "no," to a man? Is it an endurance test in which if the male does marry he suffers a kind of defeat even if he does not sin? Paul sums it up:

He who marries doeth well but he who married not doeth better.

What about she who marries doeth well but she who marries not doeth better?

Paul and Widows

Paul's attitude towards widows was punitive and fraught with the old venom of impatience he reserved for women in other areas of life. Permeating his disposal of the widow was his obsession with virginity. It is as though he is saying once out of the marriage trap you had better turn semi-virgin or else!

> "Honor widows that are widows indeed.... Now she that is a
> widow indeed, and desolate, trusteth in God, and contin-
> ueth in supplications and prayers night and day. But she
> that liveth in pleasure is dead while she liveth. And these
> things give in charge, that they may be blameless...Let not
> a widow be taken into the number under three score years
> old, having been the wife of one man, Well reported of for
> good works; if she hath brought up children; if she hath
> lodged strangers; if she hath washed the saints' feet, if she
> hath relieved the afflicted, if she have diligently followed
> every good work.... But...."   I Tim. 5:3-10

We'll get to the "but" later. To begin with, the widow who
lives in pleasure probably means a woman who lives with a
man or might just be happy. Paul considers her "dead" while she
lives. Paul's idea of how a widow's life is to be spent smacks
of masochistic tendencies, "and continueth in supplication and
prayers night and day...." What were the credentials of the
widow accepted into the community's help? Was a widow who
had been married twice rejected or studied by some board of
inquiry which must delve into her past life to see if she
measured up to Paul's idea of a "good woman?" Who can recall
Jesus ever asking for credentials of any kind from any person
before he freely gave them their need? Paul had apparently
missed the story of the Good Samaritan. Paul is a petty legalist.
He raised the roof with the Galatian congregation whom he
tonguelashed for attempting to straddle law and grace.

His directives to younger widows is even less charitable in
thought and tone:

> "But younger widows refuse: for when they have begun to
> wax wanton against Christ, they will marry; having dam-
> nation because they have cast off their first faith. And
> withal they learn to be idle, wandering about from house
> to house; and not only idle, but tattlers also busybodies,
> speaking things which they ought not."   I Tim. 5:11-13

What a poor assessment of women! He is willing to damn their souls to hell for "waxing wanton against Christ" if they remarry. Paul's enmity towards woman bristles in this shameful arrogance:

> "I will therefore that the younger women marry, bear children, guide the house, give none occasion to the adversary to speak reproachfully." I Tim. 5:14

What adversary would Paul need but his own malice? He gives with the right hand and takes with the left. First he damns them for marrying, then suggests that they do, not for any better reason than to keep out of trouble so that the "neighbors won't talk." Have you noticed there is nothing written about or to widowers?

To sum up Paul's attitudes and teachings towards widowhood let it be said that his own words condemn him:

> "Let nothing be done through strife or vainglory; but in lowliness of mind let each esteem other better than themselves." Phil. 2:3

Paul strives with woman and hardly with lowliness of mind.

Paul's Order of Creation and Woman

The serpent ever cautious, and always knowing what was in man, has used against the woman one weapon with a consistency above all others. The final card up his silver sleeve has always been *shame*. Paul, when pressed into a theological corner by his own words flips the ultimate card. The continued subjection of the woman.

> "Let your women keep silence in the churches: for it is not permitted unto them to speak; but they are commanded to be under obedience, as also saith the law. And if they will

> learn anything, let them ask their husbands at home; for it is a *shame*[2] for women to speak in the church. What? Came the word of God out from you? or came it unto you only?
>
> I Cor. 14:34-36

Why is it "a shame for women to speak in the church?" Could it be because woman might show herself to know more than males? The assumption here is that the male is naturally endowed by reason of his genitals with a superior spiritual perception with which he must lead the frail and sin-prone woman. The most blatant contradiction in this command to silence is Paul's appeal to the law. He has twice placed the woman back under the law in regards to marriage. How then do we explain his passionate outburst to the Galatian congregation that they abandon their hypocritical efforts to straddle the law of Moses and the new law of grace which Christ had instituted? Listen to what he says to the Galatians:

> "O foolish Galatians, who hath bewitched you, that ye should not obey the truth....This only would I learn of you, Received ye the Spirit by the works of the law, or by the hearing of faith? Are ye so foolish? having begun in the Spirit, are ye now made perfect by the flesh? Have ye suffered so many things in vain? if it be yet in vain. He, therefore that ministereth to you the Spirit, and worketh miracles among you, doeth he it by the works of the law, or by the hearing of faith?"
>
> Gal. 3:1-5

The next few chapters are a laborious exposition of the absolutely vital necessity of the Galatians to refrain from going back under the law if they are to be in Christ. Paul never appeals directly to the law as a weapon in any other area throughout the whole of his writings, except when he is dealing with women. Why? Because, as he quotes to the Galatians:

---

[2] Author's italics.

Cursed is everyone that continueth not in all things which are written in the book of the law to do them." And woman Paul placed under the same old curse of Eden and the ancient enmity. See what he says to his protege, Timothy:

> "Let the woman learn in silence with all subjection. But I suffer not a woman to teach, nor to usurp authority over the man, but to be in silence." I Tim. 2:11, 12

This is one of the most flagrant contradictions of Paul's teachings. Woman's so-called "sin" must never be forgiven nor forgotten. Her subjection is to be an eternal prison; a cosmic criminal.

The authority Paul refers to as belonging to males is nowhere stated in the Scriptures. Where did the tradition of male authority come from? Not from the true God who is male and female. Would a woman teaching in the church rise above a male? Is there no possibility that she would be simply raised to equality with males? And why does Paul assume woman would usurp authority? Is male ability so vulnerable to the light of honest appraisal that it must live in such fear of challenge as to smite to silence those who might question the competency of such authority?

Modern male clergymen have softened the hysteria of this command to silence and unquestioning acceptance of male rule, by appealing to the necessity of an "order" of command. In true hypocritical style, the age-old denial of the only proper order: that based on ability, regardless of sex, is taken up by those who should be the first to topple it to oblivion—but then, the church is male-dominated. Here is the basis of Paul's conclusions about authority:

> "For Adam was first formed, then Eve. And Adam was not deceived, but the woman being deceived was in the transgression." I Tim. 2:13, 14

If such is the case why did superior Adam go along with

inferior Eve? It appears that Eve had the qualities of leadership rather than Adam, since she instigated and led him. His doltish consent makes him far more dangerous. As for deception, was it not deception that led Paul to systematically slaughter Christians before his conversion to Christ? Paul accepts total forgiveness for his many crimes of murder but withholds thousands of years of forgiveness from woman for one supposed mistake in which her mate acted willingly as accomplice. How long will Christians accept his drivel as Christianity? Duplicity and hypocrisies will out in the day of judgment. Paul will answer for this, as will all who preach one thing and do another.

> "But I would have you know, that the head of every man is Christ; and the head of the woman is the man; and the head of Christ is God. Every man praying or prophesying, having his head covered, dishonoreth his head. But every woman that prayeth or prophesieth with her head un-uncovered dishonoreth her head: for that is even all one as if she were shaven. For if the woman be not covered, let her also be shorn: but if it be a shame for a woman to be shorn or shaven, let her be covered."   I Cor. 11:3-6

Now here is where Eve gets decapitated so as to hand over her head (her intellect), intelligence, and spiritual discernment to Adam. Woman has been rendered totally harmless, for what was once a whole woman has become a mindless womb. To further disfigure her body, or the memory of it, Paul suggests that her head be shaved. Have we begun to get some insights into the violence of the hatred of woman? Do we hear faint echoes of Babylon and is that blinding flash the blaze of sun-god Marduk's knife reflecting its own light as he once again poises it above the great female body for the murderous slash? Recall Deuteronomy of the Old Testament in which Moses legislated the shaving of woman's head!

> "When thou goest forth to war...and thou hast taken

captive....And seest among the captives a beautiful woman,
and hast a desire unto her, that thou wouldst have her to
thy wife; then shalt thou bring her home to thine house;
and she shall shave her head, and pare her nails;"

Deut. 21:10-12

Shame and humiliation are still the province of woman in the
Gospel of Paul and his references to the shaving of woman's
head is cruel and demeaning to them. Is the shame of woman
necessary to Paul in his own fantasies about sexual pleasure?
Modern medicine has given us deep insights into this neurosis.
He defends his argument by making an appeal to nature as infallible teacher, to support his claims:

"Judge in yourselves: is it comely that a woman pray unto
God uncovered? Doth not even nature itself teach·you,
that, if a man have long hair, it is a shame unto him? But if
a woman have long hair, it is a glory to her: for her hair is
given her for a covering." I Cor. 11:13-15

If, by his allusion to nature, Paul is appealing to nature's
lessons on maleness and femaleness as being universally expressed, then he is simply a man who does not know what he is
talking about. Nature teaches that in the animal as well as insect
world, femaleness is very often possessed of superior qualities
over Paul's idea of maleness. In the feline species the male
neither hunts as a rule, nor defends the pride. Both these
functions are the province of the female who needs the male
only sexually in order to bear the litter. The male lion's
existence is almost parasitic upon the female. Is this why Adam
named this species feline? Why then is Jesus called the "lion out
of the tribe of Judah?" Why then, in the book of Revelation are
we told the lamb comes back as the lion?

The queen bee is the center of the society, served and catered
to by males who, after having mated with her, are pushed out
of the hive to die. The other males and females in the society
work as gatherers of food. There are also many species in the

bird world where the analogy is the same. The references to
Jesus as being leonine more than support my contention that
Paul made a serious error in his appeal to the natural order as
expressed in the animate creation to support the "divine" order
of man.

Paul's imagery which resorts to the shaving of the woman's
head, is crude and arbitrary and explains more and more why
he found himself, as no other Apostle had found himself, in
serious trouble with the Corinthian congregation and others. In
relating woman's hair to her glory than re-relating it to a covering for shame, Paul is contradictory. Paul never dwells on what
the glory of the woman is. In fact he calls woman the glory of
man:

> "But I would have you know, that the head of every man is
> Christ; and the head of the woman is the man; and the
> head of Christ is God.... For a man indeed ought not to
> cover his head, forasmuch as he is the image and glory of
> God: but the woman is the glory of the man." I Cor. 11:3, 7

Observe in Paul's order woman is defined only in relation to
males. Paul thrusts males between the woman and her God
cutting her off from any direct route to God. Only males and
the male God are permitted glory.

Last but not least, we see Paul drive the last nail in the coffin
of woman in his epistle to Timothy:

> "In like manner also, that women adorn themselves in
> modest apparel, with shamefacedness and sobriety; not
> with braided hair, or gold, or pearls, or costly array; But
> (which becometh women professing godliness) with good
> works."   I Tim. 2:9,10

> "Notwithstanding she shall be saved in childbearing, if they
> continue in faith and charity and holiness with sobriety."
> I Tim. 2:15

Will we ever get out of the bedroom? Question: what about women who are virgins? How do they get saved? What about the married woman who is barren? What about the unwed mother who is child-bearing? We could go on and on, testing Paul's theology of woman chained to the bedpost.

But rather, let us consider an earnest challenge to the great Apostle:

> "...the eye cannot say unto the hand, I have no need of thee: nor again the head to the feet, I have no need of you. Nay, much more those members of the body, which seem to be more feeble, are necessary; and those members of the body, which we think to be less honorable, upon these we bestow the more abundant honor; and our uncomely parts have more abundant comeliness...but God hath tempered the body together, having given more abundant honor to that part which lacked...."   I Cor. 12:21-24

Like Moses, Paul did not practice what he preached. Who in the body could occupy a lesser position than she who is commanded to silence? Who in the entire world, in or out of the church, is so abject as woman whose only claim to glory is a hank of hair to cover her eternal shame? There are so many more contradictions in the theology of Paul in regard to woman in the church, in relation to man and to Christ, that they cannot be covered here. Suffice it to say Paul was undoubtedly a man in deep conflict about his sexuality.

One of the strangest things about Paul's fixed, authoritative theology of woman, is that he never mentions the Virgin birth. Indeed Luke and Matthew are the only two disciples who walked with Jesus who troubled to record the events that surround the birth of Jesus. Paul had every reason to use this as a persuasion in his teachings to the Romans and the Greeks, since they both had traditions that super-human persons had super-natural origins. Why didn't he use this as a theological weapon? Because he was wrapped in the shimmering coils of male pride, which blundered and blustered in theological sour grapes at the fact that woman had given birth to the Messiah, and in a manner that by-passed males completely. Watch what the serpent, petulant but powerful, substitutes for the Virgin birth: Jesus was "made of the seed of David."   Romans 1:3 To be sure, Mary was of the house of David, but Paul's own Jewish Scriptures state that the seed of the woman would bruise the head of the serpent, in Genesis:

> "And I will put enmity...between thy seed and her seed..."
> Gen. 3:15

This was the first prophecy about Jesus in the Scriptures. There is no excuse for Paul to have overlooked this. Paul was promoting the male God, made in male image, and in doing so he must have sown considerable confusion within the early infant church, since his epistle was written before some of the gospels had even been written. Was there a communication gap between those who had written accounts of the Virgin birth, (Matthew and Luke) and Paul? In view of the later difficulties that arose in the church as to the authenticity of the Virgin birth which poses problems for branches of Christendom this day, Paul, by ignoring it with ceremonious neglect, makes his major contribution. In calling Jesus the "seed of David," he is attempting to reinstate the male God in the area where he had been clearly deposed. It was particularly patriarchal, hence male, to by-pass Mary and restore the prominent male position to the carefully charted geneological records of the Jewish religion. Paul, as every Jewish male goaded by a punctured ego, had a lot to lose by acknowledgement of the Virgin birth, for this event scooped woman out from under the male ego and raised her to equality with males.

While Jesus himself stressed the necessity of faith in every walk of his earthly ministry, Paul seems to exclude the free exercise of faith in the area of marriage and woman in general. Either faith is limitless to all, or it is unavailable to all. Yet Paul sets limits for women in the strangest of ways, by appealing to the law.

Marriage is a bond. Marriage is a legal institution, and according to Paul only woman is "bound" in marriage. Back again to Paul and the law:

> "Know ye not, brethren, (for I speak to them that know the law) how that the law hath dominion over a man as long as he liveth? For the woman which hath a husband is bound by the law to her husband so long as he liveth; but if the husband be dead, she is loosed from the law of her husband. So then if, while her husband liveth, she be married to another man, she shall be called an adulteress: but if her husband be dead, she is free from that law; so that she is no adulteress, though she be married to another man.
> Wherefore, my brethren, ye also are become dead to the law by the body of Christ; that ye should be married to another...."   Rom. 7:1-4

Paul uses the analogy of marriage as bonds for woman, and the law itself as bonds for males and females. Yet he says males may come out from the bondage of the law in Christ. In other words, males may be freed from the law. How then do we reconcile Paul's tirade against women who marry after being widowed, where he consigns them to damnation if they re-marry? This conflicts with the above Scripture pertaining to woman in the bonds of marriage. Apparently marriage is a slavery under the law for woman, but not for man who is freed from the law in Christ. That being the case, once the married man is free from the law, his wife is also freed from him! Not so, says Paul. If her husband, though freed from the law while he is alive, lives, she is bound under law to him who is free while yet alive, to be freed only at his death and that to widowhood or damnation.

Now to further confusion in Paul's theology:

> "There is neither Jew nor Greek, there is neither bond nor free, there is neither male nor female: for ye are all one in Christ Jesus."   Gal. 3:26

After making all these differentiations between male and female, freeing the male in or out of marriage from the law, placing the woman back under the law in marriage twice bound to law and husband, allowing for no divorce, no remarriage, he then says there is no male or female in Jesus Christ. In other words, there is no inequality of the sexes in Jesus Christ. Then what is it to be in Christ?

To be in Christ, female version is, as Paul wrote to Timothy:

> "Let the woman learn in silence with all subjection. But I suffer not a woman to teach, nor to usurp authority over the man, but to be in silence."   I Tim. 2:11,12

Confusion again. Paul started out by setting this silence over married women who were to learn "at home" from their husbands. Here he makes no qualifications as to married or unmarried, married or virgin. So it is not just the married woman who is bound under the law of their husbands, it is every woman bound by every man who is not bound by the law himself. Is teaching in the church automatically usurping authority over the male? Could Paul have made no room for equality in women teaching? Silence is total subjection, and this command is not a safeguard against usurpation of authority; it is out and out enslavement. Once Paul has silenced her, slapped back under the law, anything goes. Here is the most flagrant corruption of the Christian faith that this teaching admits: males are placed between females and Christ. It cuts a woman off from direct approach to Jesus Christ as mediator of all men with God. It is anti-Christ. How Paul gets away with this is a puzzle for it makes Christ's mediatorship a travesty in the case of woman. It makes of woman a sub-human, placing her salvation upon the whims of the males who step between her and her God. Observe however, how the all-male God refuses to take the responsibility for her salvation:

"...whatsoever a man soweth, that shall he also reap."

Gal. 6:7

"...for we shall all stand before the judgment seat of Christ....So then every one of us shall give account of himself to God."

Rom. 14:10, 12

That has to include women or will the males take up the judgment of the silenced women of the Apostle Paul?

The basic tenet of Jesus' teachings was the exercise of faith. Paul, by placing woman under the law in marriage, and under the spiritual authority of a male-dominated church, curtails her privileges of exercising faith to whatever extent she can aspire.

Paul lists heroic examples of faith, and with two exceptions, they are all males.

Abel: offered a better sacrifice to God than Cain. Enoch: was carried to heaven by faith that he would not see death. Noah: who built an ark at God's warning and saved his family. Abraham: who left his homeland at God's command and offered his son, Isaac. Isaac: who by faith blessed Jacob. Jacob: who blessed the sons of Joseph by faith. Joseph: who mentioned the departing of the children of Israel by faith. Moses: who dealt with Pharaoh and received the Ten Commandments, etc...Gideon, Barak, Samson, David and Samuel: who "stopped the mouths of lions, subdued kingdoms, wrought righteousness, obtained promises...etc."

He finishes up the list with a grand poetic hymn of heroic praise:

"They were stoned, they were sawn asunder, were tempted, were slain with sword: they wandered about in sheepskins and goatskins; being destitute, afflicted, tormented; (Of whom the world was not worthy:) they wandered in deserts, and in mountains, and in dens and in caves of the earth."

Heb. 11:37,38

The connotation on all these grandiose endurances of hardship and heroic faith is male. And why are they male? Because there was not recorded in the male age (the Old Testament Patriarchal age) the heroism of women. Woman was recorded as only incidental to male exploits. Why did he not add to the illustrious male list the most heroic act of faith ever known to man—the conception of Jesus by the Virgin Mary? Why was Mary so forgettable to Paul? Why, to the list was not that unfortunate Levite concubine listed, who was raped to death by male sex fiends and chopped up in twelve pieces by her male owner? Why was not poor Hagar, the bondslave of Sarah, mentioned, who was thrown out in the desert with her little son with but a small keg of water and a piece of bread?

Among the women Paul included were Sarah: "through faith Sarah, also herself received strength to conceive seed, and was delivered of a child when she was past age because she judged him faithful who had promised." Heb. 11:11 So far so good but watch what he does to swing the focus back to the male hero:

> "Therefore sprang there even of one, and him as good as dead, so many as the stars of the sky in multitude, and as the sand which is by the seashore innumerable." Heb. 11:12

He had to shove Abraham to the foreground, reminding us that it was after all Abraham's male seed that counted.

The next woman is Rahab whose faith saved her from death. Notice Rahab receives something for her faith: personal salvation from death. She does not give as the males are depicted as doing. Males through the exercise of their faith "get things done." Women through the exercise of their faith "receive" things that are done.

The third reference to women in this passage, and the last is: "Women received their dead raised to life again...." Heb. 11:35

Again women receive. This is a strange inclusion under women of faith, since the gospels record a male who received his dead through resurrection in Matthew 9:18, where a certain ruler came to Jesus and said, "My daughter is even now dead:

but come and lay Thy hand upon her, and she shall live."
She was resurrected.

Is Paul scraping the bottom of the barrel in attributing to women the faith that raised their dead? What else could he do? It was most important that he separate the brave deeds of the males he listed from any contribution that the female may have made. All Paul had left was Sarah, who he is quick to point out, "received strength," to conceive, to whose deed he throws in the accomplishment of her partner Abraham. The woman shares the billing with the male in this case of active faith. In the other two references to women's faith it is not necessary to do so since they received passively from the hands of males.

One gets the impression that Paul is desperately defending males whom he believes need defending in view of the female principle's powerful creative nature. After all, when males are compared to females, what can males offer by way of superiority, in fact rather than fancy? Men die. So do women. Intellectually women are not inferior. Madame Curie is the only human being to receive the Nobel Prize twice, and she was married and gave birth to a daughter who worked with her. The sex act is pure pleasure for the male. It results in his having to support the wife and child. Woman may share equally in the pleasure of the sex act, but it results for her in confinement and the pain of birth of the child. Woman works as hard and as long as man, nurturing the child, and caring for her home and her husband. So long as woman continues to bear the children males will find it vital to the preservation of the male ego to close every other area of true creative active participation in the world's work to those who threaten his ego most: woman.

This perhaps explains the chronic frenzy of male theology of the third and fourth centuries, and Paul himself, in attempting to balance the scales between the powers and contributions of both sexes which tip heavily in favor of the female. Paul, like the patriarchs, cuts off his nose to spite his face when he, once again, relegates woman to her salvation through child-bearing:

"Notwithstanding she shall be saved in childbearing, if they
continue in faith and charity and holiness with sobriety."
I Tim. 2:15

By enslaving her to her traditional role, Paul enslaved himself
to his own self-made prison of jealousy and pride, which is at
the root of the Edenic enmity.

Taking theological swipes at Paul is a dangerous business in
the church. To the church, afflicted as she is with biblicism,
making of the Bible an object of idolatrous worship, we tread
dangerous ground. Man's tendency has always been to settle
down comfortably into a new truth as an inspired virgin, and
worship her pristine light as coming from a fixed eternal star.
She ultimately ages to a harlot; set in her ways and in love with
her ease, battling the wrinkles of time, to the neglect of her soul
within her. Just as change is the harlot's greatest enemy, so is
change the enemy of male idolatry within the church that
worships this present age of "grace" as the "be-all and end-all"
of the ages to come. Yet the Bible itself warns that the end of
this age will be of such cataclysmic proportions, in the physical
and spiritual world of ideas, that it should not be as difficult to
accept the explosion of Paul's star.

How do we reconcile Paul's error with the divine inspiration
of the Scriptures? First of all we cleave to its author as the
Creator. If we concede that purpose is indigenous to creation,
then we must allow for ordered steps as the dynamic of the
creative *process*. Paul, like Moses, was an ordered step.

We wince at the morality of the Old Testament mentality, are
repulsed by the harshness and violence of the jealous Jehovah.
We have marveled at the naivete of the male conception of
God: Samson, striding towards God by way of infantile political gyrations, bringing death and destruction to animal and
man; egocentric Abraham plunging to the very brink of murder
of his beloved son, in an act of faith; David, seducer, adulterer,
murderer and liar and destroyer of the life of innocent Bathsheba, more playboy than hero; Jacob, expert of opportunism,
cheating his way through life and wrestling with an angel to get

a blessing, again, more huckster than hero; Elisha and the bears and Moses, hypocrite but "anointed of God," excusing himself from his own ordinances and heaping upon himself the distinct honor of introducing to the "people of God," human slavery, legalized pimping and prostitution as well as the double standard—all these must be reconciled with a good God. There is no reconciliation outside of the acceptance of a God who is in *process*. Such is the humility man is called to.

We could call the Old Testament epoch a rampage of innocence if there were not one inescapable factor that forbids it: the subjection of the woman. The male principle is an ordering power. Only males ordered the revelation of God to the males of Moses' era, woman was silent. As is usual after each revelation of God to man, man, through exercise of his free will, develops or interprets that literal dispensing of knowledge in his own way. At the point that the revelation is made, man is innocent. But from there on, innocence becomes culpable as ignorance, due man's hard-heartedness and sin. By excluding the female principle, which could guide him, he must bear the responsibility for most of the agony of mankind's odysseys into error. Woman's culpability is her abject passivity in allowing males to cow her by threats, intimidations, and Babylonian blandishments, which not only permit the disobedience of the male but worship him as he indulges in it.

Moses' age was a male age. The male principle brought its heel down hard upon the neck of the female principle. So, we read and wince but do not wonder, for we know the "mystery of iniquity" that has been at work since the Edenic expulsion. Moses' sun set. Jesus' rose and was eclipsed by Paul's, who took up the cudgel from Moses. Jehovah dispensed to man once more, this time coming to men in flesh in the person of Jesus. He walked briefly among us, lived, taught, and died at the hands of the male leaders who expected a Messiah armed with the jawbone of an ass, or a Joshua with a blaring trumpet. He came more as a woman than a man. Jesus was the embodiment of a female pentecost. He came to introduce the male god to his female half. Jesus' age was feminine. It flashed and was gone, as

Jehovah's finger of fire had flashed on Mount Sinai upon the stone tablets, then left. As Moses strode down his mountain, Paul too, strode down his, clutching to his breast the new stones of a new male age.

The transition between the two ages was traumatic, to say the least. In the male patriarchal age, a male believed he could sacrifice all other men to his own ends, in his expression of faith towards God.

However, in the new age, Jesus taught men that one man must sacrifice *himself* to all other men, as his expression of faith towards God. It was diametrically opposed to the male age. It was female.

A reconciliation was necessary. The tree of life stands, as the tree of good and evil, in the middle of the garden. The truth lies somewhere in the middle. Only a creative act can make the reconciliation. Paul, in spite of his proclivity to sin, had the courage and faith to make it. For that we love him, in spite of the agony he helped bring upon woman.

Paul was a bridge builder between the male God and the female God. The uniqueness of his ministry depended, in large part, upon his Jewish maleness. Jesus had plunged the all-male God from the hot water of the patriarchal pride, to the cold water of matriarchal humility. Paul scooped the shocked male out of the icy cold and gave him new fig leaves to cover his nakedness.

To cling, as the male dominated church does, to the Gospel of Paul rather than the Gospel of Jesus is the grossest idolatry of this age, at its close.

Actually, Paul was a thirteenth wheel, so to speak. After the death of Judas, the apostles drew straws to replace him and the lot fell to Matthias. Motivated by typical male adulation of Paul, some Bible scholars have tried to place Paul among the twelve. Acts 1:26, shatters this delusion. Paul was selected as "devil's advocate" in the Edenic issue; commanding women to silence and placing them under subjection to male pride so that, by way of the evil, they would learn the good. Just as the early Jews were commanded to evil by Moses, so too were women commanded by evil by Paul. The disciples were not immune to deception, before or after Pentecost.

Before Pentecost, Peter was satanically inspired to insist that he would not allow Jesus to die. Jesus said to Peter:

> "...Get thee behind me Satan: thou art an offense unto me: for thou savorest not the things that be of God, but those that be of men." Matt. 16:23

On another occasion he said to Peter:

> "...Simon, Simon, behold, Satan hath desired to have you, that he may sift you as wheat: But I have prayed for thee...." Luke 22:31

After Pentecost, Paul had a falling out with Barnabas about the young Mark. Barnabas wanted Mark to accompany them to Cyprus, but Paul preferred Silas as their aide.

So, Paul set out to bridge a chasm, 2000 years ago. The chasm he confronted from without was no less formidable than the chasm he confronted within, for it was difficult for Paul to make all the reconciliations between male and female that he knew must be made. We hear a pathetic cry from him:

> "I find then a law, that, when I would do good, evil is present with me. For I delight in the law of God after the inward man: But I see another law in my members, warring against the law of my mind, and bringing me into captivity to the law of sin which is in my members O wretched man that I am! who shall deliver me from the body of this death?" Rom. 7:21-24

For Paul, the Female Pentecost would be a crucifixion of the male ego. Males would undergo the rod that had been laid to the back of woman. Like the all-male God of his inherited religion, Paul had built his superiority upon the inferior sands of his victim. Where would the male ego now take its heroic fantasies of conquest? Where would he now sink his knife?

In the two Gospel accounts of Matthew and Luke, the Creator begins the great humbling process, when He carefully records, through the births of Jesus and John the Baptist, that the male God had played no part in the siring of the Messiah.

The peace of man's religious Eden once more would totter on the brink of a new catastrophe. Moses, like Adam, content to "dress and keep" the Patriarchal Garden, had wrapped himself in an old innocence. But the woman had grown discontent with the cascades of mystery that once again laved her soul with the sweet "waters" of the need to know. The woman wondered, pondered, dared and reached out once more, to pluck the fruit that would signal a new thrust from an old womb.

Though Moses had primped and pampered the patriarchal landscape to perfect linear symmetry of the law, the woman sat among the wild untrimmed saplings at the outskirts of the sanctuary and dreamed a dream. The peace of Moses' paradise was about to be shattered in a new chaos. The Virgin was coming. Moses' and Paul's Garden would go wild with advent of the Virgin.

Who is she, this virgin mother of Jesus? Catholics call her "The Mother of God" and contrary to their denials, they have worshipped her with a devotion at times more passionate than that reserved for Jesus. Artists, musicians, sculptors, philosophers and theologians have drawn and drunk from the endless wells of her inspirational waters to produce some of mankind's most profound and beautiful works of art and literature. She has borne all manner of titles, "Queen of Heaven, Queen of Sorrow, Virgin Queen, Mother of God." Her virgin purity has been discussed and argued throughout the religious and secular worlds, with both derision and honor. She has attracted the faithful with the warmth of her human suffering, and repelled them by the remoteness of her sanctity. She is the only woman of prominence in the Bible, with the exception of Eve, and unlike Eve, she has been a mystery to be persistently probed.

The mysteries of Mary have risen like a tower of Babylonian confusion equaled only by the ziggurats of confusion that males have erected to Eve. The Catholic Church has been the repository of the myths of "The Blessed Virgin Mary" out of whose cumbersome masonry the faithful have chiseled and chipped the thousands of statues and grottoes to her honor that punctuate the highways and by-ways of the planet.

Writing this chapter it seemed prophetic to me that Pope Paul issued a document calling for increased devotion to the Virgin Mary, declaring that such action is fully in keeping with the modern women's rights movement, and the search for Christian unity. In this new major exposition of the Virgin's role, the Pope said, "The modern woman will note with pleasant surprise that Mary of Nazareth, while completely devoted to the will of God, was far from being a timidly submissive woman or one whose piety was repellent to others." In a 30,000 worded document entitled, "Marialis Cultus," or Marian Devotion, the Pope described the Virgin as the "new woman, one whose example supports the liberating energies now in motion in the world."

"Mary," he says, "fully and responsibly accepted the will of God, because she heard the word of God and acted upon it and because charity and a spirit of service were the driving forces of her actions."

It is a persistently strange phenomenon that males have always made pronouncements after the fact, as though the startling new idea has come to them and them alone. This liberation of the Virgin Mary has not been won by males for women. It has been fought for and won by women, in spite of males.

Eve and Mary. Eve; innocent until disobedience plunges her and her companion into the godsome burden of the knowledge of good and evil, resulting in sin and death and Mary; not innocent, but obedient, birthing through the instrumentality of her human body, the male child Jesus. Two women seeming opposites, who are poles apart, and different as day from night. But are they?

Between the so-called seduction of Eve in the Garden and impregnation of Mary by the Holy Ghost, there lies some 4000 years of law and blood sacrifice of the age of Moses, where the male principle had prostrated the female principle beneath the heel of pride. Eve was woman, to be feared and controlled. Mary was she who conceived "immaculate." Eve was woman whose body was "used" as a tool by males for procreation through force and law. Mary was woman whose body was used as a tool for procreation through spirit and obedience.

How do they differ? Mary the virgin, introduces a new concept to the world. In the ancient Babylonian and Sumerian creation accounts, which support in principle the Genesis accounts, the great female dragon, Tiamat, is slain by the heroic male sun-god Marduk. Tiamat's great fish body is taken by force of violence and hate; ripped open, flung heaven- and earthward and reordered to a new creation. The story of the Levite concubine in the Book of Judges, is an allegory on this Babylonian slaughter of the female, who was raped to death by a pack of homosexual males, who desire to "know" her Lord, the Levite priest. The Levite priest hacks her dead body into twelve parts and sends them to all the tribes of Israel as proof of the "lewdness and folly" in Israel. Is it difficult to see Eve as the prototype of the Levite concubine, or as Tiamat? The use of woman's body as the raw material of creation is rooted in the Genesis accounts as well. But what have we in the Virgin birth? We see the same drama, only the cast is different and the script rewritten to take the violence out. Woman, in the person of Mary, is still the ancient Tiamat. Gabriel is the new Marduk. Instead of slaying her with a knife, Gabriel asks if, by her own consent, she will allow her body to be used as the raw materials to create the new male: Jesus. Mary submits or agrees willingly and we have another "Incarnation." Something else is introduced to man in the advent of the Virgin. We have for the first time a female myth or conception of an ideal male formed by the female! Previously myths had been formed by males about females. Here we see the reverse. This was Mary's Immaculate Conception." Like Jehovah's immaculate conception, Mary's Immaculate Conception of the finished product of the ideal male was Jesus. Like Jehovah, Mary made a sweeping original conception but in the process of the actual creative steps involved, there would be a long, hard road of suffering, trial and error, and thousands of years of slow development before the ideal was realized. The "Immaculate Conception" of Mary was the *female genesis.* The all-male God has at last learned humility and forsaken his weapons of murder and rape. Goodbye, Marduk! Hello, Gabriel!

Yet males have been slow to learn. They cling to the old concepts of violence and force we see today on a planet on the brink of destruction, by a male principle still on the rampage.

To Eve came the shimmering serpent. To Mary came the shimmering Gabriel. Two women hear and act upon what they hear in belief. The results? Trouble and sorrow for both. Eve saw death and sin enter the world. Mary saw her son crucified upon the cross. But there the similarity ends; for there was a marked difference between the two and that difference was in the conscience of each. To Eve, conscience brought shame, suffering, and punishment which rendered her passive to the abuse that would be heaped upon her. But to Mary, conscience brought blessing and approval and the glory her activism would shower upon her. When Jehovah pardoned and blessed Eve by making her His chosen adversary to the serpent, she flunked out because she didn't realize she had been pardoned. In short, her faith in the rightness of her course failed her. But Mary knew the rightness of her course, and her faith stood strong against all male opposition. Blessing or curse? Both women chose. Now a pattern emerges. Two women, each taking crucial steps for mankind and thereby changing the course of his life condition, history and relationship to his God. If we can free our minds from our obsessive preoccupation with the sin-factor in Eve's act, we will realize that Eve, by taking the portentous step, seized for herself the office of instigator. Mary did the same. But popular theology cringes at the use of the word "instigator," as applied to Mary. Eve; yes, but Mary was no instigator, meaning troublemaker. To Mary we have chosen to impute all that is uplifting and ennobling. We accord her the office of "inspirer." Therefore, Eve earns our anger and suspicion, while Mary gets our reverence and honor. Yet they both "initiated." However we look at them, they have this in common; that of being prime or first mover of man into any new creation or revelation of the living God.

Both women opened a new dispensation or age of revelation for man. Eve's was the age of the law of Moses, Ten Commandments, where the male principle dominated. Mary's age was the age of the spirit expressed in what can be called basically female qualities of love, mercy, compassion, etc. making her age female in principle. Eve: male. Mary: female. Polarity. If we can ignore Eve's sin, and examine the expressions of the two spirits of the ages, we see how they fall into the plan of creation.

The law must be interpreted by the spirit of love. The law is fulfilled by the spirit of love by giving it life. Therefore the spirit, like the law, is good. If Eve is the law and Mary the spirit, then Mary fulfills Eve, and Eve is Mary's reason for fulfilling. What we have here is not a ladder of descending power as Paul saw it, with God at the top of the ladder, and Christ below Him, and the male below Christ, and the woman below the male, and nobody under her. What we have is a circle, for if we bend Paul's ladder back to the Creator, God, in a cycle of endless procreation and life we have to come full circle through the use of the woman's body, again by God, to initiate that creation.

Getting back to Eve and Mary, since both the law and the spirit were good in that they contributed to the creative purposes of God, then we can absolve Eve for her so-called "disobedience" in Eden, and support again our contention that in so doing, Eve acted as the Creator had hoped she would. With this vindication of her we can scrap all that is evil and worthy of death and banishment. Eve's age served God's creative purposes, and Mary's age did the same. They are the same woman.

Eve is man's sinful earthly viewpoint of woman and woman's sinful, earthy viewpoint of herself, while Mary is the true God's heavenly viewpoint of the same woman, yet it remains for males to catch this viewpoint, clinging as they do to the ancient distrust of Eve; the "cursed" of God doomed to become, as Genesis states it, "mother of all living."

Males have missed the point of Mary because their concept of the lopsided all-male God has made it inevitable that they would. Only this can explain the rejection of Jesus, who embodied all the female qualities hitherto suppressed in the age that preceded him. It also explains the persistence with which male theologians of the third and fourth centuries continued the rampage of male superiority which continued to reject woman's archetype in the person of Mary. Just as the Jews rejected Jesus,

Christian males rejected Mary, relegating her to a position of being purely a "historical virgin," one of a kind, over and above all women.

When they killed Jesus they were, in effect, slaying the ancient Tiamat again. Male Christendom took up the gauntlet and continued the battle. Willful insanity? Yes. Just to make sure that males cannot again usurp the balance the Creator wishes to attain between the male and female principles, he has given us, in the two accounts of the births of Jesus and John the Baptist, a "fail-safe" proof that it was his intention that males have nothing to do with the birth of the Messiah.

THE BIRTH OF JOHN THE BAPTIST

"There was in the days of Herod...a certain priest named Zechariah, of the course of Abijah: and his wife was of the daughters of Aaron, and her name was Elisabeth. And they were both righteous before God, walking in all the commandments and ordinances of the Lord, blameless. And they had no child, because that Elisabeth was barren; and they both were now well stricken in years.

And it came to pass, that, while he executed the priest's office...there appeared unto him an angel of the Lord standing on the right side of the altar of incense. And when Zechariah saw him, he was troubled and fear fell upon him. But the angel said unto him, Fear not, Zechariah, for thy prayer is heard; and thy wife Elisabeth shall bear thee a son, and thou shalt call his name John....And he shall go before him [the Lord] in the spirit and power of Elijah, to turn the hearts of the fathers to the children, and the disobedient to the wisdom of the just: to make ready a people prepared for the Lord. And Zechariah said unto the angel, Whereby shall I know this? for I am an old man, and my wife well stricken in years. And the angel answering him said, I am Gabriel, that stand in the presence of God; and am sent to speak unto thee, and to show thee the glad tidings. And, behold, thou shalt be dumb and not able to speak, until the day that these things shall be performed, because thou believest not my words, which shall be fulfilled in their season." Luke 1:5-20

THE BIRTH OF JESUS

"And in the sixth month the angel Gabriel was sent from God unto a city of Galilee, named Nazareth, To a virgin espoused to a man whose name was Joseph, of the house of David; and the virgin's name was Mary. And the angel came in unto her, and said, Hail, thou that art highly favored, the Lord is with thee: blessed art thou amongst women. And when she saw him, she was troubled at his saying, and cast in her mind what manner of salutation this should be. And the angel said unto her, Fear not, Mary: for thou hast found favor with God. And, behold, thou shalt conceive in thy womb, and bring forth a son, and shalt call his name Jesus. He shall be great, and shall be called the Son of the Highest; and the Lord God shall give unto him the throne of his father David: and he shall reign over the house of Jacob forever; and of his kingdom there shall be no end. Then said Mary unto the angel, How shall this be, seeing I know not a man? And the angel answered and said unto her, the Holy Ghost shall come upon thee, and the power of the Highest shall overshadow thee: therefore also that holy thing which shall be born of thee shall be called the Son of God.

And, behold, thy cousin Elisabeth, she hath also conceived a son in her old age; and this is the sixth month with her, who was called barren. For with God nothing shall be impossible.

"And Mary said, Behold the handmaid of the Lord; be it unto me according to thy word. And the angel departed from her." Luke 1:26-38

In both these events the Archangel Gabriel is sent. In both cases he makes an announcement of great import to the two individuals. The announcement to both is identical: both will have a male child born to them who will be a great servant of God. The news is received with fear and joy by both Zechariah and Mary. There the similarity ends. What was the parting of the ways between them? Mary, though she feared, *believed*. In Zechariah's case, the news is received in fear but the Scripture says he did not believe. Because he did not believe, Zechariah is struck dumb. In other words, he does not tell anyone else, not even his wife Elisabeth, who would conceive and bear the child. Woman is not privy to God's working with the male. Let's look at what the book tells us about Elisabeth's reaction to her miraculous and unexpected pregnancy.

> "And after those days his wife Elisabeth conceived, and hid herself five months, saying, Thus hath the Lord dealt with me in the days therein he looked on me, to take away my reproach among men."   Luke 1:24,25

These remarks stand in sharp contrast to Mary's position. What Elisabeth says in essence is, God has restored her to favor with men or with her husband. It was God who told Eve that having eaten of the tree, "your desire will be *to your husband*, and he will Lord it over you." Elisabeth's desire was for *men*, not for God. Elisabeth is really another archetype of Eve. The woman of the law; the woman of the old dispensation, where males ruled females with the iron fist. Elisabeth related to God only through her husband.

Mary, the Scripture says, believed God. Let's take up what was involved for Mary in this transaction with God. There were her parents and relatives to be faced and most of all, Joseph! The angel had said nothing to Mary about his intended appearance to Joseph in a dream, where he would explain the truth of her condition. For Mary it was enough that the angel said, "fear not." The leaders of the synagogue rushed through her mind; the townspeople who would think her an adulteress! The penalty for adultery was death by stoning. Yet her faith was strong and she, in her humility, consented in perfect trust of

God. The child was conceived. But how did she discern who it was that spoke to her? By what name or power did she test the spirit of the voice that spoke to her? She could not have used the name of Jesus. All Mary had was her faith in God. But even here she is in dangerous waters. History attested to the fact that women had no spiritual standing before the all-male God. To be sure, there had been heroic women in biblical records, but they had all been greatly eclipsed by male exploits and none had dared to conceive of a Messiah. Actually, Mary was going against her religion, for the God she conceived of would not only go against Moses, but literally dethrone him. For Mary to attribute to God the voice that asked her to give birth to a Messiah who would overthrow the existing scriptures, laws, ordinances of the synagogues, and the priesthood, was a fantastic act of faith. Mary entered a covenant relationship with God in a highly private manner that, like Abraham's sojourn to unfamiliar lands, demanded absolute faith and trust that she was approved and blessed. It demanded that she *believe* that the voice which said, "hail, thou that are highly favored..." was the voice of God. Mary was at odds with the all-male God. Everything conspired against Mary's conclusion that she had not been deceived, as Eve had been deceived. The key to her "blessing and favor" was that she believed. Therefore, the voice could be none other than the voice of God's Gabriel. To the male-dominated woman who places her husband as her "head," such a voice would always be the insidious hissings of a Satanic Devil. To the male-dominated woman such promptings would recall the scriptural accounts of the Edenic expulsion. A cacophony of stern male voices would drown out the dulcet tones of the angel—her husband's voice, Moses,' Paul's, her priest's, her rabbi's, her minister's voice would all rise above the voice of any annunciation of her God to her.

Perhaps more in this way than in any other, we can begin to grasp the portentous risks involved in the great acts of faith for she, who would enter fully into the creative adventure with her God, will always find herself at dangerous odds with the existing order.

Our contention at the beginning of this section was that God was to show males, in the Virgin birth, that woman has been his instrument for initiation and that the serpent pride of male ego has erroneously usurped the divine balance between the male and female principles. The Scriptures present a well documented prosecution of the case in its accounts of two people to whom the angel Gabriel made his announcements. The Scripture plainly says that Zechariah has prayed for a son. In other words, he had asked God for a specific blessing. Like most prayers, it was a selfish prayer:

> "...Fear not Zechariah: for thy prayer is heard; and thy wife Elisabeth shall bear thee a son, and thou shalt call his name John."   Luke 1:13

Observe the reasons the angel had been sent to the two of them. In Zechariah's case it was in answer to a request to God. In Mary's case it was simply that God had selected her. Could it have been that Mary's spirit was so in line with God's desire that He privileged her with the honor of instrumenting the strongest yearnings of her own spirit: a son in the image of God? Is it not a simple deduction that Mary, like all women trapped in the abuse of the female suppression of 3600 years, conceived a new kind of male, willing to surrender the sub-human concept of woman, and a new woman unwilling to submit to it? And does not the obvious reversal of the Baby-lonian concept of the violence that had previously been employed in the use of woman's body indicate that Mary had yearned for a new Marduk?

Why had not the male, Zechariah, found such favor with God? The most important aspect of the advent of the Virgin Mary is that for the first time since Eve, a woman has entered a similar covenant relationship with God. She is "God's friend." Christianity has taken Mary as an historical individual rather than a symbol of woman per se, just as they have divorced Jesus from identification with all males through the semi-anonymity of history. In the theology of the early church fathers, Adam is thought of as having been the perfect "son of God," whom Eve led into sin. In selecting Mary over Zechariah's wife, Elisabeth, (who could have been used) God was leaving nothing to doubt that he was favoring females over males in this issue.

The great pains he takes in recording the accounts of the two births, (Jesus and John the Baptist) is justified in his accurate anticipation of the male-instigated arguments that God would have had to use a woman, no matter what, in the birth of the Messiah. But he did not use ANY woman. The woman he did use was a woman who was not in subjection to any male, who had taken God as her head. The all-male God was by-passed. The Apostle Paul himself would have to conclude that God was at last, in Mary, commanding women to break the yoke of male subjection by dealing directly with God. God was equalizing the sexes; liberating woman!

Zechariah and God dealt directly, and the transaction was unknown to Elisabeth. In Mary's case, the male in her life, Joseph, was not consulted at all. He was not asked if he would consent to his wife being used of God, but was told *after* she had given her consent of her own volition.

Flash back to Eden and re-inspect Eve's act, performed alone, without the knowledge or consent of Adam. Are not the two incidents the same? Does this not prove my premise that Eve acted rightly and in accordance with God's will, losing out only because after she did it, she lost faith? What should have been approval became to her a "curse." Mary is Eve with a second chance, and this time she does not doubt the rightness of her course. Eve and Mary; one woman. Elisabeth and Mary; one woman, as we see in this passage:

> "And Mary arose…and entered into the house of Zechariah, and saluted Elisabeth. And it came to pass, that, when Elisabeth heard the salutation of Mary, the babe leaped in her womb; and Elisabeth was filled with the Holy Ghost: And she spake out with a loud voice, and said, Blessed art thou among women and blessed is the fruit of thy womb. And whence is this to me, that the mother of my Lord

should come to me? For, lo, as soon as the voice of thy salutation sounded in mine ears, the babe leaped in my womb for joy. And blessed is she that *believed*:[1] for there shall be a performance of those things which were told her from the Lord."   Luke 1:39-45

Why had it not been Zechariah who would speak such words as to make the babe in his wife's womb to leap for joy. He did not believe. Elisabeth did not yet know that the baby she was carrying was a child marked for God. She knew it only when Mary spoke.

Mary's Song—The Magnificat

"...My soul doth magnify the Lord, and my spirit hath rejoiced in God my Saviour. For he hath regarded the low estate of his handmaiden: for, behold, from henceforth all generations shall call me blessed...he hath scattered the proud in the imagination of their hearts. He hath put down the mighty from their seats, and exalted them of low degree...."   Luke 1:46-48; 51, 52

"He hath regarded the low estate of his handmaiden," that puts it pretty plainly doesn't it? Now all generations shall call her "blessed," not cursed. Mary and Eve have at last come together as one woman. At the time of these events there were no female rulers, so Mary could not have been talking of any females "put down from their thrones." "He hath put down the mighty" could only refer to males in that society and "exalted them of low degree," could only refer to woman herself!

At that moment, the all-male God made in male-image, suffered total eclipse and the female side of God's personality rose...at least temporarily, for we know Jesus was hated, rejected, and killed by male religious leaders.

---

[1] Author's italics.

The Apostle John put this appendage at the end of his gospel account:

> "And there are also many other things which Jesus did, the which, if they should be written, every one, I suppose that even the world itself could not contain the books that should be written."   John 21:25

John's appraisal of the literary frenzy to discover who this Jesus was, was second only to the frenzy to discover who this "woman" is, for both "subjects" have preoccupied the minds and pens of males, with almost equal intensity. The mystery of woman, as "subject" and Jesus as "subject" are strangely related, for when one studies the theologies of males throughout the millenia since the Edenic expulsion, no one has ever satisfactorily solved the mystery of either. Woman today, just as Jesus today, remains shrouded in the old miasmal mists of a Christianity determined to attain to the kingdom of God, through super piety and naive biblicism, dedicated to the idolatry of an all-male God.

Jesus is deeply entwined within the female principle, for he was a hybrid of both male and female, in a divine co-regency within. They have missed him, as the Jews missed him. They sought a token tempering of the old Mosaic male astride the horse, woman trudging six paces behind her lord. Thus have they been thrown into the confusion of power that bred the tortured theologies of Augustine and the brutalities of the dark ages. Rather than surrender to a restored male and female Godhead, by castrating Jesus, they sought to present the amputated genitals to their male god in a trade for "business as usual." It hasn't worked.

At last we get to the scriptural record of Jesus and woman, in which we explore every account of His dealings with them. The pattern that emerges in Jesus' dealing with woman, as related to the ancient enmity, is precise and clear. Jesus did not reserve compassion and praise for woman alone, for He healed many men. He even praised a few. However, we touch upon several peculiar aspects of Jesus' ministry with women, as compared to men. True, He did reserve His harsh words for males alone, but strangely enough, they were not all directed towards the religious Jewish males, for many of His censorious remarks and exhortations were directed towards His own disciples, whom He upbraided on several occasions.

If we take even a cursory glance at Jesus' dealings with males as compared to females, we obtain better insights as to the roots of the problem between them. Scripture, contrary to popular opinion, is not a conglomeration of unrelated details, recorded for the sake of keeping an accurate historical record. Whole doctrines have been built upon a single line, and conversely, whole doctrines have been built upon the exclusion of a line, by way of implication. We cannot ignore, in view of this selectivity, the fact that a case against the male principle is being presented, and most often hinges upon what appears to be single, innocuous lines. The case against the male is, at the same time, the case for the female. Since the Bible was written from the male point of view, it is to be expected that female vindication and instigation would remain hidden to the casual observer.

We have discerned, in the dealings of Christ with males, some aspects that are peculiar to males alone. For instance: in the case of the rich young ruler, we see a male who fails with his God, choosing his riches over all else. We have no such record of a woman in the New Testament to correspond to it. Women always obeyed the call. Another peculiarity is found in Jesus' practice of commanding males to refrain from telling others of their healings. They often disobeyed. Is Jesus testing them for obedience? Or is he testing them in faith? Is Jesus saying, faith amends disobedience? There is no record of a female disobeying Jesus' commands to her. The owner of the swine which perished in the sea at the deliverance of the Gaderene demoniac, is so incensed that he actually asked Jesus to leave town and take His good works elsewhere. Where do we find such a record in the female biblical legacy?

The Homeric epic of contention, however, is in the issue of faith. In this issue, woman gets a perfect score, for every woman who approached Jesus got what she had come for, except two. One was Martha, sister of Mary of Bethany. Strangely enough, she was pitted against another woman, but in a male fashion. Her request was that Jesus command Mary back to the traditional role that males assigned her. She was refused. The other was the mother of the "sons of thunder," who asked Jesus to assure that her two sons were placed at the left and the right of God, during the kingdom rule. Jesus refused her also. Both of these women represented the male establishment, espousing male desires and male ambitions for themselves. This is powerful commentary to uphold our premise.

Women of faith achieved, while Peter almost drowns when he attempts to walk the waters of Galilee. Jesus publicly berates His disciples for failing to heal the epileptic boy through lack of faith. Zechariah is struck dumb by disbelief in the male "annunciation" to him, preceding the birth of his son, John the Baptist. James and John are rebuked when they wish to call down fire from heaven, Elijah style, to teach the Samaritans a lesson.

Do we conclude from this that Jesus simply expected more from males than from females, thereby conforming to traditional Christian theology, which assigns to woman a metaphysically fixed passivity? It is true, women did not attempt to walk on water or cast out strong epileptic demons before Pentecost, but they received the power to do so later, at

Pentecost, along with males. How does one differentiate between female and male expressions of faith? Was Peter's derring-do in his marine walk any more sensational than Mary's uncalculated risks, in consenting to the Immaculate Conception? If we choose to compare undertakings, then we must compare results, for while Mary succeeded, Peter failed.

In the three days of Jesus' ordeal, women before, during and after the Crucifixion were used as vessels of faith and supernatural revelations which the male rejected. We do not imply that males are to be led by the noses by women, or that they must take every whim of woman as coming from the realms of spiritual perception. We agree that ideas must be ordered by intellect.

The male proclivity to reason is necessary and good. Intellect must carefully scrutinize what the imagination presents, in the creative act. What we contend with is the jealousy that pervades male rejection of woman's authentic inspirations as "idle tales," and the petty plagiarism that motivates their final embrace of her instigations as primarily their own.

Making these comparisons between Jesus' encounters and dealings with woman and males, we are forced to conclude that, of the two, men are the weaker vessels in faith, slower to learn, and definitely covetous of the female's more highly developed spiritual gifts.

The explanation of woman's superiority lies in her history at the hands of the jealous male God. The severity of her oppression literally commanded her to cultivate strengths and virtues, not as pseudo-pious Christian males have done in a show of spiritual pride, but as a weapon of survival against His hand.

Perhaps woman is the living prototype of the Sermon on the Mount, for if spiritual poverty, meekness, mercy, hunger for righteousness, revilings and persecutions are the qualifying experiences for obtaining the "blessedness" which prefaces each beatitude, then woman's history, under the heel of male pride has indeed made her most blessed among all men.

Martha and Mary

Jesus had a good friend named Lazarus who lived with his two sisters in Bethany. Lazarus' doors were always open to Jesus. If He needed a little peace and quiet, a good hot meal, or a comfortable bed, He got it here, for Martha, one of Lazarus' sisters, would see that He did.

Martha was deeply devoted to Jesus, as was her sister, Mary. But there were marked differences between the sisters. Martha was the epitome of the thoroughly domestic woman; efficient, energetic and probably an excellent cook. Mary, on the other hand, was a mental woman. Martha's world was leavened with the yeast of bread dough, which she kneaded and plumped into succulent loaves to feed the hunger of men's bodies. Mary's world was leavened with the yeast of ideas, which she rolled and patted into dreams and visions that would feed men's souls.

Jesus was well aware of the differences between them, and the mutuality of the bonds of real affection among the four is testimony to the respect He had for the personalities of each. A delightful story of an occasion when Jesus' presence triggers a rivalry between the sisters is recorded in Luke. Its inclusion in the biblical record is not for reasons of entertainment or, as most have thought, to depict the democratic indulgence Jesus had for female rivalries. It goes much deeper. It is an indisputable commentary on the traditional role of woman, as being incompatible with the concept of woman as a full human being. The occasion was like many others. Jesus had probably arrived suddenly and unexpectedly to work out the kinks of a hard day:

"Now it came to pass, as they went, that He entered a certain village: and a certain woman named Martha received Him into her house. And she had a sister called Mary, which also sat at Jesus' feet and heard His word. But Martha was cumbered about with much serving, and came to Him, and said, Lord, dost thou not care that my sister hath left me to serve alone? bid her therefore that she help me. And Jesus answered and said unto her, Martha, Martha, thou art careful and troubled about many things: But one thing is needful: and Mary hath chosen that good part, which shall not be taken away from her." Luke 10:38-42

So Martha scurried to get a meal ready for the unexpected guests while Mary, preferring the company of Jesus and the others, probably sat outside in the yard to drink in the exciting news of the day's work. Martha saw it otherwise, and probably grew more and more irritated with Mary's attitude towards the business of feeding the hungry men. She finally exploded and dragged Jesus into the issue by asking Him to send Mary packing off to the kitchen, where tradition said she belonged. He refused. Gently, He reminds Martha that her commendable domestic virtues are not the whole pie of her existence.

Mary was a biblical woman's Liberationist. Today she would have perhaps been a writer, an artist, an actress, and haven't the good, solid Marthas of the world always made it rough on the Marys, withholding full sanction of their womanhood if they refuse to define their humanity in terms of their sex and the traditional roles that males had cast them in?

Jesus lifted and defended woman in this episode, not only against males who would chain her body to service by divesting her of her mind, but also against the females who aid and abet them in doing so.

THE WOMAN AT THE WELL

We could compare this incident to a male counterpart of it in the rich young ruler, who came to Jesus for salvation. This wealthy young man was told that to inherit the kingdom of heaven, he would have to distribute his riches to the poor and follow Christ. He went away saddened.

The woman we read of here accepted Jesus' teachings with joy. One of the strangest aspects of this story lies in the directive Jesus gave to His disciples to refrain from entering or preaching in Samaria. The Jews had held the Samaritans in contempt since their schism, along with the ten northern tribes who had refused to acknowledge Solomon's son as king. He was passing through on His way to Galilee.

It was hot and the walk had been long. He grew thirsty. He stops at a well, remembered to be Jacob's well. A lone woman is drawing water into waterpots. It is noon, the hottest part of the day. A lone woman was unusual. Women customarily came to the wells early, while it was still cool. Drawing the day's rations of water was a time for the women to gossip, and discuss problems as each took her turn at the well. It was obvious that this woman was an outcast among the village women.

Jesus asks her for a drink. She is surprised that He asks, in view of bad feeling that had existed between Jews and Samaritans. Jesus explains:

"...If thou knewest the gift of God, and who it is that saith to thee, Give me to drink; thou wouldest have asked of Him, and He would have given thee living water." John 4:10

She is puzzled and defends her religious heritage, calling Jacob her father, and asking him if he considers himself greater than Jacob. He replies:

"...whosoever drinketh of this water shall thirst again: But whosoever drinketh of the water that I give him shall never thirst...shall be in him a well of water springing up into everlasting life." John 4:13,14

She says: "Sir, give me this water."

Now Jesus bluntly says:

"...Go, call thy husband, and come hither. The woman answered and said, I have no husband. Jesus said unto her Thou hast well said, I have no husband: For thou hast had five husbands; and he whom thou now hast is not thy husband: in that sayest thou truly." John 4:16-18

She is struck by the intimate knowledge He has of her life.

"...Sir, I perceive that thou art a prophet. Our fathers worshipped in this mountain; and ye say, that in Jerusalem is the place where men ought to worship." John 4:19,20

She answers him truthfully, admitting that she is not a religious person. She can neither accept her lot as a daughter of

Jacob nor as anything else the male religion said she was. She had given up on marriage because she had given up on men. This woman was a renegade, but an honest one. She was also perceptive, seeing through the hypocrises of her ancient religion, and those who practiced it. Why had Jesus singled her out among all the women in the village? He saw a deep spiritual need, coupled with an honest heart. He agrees with her appraisal of religion:

> "...Woman, believe me, the hour cometh, when ye shall neither in this mountain, nor yet at Jerusalem, worship the Father. Ye worship ye know not what: we know what we worship..."   John 4:21,22

She would like to believe what this stranger says to her, for it agrees with her own heart. Her truth had been to reject the religion of the men she had lived with; who had bound her to an all-male God. A simple statement of faith opens her to a privileged position with Jesus:

> "...I know that Messiah cometh, which is called Christ: when He is come, He will tell us all things. Jesus saith unto her, I that speak unto thee, am He.   John 4:25, 26

She runs, forgetting her waterpots, into the city:

> "...and saith to the men, Come, see a man, that told me all the things that ever I did: is not this the Christ? Then they went out of the city and came unto Him."   John 4:28-30

What was the explanation of her instant acceptance of Jesus as her Messiah and the fenzied enthusiasm that resulted? In an instant, she became not only a female evangelist, but the first Samaritan to preach. Why did she not rush into the city to preach her first sermon to the women? Because in what transpired between Jesus and her, she found herself and thereby found her God who was both male and female. Jesus had confirmed to her what she had always known: that the male pride that lay at the root of her father's religion could never change the world unless it was humbled, as woman had been humbled these millenia; as she had been humbled. She received the divine commission. She met the Christ and ran, like Mary Magdalene, to tell the men, the symbolic husbands she had never before challenged.

It was inevitable that this woman, as most women, should meet with male scepticism. The text continues to its conclusion by saying that many believed in Him because of her testimony. He was, because of her evangelistic fervor, invited to stay on with them for a few days.

This particular story relates more powerfully to the Edenic issue than perhaps any other, for it exposes woman's tragic displacement in the creative dynamic.

The popular Sunday sermon on this incident has generally been conceived in the tables of the law, focusing upon the morality of this woman's succession of lovers. But these have missed the point. In the first place, Jesus says nothing to the woman about making her latest liaison legal. He does not tell her, as in the case of the woman caught in adultery, "to sin no more." As in the utterances to the women who followed Him to the cross, and other incidents, Jesus addresses Himself to universal issues: the Edenic issue for one, and the subjection of woman for another. He also addresses himself to Pauline doctrine, for it is not coincidental that, in opening up a new territory. He selects a female to become His first evangelist. He could not have elected a woman in a province where orthodoxy reigned, for women were not allowed to either preach or teach males. But in Samaria, a province that had fallen into schism with Jerusalem, He could break with tradition as a teaching to the church, which would come later, laden with misconceptions of what He had taught.

The Samaritan woman is a picture of Eve, having failed to trust in her supernatural prompting of the Holy Spirit; cowed and rejected by males. Jesus broke the bonds of passivity and faithlessness, and she found those inner wellsprings that would flow up in everlasting life, to ultimate freedom for males and females alike. In having no husband, this woman had made the right motion. But she failed to find her rightful place as initiator to males, from God. Jesus pointed the way.

Jesus and the Little Children

"And they brought unto Him also infants, that He would touch them: but when His disciples saw it, they rebuked them. But Jesus called them unto Him and said, Suffer little children to come unto me, and forbid them not, for of such is the kingdom of God."   Luke 18:15, 16

Who would bring infants and little children to Jesus for a "touch blessing" but women? Even in this little Scripture, the old enmity rears. In the closed circuitry of the male establishment, children are consigned by males exclusively to the province of woman. Again we see a rejection of any thing female by the male disciples, for they told the women to leave them alone.

Jesus, in turn, rebukes the disciples, reminding them that women and children have their rightful place, not only in His time and attentions but in the coming kingdom.

The Widow's Mite

Who was more vulnerable to poverty in the society of Jesus' day than a widow? Whose life more desolate than a widow alone? Forbidden the ballasts of a skill or a trade to hoist against the winds of adversity, woman lived on the outskirts of hope. Her womb was no longer a valuable commodity in the market place. Like most women of her day, she had little to cast into life's treasury, but her body.

The account is short and speaks for itself, describing how the rich passed by casting in great and impressive amounts against her pittance of two farthings. But Jesus, knowing her social and racial destitution says:

"...Verily, I say unto you, That this poor widow hath cast more in, than all they which hath cast into the treasury: for they did cast in of their abundance; but she of her want did cast in all that she had, even all her living."   Mark 12:43, 44

The Woman Taken in Adultery

The double standard is probably the most damning evidence of the peculiar schism in the male mind that sets chastity and self-control in woman's east, and male incontinence, in the far west.

Life and literature overflow with pathetic women crushed under the weight of the terrifying social consequences of the "fallen woman" syndrome that have plummeted the Anna Kareninas of our world to their tragic fates. Our methods of inflicting punishment upon woman have grown in subtlety. We have laid down our David-stones and taken up spiritual ones. Still, though our weapons have become less obvious, they have been every bit as deadly.

In biblical times men were less concerned with subleties. Although the lethal undercurrents of the double standard were no less strong, its hypocrisies pulled men down in the same deadly earnest. Death by stoning is a terrible thing, yet in this story of the woman taken in adultery, we see that the literal flow of blood was no deterrent to the duplicity of this primarily male aberration.

The Scribes and the Pharisees brought a woman to Jesus, whom they accused of having been taken in adultery, "in the very act." John 8:4

The text says they said this, tempting Him, so that they might accuse Him. With one victim in hand, they thrust home at the other one: "Now Moses in the law commanded us, that such would be stoned; but what sayest Thou?" John 8:5

Jesus stoops down and writes with His finger upon the ground. He lifts Himself up and says: "He that is without sin among you, let him first cast a stone at her." John 8:7

Something terribly important had happened here that male Bible interpreters have failed to see, literally, for Jesus' act of writing on the ground had to do with their willing blindness. In claiming to have caught the woman in the very act of adultery, she was apprehended with her male partner. Where was the male?

Only after He challenges them verbally, "let him who is without sin..."do they turn away:

"And they which heard it, being convicted by their own conscience, went out one by one, beginning with the eldest, even unto the last...."   John 8:9

They heard, but they did not see, which means that they had missed the point, just as most sermons preached on this incident have missed the point.

This is how they missed the point: They were reached only by an appeal to an honest admission that they were not sinless, but, within the context of the universal issue of irrational male enmity towards woman, they remained blind. It was a mixed victory for Jesus.

This is one of the strongest statements in the Bible against the war upon the female principle, because the serpent rears most venomously, in issues of woman and her sexuality. If this incident weighed upon the consciences of these religious leaders at all, it would not be through the memory of the beleagured woman they arrayed themselves against. It would be in the accusing memory of her cowardly male partner whom they had let go, for he was the symbol of their own escape from truth.

The Female Entourage of Jesus

Tucked away in an isolated biblical corner, is a tiny Scripture, which has embarrassed male expositors like few others, and will startle the studiously pious when analyzed with a little imaginative arithmetic.

Here are twelve men; assorted Jews and Jesus, a healer of rapidly expanding reputation and popularity, who drew crowds wherever He went. The Scripture says:

"He went throughout every city and village, preaching and showing the glad tidings of the Kingdom of God: and the twelve were with Him, And certain women, which had been healed of evil spirits and infirmities, Mary called Magdalene, out of whom went seven devils, And Joanna the wife of Chuza Herod's steward, and Susanna, and many others, which ministered unto him of their substance." Luke 8:1-3

Most of the disciples were married men. Some of the younger males were single, like James and John. Jesus probably had an enormous attractiveness, physically and in every other way. When our young people took to the roads in hippie bands, in mixed or single company, we took it hard.

In Jesus' band of nomadic females, there were single and married women, some of not too savory a reputation. In a day like that day, where women were still considered the personal property of males, this was serious anti-social behavior. It was the skeleton of scandal. Joanna must have been an extremely attractive women; well-dressed as befit her station in life as the wife of one of Herod's right arms. Mary Magdalene, to whom tradition imputes the pursuit of the oldest profession could hardly be said to ornament the band with respectability. Susanna we know nothing about, except that she was devoted and who knows what the other were like? We are told the names of only three of the women; one a prostitute, the other a married woman of high position. The point was to carefully include, even if in a minimal way, enough pertinent data so that we can make the proper inferences and draw accurate conclusions. One of the proper conclusions is that the presence of Joanna symbolizes the totally emancipated woman. For one thing, she was married and she was a Christian. There must have been some heated discussions between Joanna and Chuza about her traipsing around the countryside after a band of lunatic-fringe males. His position at the court was certainly embarrassed because of it, and his home seriously disrupted. Were there children involved? We don't know. Chances are good that there were. Court gossip must have abounded whatever the case. Not only behind these women, but behind the men, must have lain seriously disrupted homes. Peter was married. The younger males were probably needed by their families.

How they lived isn't difficult to surmise. In those days the average person walked everywhere. Ten to twenty miles a day was not unusual and we can assume they covered a lot of ground daily. They must have slept under the stars, and the "ministering" women must have cooked over open fires or at community ovens to feed the entourage.

Perhaps this period was the one in which Mary Magdalene and Jesus became fast friends.

It is exciting to observe how carefully the Scriptures bury gems against the day of famine, for this Scripture if mined, addresses itself powerfully to the spirit of this decade.

The revolutionary impact of this group upon the moral and ethical, as well as religious mentality of its time was considerable, but the greatest commentary it would make would be to the future oppressive doctrines of the Apostle Paul. Jesus did not forbid these women. It is obvious that they did not care what their husbands or fathers thought about their loyalty to Jesus, and neither did He. The point of including this Scripture in the record is to restore to woman her equality before God in spiritual matters, placing her spiritual dedication to God before husbands, fathers and even children, if so led. It is a *lifting* of the Edenic prophecy to Eve,"…and your desire will be for your husband and he will rule over you."

THE WOMAN WITH ISSUE OF BLOOD

This story has a double aspect—that of a man and a woman at the same time. The issue, as always, is that of faith.

Jesus returns from a teaching trip to be greeted by a huge crowd waiting for Him. The ruler of a synagogue seeks Him out, imploring Him to heal his twelve-year-old daughter, sick to the point of death. He requests that Jesus come to his home and lay hands on the child. Jesus agrees. As they make their departure, they are pressed about by the great throng of people seeking help from the Healer. A woman who had suffered bleeding from a female disorder for twelve years was in the throng. Her chances of receiving healing appeared slim, seeing the crowd in competition, and knowing that Jesus has Jairus's daughter on His mind. Believing that if she just touched the hem of His garment, she would be healed, she presses her way through the throng, and touches His clothing. She is healed instantly.

"And Jesus said, Who touched me?"   Luke 8:45

Peter is bewildered by Jesus' question. It seemed a strange question seeing they were all encased in human body contact, as they struggled to get out of the crowd. But the touch Jesus referred to was a spiritual touch. He repeats: "Somebody hath touched me, for I perceive that virtue is gone out of me." Luke 8:46 Other translations render the word "virtue" as "power." Whichever the case, the faith of this woman was so strong that her spirit drained from Jesus the healing power she needed.

But His question as to who touched Him frightened her. Perhaps she was too sinful to have been healed by the Master. Trembling, she confesses her presumption. Jesus replies: "Daughter, be of good comfort: thy faith hath made thee whole; Go in peace."   Luke 8:48

In the meantime, a messenger from Jairus's house presses through the crowd to tell him not to bother Jesus further. His daughter has died. Jesus comforts the father, telling him she is not dead but sleeping.

Peter, James and John accompany Jesus to Jairus's house. Exhorting them not to fear, but believe, he puts everyone out of the house except His disciples and the parents of the girl. He speaks the words and she arises: "And her parents were astonished: but he charged them that they should tell no man what was done."   Luke 8:56

The point we wish to make in recounting the story of Jairus's daughter in connection with the woman who touched the hem of His garment, is the very point the Bible wishes to make. This woman's faith was far greater than Jairus's was. It broke through the faith of every other person in that huge crowd, usurping even the faith of Jairus and the preoccupation of Jesus with him. The crisis of Jairus's dying daughter certainly outweighed the crisis of this woman's ailment, if we speak in terms of natural knowledge; but in terms of faith, the woman was driven to a greater intensity than the distraught father. Her faith surpassed his. In the annals of faith, this is one of the great acts and one of the most ingenious. A woman's faith contends with a male's and gains the victory.

The Canaanite Woman

At first glance this story seems to impute a harsh rejection of a woman by Jesus. But, if we know the political situation and the antipathy between the Jews and the Syrophoenicians, we get a different picture, and a penetrating insight into Jesus' knowledge. It seems that this woman had been irritating the disciples. She had apparently approached Jesus, begging Him to deliver her daughter from a "devil that vexed her grievously." Jesus, to all appearances, ignored her: "He answered her not a word." From there she approaches the disciples until they finally ask Him to get rid of her. Jesus seems to agree with them, saying He was not commissioned to minister to any but the "lost sheep of the house of Israel." Determined to have her interview with the Healer, she gets through the security around Jesus and falls to worship Him, at the same time pleading with Him to rid her daughter of the evil spirit. Why did He ignore her the first time? Was He testing her faith? He knew His disciples had a natural aversion to the woman because she was a Canaanite. He also knew that the enmity was two ways. This woman was to undergo one last test of her faith before she would get her wish. Jesus cuts her down with: "It is not meet to take the children's bread and to cast it to dogs." The barb must have caused even the prejudiced disciples to wince. She thrusts back swiftly, "Lord: Yet the dogs under the table eat of the children's crumbs." Mark 7:27, 28. Her reply was as shocking as His, for it was cunning, quick-witted and pugnacious. It was almost a challenge. The two had sparred verbally and intellectually and Jesus concedes to her determination with praise and admiration: "O woman, great is thy faith, be it unto thee even as thou wilt."

This exchange almost amounted to an argument between them. It is heartening that Jesus didn't chide her for her pluck, but took an instant delight in her resourceful determination and earthy wisdom. Her daughter was healed, the Scripture says, "from that hour."

This is one of the great acts of faith and another of the most ingenious. Woman vies with a male and again wins out.

MARY THE SINNER

Tradition attributes the identity of this woman to the same Mary of Bethany who was the sister of Martha and Lazarus. The motivation of this Mary's actions could be compatible with the personality of that Mary. The ritual of love this woman performed over the body of Jesus could only have emanated from a sensitive, expansive soul and a highly intuitive one.

She knew Jesus was going to die, perhaps even before He did, because we know He predicted His death only later on in His ministry. She certainly knew it before His disciples. If this woman was the same Mary of Bethany who sat at Jesus' feet, we already have an insight into the emotional make-up that prompted this extremely impulsive act. She was not only a mental woman, given to artistic tendencies, but also a maverick from the traditional domestic arts that women were expected to cultivate. She had, no doubt, suffered for her non-conformity, especially at the hands of her sister, Martha, who disapproved of her discontent. Where could a woman go for approval? Jesus had approved her longing to participate in the world of ideas and self-expression which had primarily been a male prerogative. She longed to give Him something intensely personal, not as Martha would give; a meal, a bed, a comfortable chair. She longed to present to Jesus something beautiful; something that would touch not His body but His soul.

Perhaps the only valuable possession she had was a jar of

perfumed ointment. This was a very expensive commodity in those days. It was used to anoint the dead for burial.

It was a rather formal occasion. The invitation to Jesus to dine with a Pharisee promised to be an occasion already fraught with tension.

From what the account says, Mary, carrying the precious jar of ointment, literally bursts into the room. Perhaps her impulsive act was the instantaneous result of a sudden flash of intuitive insight that told her Jesus would die soon. In a panic of frenzied devotion she could think of only one thing: to tell Him she cared, but to tell Him in her own way.

> She "...stood at His feet behind Him weeping, and began to wash His feet with tears, and did wipe them with the hairs of her head, and kissed His feet and anointed them with the ointment." Luke 7:38

In the moments of shocked silence that must have transpired Simon, the Pharisee, probably had some uncharitable thoughts about the intrusion, which Jesus read, for He defends the woman by citing a parable:

> "...Simon, I have somewhat to say unto thee.... There was a certain creditor which had two debtors: the one owed five hundred pence, the other fifty. And when they had therefore, which of them will love him most? Simon answered and said, I suppose that he, to whom he forgave most. And he said unto him, Thou hast rightly judged.
> And he turned to the woman, and said unto Simon, seest thou this woman? I entered into thine house, thou gavest me no water for my feet....My head with oil thou didst not anoint: but this woman hath anointed my feet with ointment. Wherefore I say unto thee, Her sins, which are many, are forgiven; for she loved much; but to whom little is forgiven, the same loveth little." Luke 7:40-47

The parable is self-explanatory as is Jesus' defense of the woman. It is a woman Jesus uses to rout male pride and religious legalism, to her everlasting glory, for Matthew records Jesus as saying:

"Verily I say unto you, Wheresoever this gospel shall be preached in the whole world, there shall also this, that this woman hath done, be told for a memorial of her."

Matt. 26, 13

Jesus bestowed no such honor upon a male.

THE WEDDING FEAST IN CANA

In this story there are probably more universal symbols used and more universal truths than in any other events in the New Testament, short of the events leading up to, and during Christ's death. References to the Edenic issue abound as well, for it winds like a serpent around later events at the Cross.

This occasion has been analyzed exhaustively by Catholic theologians, who have drawn much of their Mariolatry from it. Most of their emphasis, at least in the past, has been upon the mother-son relationship; a sort of saccharine idealization of Jesus' filial devotion to his mother, who gave Him His fleshly body, being therefore worthy of token acknowledgement. It carries with it all the old familiar, cliché-ridden concepts of male semi-reluctant indulgence to female whim. In this theology, Mary is all mother; her identity totally swallowed up in maternal instincts. Her son however retains his individuality as a male. There is no connotation of fatherhood accommodated to Jesus. This is one of the gross distortions and base injustices perpetrated upon womanhood, relegating her to the realm of patroness of the myriad, daily bulletins woman receives from the uninteresting world of practical human needs. It is abjectly simplistic and spiritually chauvinistic.

Here's what the account says:

"And the third day there was a marriage in Cana of Galilee;

and the mother of Jesus was there; And both Jesus was called, and His disciples, to the marriage. And when they wanted wine, the mother of Jesus saith unto Him, They have no wine. Jesus saith unto her, Woman, what have I to do with thee? mine hour is not yet come. His mother saith unto the servants, Whatsoever He saith unto you, do it. And there were set there six water pots of stone, after the manner of the purifying of the Jews, containing two or three firkins apiece. Jesus saith unto them, Fill the water-pots with water. And they filled them up to the brim. And he saith unto them, draw out now, and bear unto the governor of the feast...."

John 2:1-8

The account goes on to say that the wine was so excellent that the ruler of the feast proclaims the last wine to be better than the first.

The presence of Mary, Jesus and the disciples is an interesting detail. When Jesus says, "...mine hour is not yet come," we are informed of two things: that His hour to work miracles had not arrived in His estimation, and that His "hour" with woman had not arrived.

This is a play on the Edenic drama. Adam apparently, like Jesus, did not think the hour had come to move out of the Edenic innocence in a move towards knowledge. It was to Eve that the decision was left. She took the first step without consulting Adam whom she instigated and then involved. Mary does the same. She recognized a need. She shares the vision with Jesus. In Mary's mind, Jesus is ready to come out of His obscurity and begin His public ministry. Jesus, like Adam, demurs. Mary, nevertheless, takes the fateful step in spite of His reluctance, as Eve did.

Look closely at Jesus' reply. It is really a question, "Woman, what have I to do with thee?" Mary answers and shows Him. She is to perceive and initiate. He is to perform. Notice Mary, after instigating Jesus, then speaks to the servants, telling them to obey her son. Paul's theology again suffers very badly in this whole transaction, for Mary operates in exactly the manner that Paul forbade women to operate.

So, the marriage at Cana is a vignette of Eden. The cast is the same, for the Bible calls Jesus, "the new Adam." Mary then is the new Eve. The universal concepts involved in this story are the Edenic issues, not the sentimental mother-son relationship of traditional Mariolatry which is rooted in the doctrine of the subjection of woman as an extraneous sprout of the male God. This exchange between Mary and Jesus indicates also the hesitance common to both Adam and Jesus to respond to the female prod. Jesus however, unlike Adam, did not rebel through jealousy or pride against Mary's swift insights into the pressing need of the situation. Though He questioned her timing, He did obey her with trust and humility, and changed the water into wine.

The presence of the disciples is interesting. Since the Scripture later indicates that this prod from Mary signalled the beginning of Jesus' public miracle ministry, we can assume that this was also the key to the disciples that He was the Messiah. This too, must be credited to Mary's perceptive timing. It also shores up the fact that neither Jesus, nor the other males, had the spiritual insight to perceive a real human need.

Jesus' reply to Mary, "Woman, what have I to do with thee? mine hour is not yet come," is directly addressed to woman as instigator. In posing it in the form of a question, He is saying that in His opinion, it is not time for Him to act. He is, at the same time, referring to those hours before and after His trial, when woman would play her dramatic role, for they both knew that His embodiment of female qualities would ultimately trigger the wrath of male Jewish leaders. In that "hour," He would have everything to do with her, for in killing Him, He knew they would be killing her by way of the ancient enmity.

When we look back to woman's exile from the Godhead in the age of Moses and the patriarchs, we understand Mary's "Immaculate Conception" of Jesus as a new Adam; the ideal male. The self-righteous idiocy of a Samson and the egotistical craft of a Jacob, were deleted in her concept and replaced with a reverence and recognition of woman, not as a cursed creature to be feared, but as a blessed servant to be acknowledged and honored. Jesus did not turn against Mary at the Cross in anger and pride. He accepted with courage the confrontations it demanded of Him. But the old Adam reacted in hatred of her, too frightened to ever trust the voice of his "wife" again. The old Adam could never have gotten to the Cross. He protected himself against it by shutting out his wife's voice. Jesus listened and obeyed, and went in humility to the Cross and won, for women and men, the victory over death.

Ahead for the new Adam were the mighty miracles of healing, deliverance and teaching, and the overthrow of the old laws that bound men not only to the letter but the vicious hatred of the religious leaders because of it. Jesus' greatest hour with woman would come at Calvary, for Jesus and women were one.

THE CRIPPLED WOMAN HEALED ON THE SABBATH

The synagogue on this Sabbath day was crowded. People were solemn in mien and reverent in manner; men on one side; women and children on the other. The religious pecking order ordained that the most prominent members of the community, in their most impressive finery, should be seated ceremoniously in the front pews. Behind them, in diminishing octaves of importance, sat the remainder of the congregation. On the men's side a mosaic of caps, turbans and headscarfs, and on the woman's side, plaited hair, head mantles, fringes, rings and bracelets. The tradition of color in dress to express the state of mind, or the spiritual posture before God, signaled a polygot human spirit, in contrast to the monotone austerity of the ritual fixed by ordinance and law. Like embalmed Patriarchs, the sacred books, encased in awe, dominated the reading platform between the lamps and trumpets and leaders who conducted the services.

It was customary that no one person was appointed to preach. Any competent worshipper might be invited by the ruler, to give the sermon. That day it was Jesus. From the lectern, Jesus spied a woman, perhaps an arthritic:

> "And he was teaching in one of the synagogues on the Sabbath. And, behold, there was a woman which had a spirit of infirmity eighteen years, and was bowed together, and could in no wise lift up herself. And when Jesus saw her, he called her to him, and said unto her, Woman, thou art loosed from thine infirmity...and immediately she was made straight, and glorified God. And the ruler of the synagogue answered with indignation, because that Jesus had healed on the Sabbath day, and said to the people, There are six in which men ought to work: in them therefore come and be healed, and not on the Sabbath day. The Lord then answered him, and said, Thou hypocrite, doth not each one of you on the Sabbath loose his ox or his ass from the stall, and lead him away to watering? And ought not this woman, being a daughter of Abraham, whom Satan hath bound, lo, these eighteen years, be loosed from this bond on the Sabbath day?"   Luke 13:10-16

There are many symbolisms employed here. The deep symbolism present is of woman, so bent with the burden of her lowly condition that she cannot raise herself up to cast her eyes to the heavens above her. "She could, in no wise, lift herself up," has more significance then pertaining to her disease alone.

She must have been a pathetic figure, her walk from her seat to the lectern as painful as it was tedious. What went through her mind as she hobbled her way up the aisle, amidst the intermittent waves of astonished whispering and dead silences?

Once at her destination the hush of suspense was broken by Jesus' words; "Woman, thou art loosed from thine infirmity."

Sobs of release and gratitude must have collided with gasps of astonishment from the congregation. Heads must have leaned together and eyes blazoned toward the leader, whose censure of Jesus was more than verbal. He literally asked Him to leave the platform for the account says that he lectured the people on the illegality of such an act on the Sabbath and that it was delivered with "indignation."

It is only natural that a woman would bring this religious boil to a head for woman was, perhaps, most in need of loosing to the waters of abundant life, whether on the Sabbath or not. But there's more treasure here than Jesus' unsolicited compassion for a woman in need of healing. In comparing her to an ox or an ass, He defines woman's condition as a result of the Edenic split. The ox or ass is revealed to us as woman's symbol which we can apply to other passages in the Bible where these symbols are used. The beast of burden is compatible with woman, while another animal is applicable to males, as demonstrated in another companion story:

The synagogue is once more the scene, and again it is the Sabbath. On this occasion, Jesus heals a man with a withered hand. The same outrage accompanies the miracle to which Jesus offers the same argument. This time, however, He uses an animal symbol placing an entirely different connotation upon the male: "What man shall there be among you, that shall have one sheep, and if it fall into a pit on the Sabbath day, will he not lay hold on it, and lift it out?"   Matt. 12:11

The differences between a sheep and oxen or asses are obvious. First, a sheep is not a beast of burden. It is a highly dependent creature and in need of solicitous tending. Sheep are classed as extremely innocent animals, too naive to even know when its enemy, the wolf, is nearby. While the tethered oxen must depend upon her owner to water her, the sheep may move freely, connoting the comparative freedom of males to females. However, because of its lack of awareness and trust in the shepherd, it is apt to fall into a pit, should it wander out of his sight. The sheep, in need of rescue, symbolizes not only the male proclivity to lead, but its equal penchant for falling into error. These two companion stories are equations of the male and female dynamic, which confirm our assessment of the tethered woman and the error-prone male who wanders away.

Jesus loosed the oxen from her stall and led her to water. He continues to rescue error-prone sheep.

Prologue

Jesus' "hour" with woman had finally struck. It was to be an hour of chaos; a moving of God's spirit across the face of a new deep, a prelude to another Genesis.

Once more a woman, the female principle, would detonate a new holocaust upon the world of sinful men destined to explode to hatred around him, who was so much like her. With woman's ancient passivity, Jesus would surrender His body to the violence of the ancient Marduk. This time his knife would be fashioned in the shape of a cross; a grim contradiction of wooden beams, flung between heaven and earth, as Tiamat's body had been flung heaven-and earthward. Like Tiamat, He too had become the symbol of ominous darkness; a chaotic treachery of disorder to the male godhood of Moses and the Jewish religious leaders. Babylon dispatched a new memo to men with an old message: creation through rape and violence against the female principle was still the universal dynamic of creation.

Woman knew what was about to transpire. Had she not drunk the same cup at the hand of the all-male God? She identified with this Saviour who had lifted female virtues to a hitherto unsuspected glory. Still, she had thought the ancient atrocities had been peculiarly her own until He took them to Himself in this strange immolation of body and soul.

But what was this paradox? Was it Eden revisited? Was the ancient drama to be relived again? Was this a prelude to another fall; a prelude to another rise?

The hour of the lamb, the ox and the serpent had arrived again. Woman, the ass upon whom He rode to triumph a few days ago, would now walk to the Cross with Him and together they would hang—an absurd hybrid of the old Gnostic grafitti of male and female; a jackass fastened to a crucifix.

Woman at the Trial

The impending events of Christ's death orchestrated the Machiavellian enmity between the male and female principles like the somber melancholy of a Wagnerian overture to tragedy. But the lonely flute of Pilate's wife absconds with the melody and the tone is pure and the melody beautiful. Only the spiritual ears can attune to woman's voice above the din of male brass:

> Pilate said..."Whom will ye that I release unto you? Barabbas, or Jesus which is called Christ?   Matt. 27:17

The question has flung the bells of past history against the present, as the good men among us have trekked to their Golgothas and died the death.

Still, the voice of woman surges above the shouts of, "Give us Barabbas!" It surges for one moment in golden possibility. It glows for a moment, then goes:

> "...Have thou nothing to do with that just man: for I have suffered many things this day in a dream because of him."
> Matt. 27:19

God sends one prophetic dream to men. He does so through a woman who hears, and obeys. She is rejected and banished to silence—an exile from the split Godhead. Male schizophrenia will embark on its greatest hour.

Women on the Way to the Cross

> "And there followed Him a great company of people, and of women, which also bewailed and lamented Him. But Jesus turning unto them said, Daughters of Jerusalem, weep not for me, but weep for yourselves and for your children. For, behold, the days are coming, in which they shall say, Blessed are the barren, and the wombs that never bare and the paps which never gave suck."   Luke 23:27-29

The uncanny silence which Jesus maintained throughout the ordeal of His trial and enroute to Golgotha, was broken only twice, once before Pilate and again in this terse, prophetic utterance on His way to the Cross. His only recorded utterance was to woman.

We reasonably conclude that men as well as women shouted words of comfort and loyalty to the doomed teacher, but it was to woman that Jesus spoke the words that shattered like glass against the unyielding rock of that hour. It is to her future agony He addresses His prophecy. Why was there no admonition to males? Were not the events themselves ample testimony to the male establishment? What He says to woman, His companion in passivity and persecution, is more like a call to battle than a word of comfort. That is exactly what it was:

> "Behold, the days are coming in which they shall say, blessed are the barren, and wombs that never bare and the paps which never gave suck."

It was a battle slogan for the day when the passive ox would break loose from her tether and shrug off the yoke of her male owner. But before that day, (which is our own!) the Lamb would suffer, "at the hands of evil men."

WOMAN AT THE CROSS

The terrible ceremonies of hammer and nails are completed. For a time the small gathering of observers and comforters reel in a drunken confusion between sight and sound. Before them hung Jesus. Behind them, the persistent echoes of hammer blows that rose and dropped in their memories like up-draughts of disturbed air, lifting and falling like the hope and despair this man had brought into their lives. For an instant they stood between two dimensions of time.

The faithful were there and the record takes pains to mention only women, some by name. Why? Because, as in the case of

Pilate's wife, woman with whom Jesus identified in an intimate way, was to share in His agony before His exoneration.

Mark lists Mary Magdalene and Salome and "many other women who came up with Him unto Jerusalem." A trio of women stood by the cross; His mother Mary, and Mary's sister, wife of Cleophas, and Mary the Magdalene. Only one male is prophetically included within this female representation, the young apostle John, who would later write the Apocalypse while in exile.

Again, Jesus breaks the seal of His thoughts and addresses first a woman. He says to Mary: "Woman, behold thy son! Woman, look upon the Son you conceived as the ideal of humanity. Though your conception was inspired of the true God, look upon the evil that sinful men have laid upon me. You are my mother. Woman is the mother of all men, having power to shape their souls. So long as you fail to exert your influence over the hearts of males, a cross will always be the end of those who lead the way among us. You, as instigator of God, are called to a special privilege. Your spiritual perceptions can guide and strengthen men but you must lay down the passivity which has tethered you to men's weaknesses, rather than God's strengths."

His next utterance is to John, the disciple He loved: "Behold: thy mother!"

He now completes the circle. To John, His chosen among the disciples, most akin to His own spirit, He presents Mary, symbol of woman, eternally crushed beneath the same weight of evil that had nailed Him to Golgotha's cross. John would stand between the woman and all men who, in the phantasms of their own ego and pride, would reject her perceptions and despoil her nature, to shape the world to their own image. Now the circle is complete. The Scripture says that: "...from that hour that disciple took her unto his own home."   John 19:27

This signalled the prologue to a future drama for the disciple "Jesus loved." It would be a new beginning for woman, for it would be to John that the great revelations of the Apocalypse would be given, in which the glory of redeemed woman would be revealed to mankind. Mary could be entrusted to no other.

The remaining incidents of Jesus' sufferings upon the Cross flowed from the unrestrained hands and lips of males. The crass gambling for His clothing, the vinegar sponge; the jeers and taunts and the spear in His side, were samples of the male principle on the rampage against passivity and innocence. Every thrust, every indignity, would be a thrust into the soul of woman.

One last remark is monument to the tragedy of unrestrained male pride, which dooms the all-male God to the catastrophes of hindsight. When Jesus breathes His last, a soldier declares:

"Truly this was the son of God."   Matt. 27:54
The lonely strains of a flute rise again, for an instant, above the brass:

> "Have nothing to do with this just man, for I have suffered many things, this day in a dream, because of him."

WOMAN AT THE CROSS AND THE TOMB

Matthew, Mark and Luke were present during the anguished panic of the trek to Golgotha and the soul searing Crucifixion, but it must have been from a distance. Peter was absent. It would be only natural that those who had participated in Jesus' trial and Crucifixion would undertake the tasks of preparing the body for burial. With the exception of the rich man, Joseph of Arimathea, who unwound the red tape of legal claim upon the body, it was woman who claimed His soul. It was her loving hands that would perform the tragic task of anointing the lifeless body with the sweet savory spices of preservation.

Mary Magdalene appears at the tomb:

> "The first day of the week cometh Mary Magdalene early, when it was yet dark, unto the sepulcher, and seeth the stone taken away from the sepulcher. Then she runneth, and cometh to Simon Peter, and to the other disciple, whom Jesus loved, and saith unto them, They have taken

away the Lord out of the sepulcher, and we know not
where they have laid him...."   John 20:1, 2

Peter and John hasten to the tomb. They likewise find it empty.
A pattern emerges of woman as the spiritual and earthy eyes of
males who at her report must see for themselves.

Peter and John leave, as ignorant of what had transpired as
Mary Magdalene who stays behind, whipped to tears by a new
sorrow. She had not realized how comforted in her grief she had
been by the shred of His body. Now, even that small comfort
had dissolved in what seemed to be a relentless cruelty of disap-
pointments. She stoops to look in again, as if to adjust the old
knowledge to a new reality. She sees, not an empty tomb, but
two angels in white:

> "...sitting, the one at the head, and the other at the feet,
> where the body of Jesus had lain. And they say unto her,
> Woman why weepest thou? She saith unto them, Because
> they have taken away my Lord, and I know not where they
> have laid him. And when she had thus said, she turned
> herself back, and saw Jesus standing, and knew not that it
> was Jesus....She, supposing him to be the gardener, saith
> unto him, Sir, if thou have borne him hence, tell me where
> thou hast laid him, and I will take him away. Jesus saith
> unto her, Mary. She turned herself, and saith unto him,
> Rabboni, which is to say, Master."   John 20:11-16

He tells her to run quickly and tell the disciples that she had seen
Him and what He had said.

There are so many testimonies in this one passage alone, to
the consistent pattern of woman's initiatory role in God's
revelation to man and her instigatory role in passing it on to
males. It undergirds the whole of the New Testament and
absolutely confirms this book's premise that the true God is a
male and female God and, more important, that Eve's act was
to her everlasting glory.

To begin with, the vision of the angels was denied to Peter

and John. Though their grief was probably as intense as the women's, it failed to motivate their spiritual powers to see what Mary Magdalene was privileged to see. Nor did it honor them with hearing what she heard. Her conversation with the angels would, in itself, be enough to credit womanhood in the person of Mary Magdalene as being "highly favored" of God in spiritual perception. But her discovery of Jesus and her subsequent recognition of, and conversation with Him, serves as absolute proof.

We have always taken it for granted that His followers knew He would rise from the dead. They did not, which accounts for much of the despair of His male disciples. But, it also contributes to woman's glory, for she was the first to come to this knowledge through faith alone.

Woman is possessed of a hunger to know, though males have relegated her to the realms of feeling alone. True, the mechanism through which she gains her knowledge is not based on reason only. Observe her obedience in running to tell the disciples what Jesus has told her. Observe also the sad and expected rebuff by the males she is commissioned to instruct. They refuse to believe her!

> "And she went and told them that had been with Him, as they mourned and wept. And they, when they had heard that He was alive, and had been seen of her, *believed not.*[1]
> Mark 16:10,11

Luke throws more light on the issue when he records the same event, adding the further evidence that it was only after Mary's testimony that:

> "And they remembered His words...[that He would rise again], And returned from the sepulcher, and told all these things unto the eleven, and to all the rest." Luke 24:8,9

---

[1] Author's italics.

Sounds familiar doesn't it? Women do the spade work and males seize the revelations of the woman and broadcast them as their own, in the eternal re-enactment of that universal plagiarism that has typified male ego and pride, from the beginning. The Scripture seals the evidence by reiterating the sorry truth:

> "It was Mary Magdalene, and Joanna, and Mary the mother of James, and other women that were with them, which told these things unto the Apostles. And their words seemed to them as idle tales, and they believed them not."
> Luke 24:10, 11

Luke appends Mark's account by adding that to the Apostles the women's report seemed to them as, "idle tales," overworked imagination, the strange proclivity of woman, like Pilate's wife, who dreamed a dream.

> "Then arose Peter, and ran unto the sepulcher; and stooping down, he beheld the linen clothes laid by themselves, and departed, wondering in himself at that which was come to pass."
> Luke 24:12

At any rate, Peter is at last driven to wonder. Woman has made her first convert in the person of Peter. The ice is broken in the male heart, the great thaw begins, and the way is paved for Jesus' first resurrection appearance to males.

The first appearance is granted to a couple of disciples as they walked to Emmaus, forlorn, disappointed and rehashing the recent events:

> "And it came to pass, that, while they communed together and reasoned, Jesus himself drew near, and went with them, But their eyes were holden that they should not know him."
> Luke 24:15, 16

They walk and talk with this stranger, relating the recent tragedy. They admit their doubt of Jesus' Messiahship when they say, "But we trusted that it had been He which should have redeemed Israel, and besides all, today, is the third day since these things were done." They relate the women's claim to having not only found that the body was missing, but were privy to a vision of angels declaring Him raised. They then reluctantly fall back into unbelief:

> "And certain of them which were with us went to the sepulcher, and found it even so as the women had said: but him they saw not."   Luke 24:24

A simple act of Christian charity saves the day for their despair. Jesus, the account says, made as if to continue on His journey after they came to their destination. They constrain the stranger to spend the night with them since it was getting on to evening. He accepts, and after sitting down to the evening meal they experience their long awaited theophany when Jesus performs the breaking of the bread: "...He took bread, and blessed it, and brake, and gave to them. And their eyes were opened and they knew Him; and He vanished out of their sight."

> Luke 24:30, 31

After this they reassess how their "hearts burned within us, when He spake?" Male hindsight over female foresight. They are so excited they rush all the way back to Jerusalem to tell the others.

The final revelation came to them by way of a symbolic gesture which is in keeping with male principle or solar energy or intellect, which works through the ordering of symbols. Finally He appears to the eleven:

> "...as they sat at meat, and upbraided their unbelief and hardness of heart, because they believed not them which had seen Him after He had risen."   Mark 16:14

There still remains their fright in seeing what they believe is a ghost. Jesus has to smooth their fears away by taking something as real as a fish and honeycomb and eating them before their shocked eyes. There still remains the doubt of Thomas, before belief comes full circle. Only then do the male disciples of Jesus rejoice in a risen Saviour and an accomplished redemption.

His "hour" with woman had arrived. She followed Him to His death, as much as her own as His. In the hours that would lie between the death and Resurrection she would mourn a new barrenness of womb. Rachel, once more barterer for mandrakes, and beautiful Tamar wept and wandered, stunned among the treacheries of a new rape. But there was a rising also, against which the gates of hell did not prevail. In that hour, woman rose with Him as privileged apprentice, instigator, initiator, restored goddess to an all-male Godhead.

But her hour would be brief. The wolves were even then sniffing out the fold. The teachings of the Christ, would be entrusted to the hands of ignorant, sinful males, even those within His own sheepfold. The goats in sheep's clothing would continue to reject woman as Jesus had been rejected. Paul would silence her in the chains of Jewish law, sever her head from her body and command His spirit into subjection to an all-male god. For the next 2000 years, her ancient adversary would take no holiday from her persecution.

John, the "beloved," would stand between her and the wolves, privileged to the single task of revealing in his great revelation from God, her terrible predicament until the return of Christ. Her brief Pentecost would flash for a moment like a brilliant comet, only to sputter out in the void of male enmity. Woman would wander the heavens until that promised, latter day Pentecost which would herald the end of history...and the beginning of eternity.

Chapter 8
"AH! WILDERNESS!"

No book has so teased, bewildered and mystified Christians and theologians as the 66th book of the collected biblical library of the two Testaments. One reason for this is that most people have approached the book of John's revelations, sometimes called the Apocalypse, from a purely materialistic point of view. To be sure, it describes great upheavals upon the earth which will manifest visibly to men's eyes, but it is also an account of great upheavals in the world of spirit which precedes them.

The Book of Revelation literally drags us by the scruff of our necks into heaven, to witness the horrendous war of ideas that will break above our heads in a cataclysmic ideational Armageddon that triggers earthly phenomena before our eyes.

One of the most mysterious characters of the book is a male. His identity is concealed and symbolized by the number 666. John says this man will be revealed to the "wise" and those with spiritual vision at the end of the present age. The number 6, in biblical numerology, stands for imperfect mankind. Triple, it stands for diabolical imperfection which this man will personify. What then, is signified by the Bible's books being set at the number 66? Wouldn't that imply that the Bible is an imperfect book? Exactly! The number 7 is the number of spiritual perfection in biblical numerology. To bring the Bible to perfection, one more book would have to be added to make 67. Jesus called this 67th book, the "book of life." Obviously this means that life itself brings the Bible to perfection and that each man writes his own book as an individual, while the world writes its book as a collective.

This concept delights in a final vision of man entering heaven at last, to rest on his laurels, all struggle over. But the Book of Revelation says otherwise. In the context of woman, Revelation is opening like a flower filmed in slow motion, and woman's final vindication and release are becoming visible. Woman stands within its pages, at first, in all her agony. She finishes within its pages glorified and liberated from the universal forces of violence and hatred that have toyed with her so savagely since the Edenic expulsion.

The average reader is overwhelmed by the richness and profusion of the symbolism in what appears to be an irrational sequential pattern, shifting between heaven and earth, from actor to actor, among a cast of thousands.

The plagues poured from the angel's vials are a cascade of ideas, "immaculate conceptions" from above, born of the hunger in the human spirit to shake off the old, outworn institutions and ideas that stunt our growth and destroy our freedom. We all envision a better life, a more abundant life.

Another key to understanding the Book of Revelation is to realize that there is a dichotomy of persons and viewpoints. The writer, John, swings from left to right, up and down, in a multidimensional view of the forces at play. Unenlightened Christendom has invariably attempted to interpret this book in a one dimensional manner. So, the church drags us into the deserts of idolatry and false doctrine that have fixed her God like a dead moon circling a dead planet, beyond any new Genesis.

For this reason, we slip another key onto our keychain and unlock another door to the mysterious world of Revelation in the secret of multi-dimensional time. Everything pertaining to God is triune in nature. Time is also triune. Revelation employs a trinity of time, referring to past, present and future aspects of persons and places. We see the old and the new, the past and present, and finally, projections of the future.

Within the context of our subject of woman and the climax of her mystery in the past two dispensations, it is necessary to keep in mind that the portraits of the three women in Revelation are not only depictions of the plight of the individual woman but the plight of every character in the Bible which falls under the female principle. The nation Israel falls under the female principle as a nation, called to be Jehovah's wife. The church, the "bride" of Christ, is another. The Holy City, New Jerusalem, is called "the bride of Christ" and the physical creation itself is classed as female. Deeper excursions into symbolism reveal the sun or solar energy being blessed as male; and moon, lunar energy, classed as female. When we read the book and the accounts of the three women, we should apply the details of their situations to all the female principles that fall within the particular time period spoken of. Without a multidimensional viewpoint, we are doomed to confusion. The male-controlled theological arm of the church has separated the female symbols in the book, attributing to the three women only one of the many female characters which fall under the female principle. Thus they have lost the identification of one with the other which would ultimately filter down to the individual woman and which would speak to the human heart on the human level. When Israel is separated from Mary, and Mary from the church, and the church from every woman, the book fails to speak to people. Males have not, however, withheld from themselves an individualistic connotation in male characters presented. They claim anti-Christ for their own and the person of Jesus, as appropriate to males individually. Such is the male ego dealing with the egoless female. Perhaps this is the reason Jesus was so highly selective in choosing to gift John with the Revelation over the other male disciples. He knew John could be trusted to remain obedient to the vision without adding male flourishes of his own. John wrote the only theology of the woman with the exception of Paul's. Having entrusted Mary to John's care, who else could have written it?

The issue of woman is settled in the apocalyptic vision of John. In it we witness a panoramic sweep of woman's past, present, and future plight, during the millenia of serpent-inspired persecution and her deliverance from it. The Book of Revelation is God's closing of the Edenic issue. It is His last word to the male sun-gods of this age, who like Marduk of old, would continue to create through violence.

THE WOMAN AND THE DRAGON

The first of the triune women of Revelation is depicted in a duet of the Virgin Mother. John calls her "a great wonder that appeared in "heaven:"

> "And there appeared a great wonder in heaven, a woman clothed with the sun, and the moon under her feet, and upon her head a crown of twelve stars: And she being with child cried, travailing in birth, and pained to be delivered. And there appeared another wonder in heaven; and behold a great red dragon, having seven heads and ten horns, and seven crowns upon his heads. And his tail drew the third part of the stars of heaven, and did cast them to the earth: and the dragon stood before the woman which was ready to be delivered, for to devour her child as soon as it was born. And she brought forth a *man*[1] child, who was to rule all nations with a rod of iron: and her child was caught up unto God and to His throne.
> And the woman fled into the wilderness, where she hath a place prepared of God, that they should feed her there a thousand two hundred and three score days."   Rev. 12:1-6

Woman has come full circle from Eden to Revelation. Eden echoes:

> "...I will greatly multiply thy sorrow and thy conception; in sorrow thou shalt bring forth children; and thy desire shall

---

[1] Author's italics.

be to thy husband, and he shall rule over thee." Gen. 3:16

It isn't enough that this woman agonizes to birth the child, but she does so in terror that the dragon will devour it at the moment of birth.

One of male Christendom's biblical aberrations had been to claim this "man child" to itself exclusively. This is ridiculous, for the use of the term "man" is meant to denote mankind, which embraces both male and female. The old delusions of the male Godhead rampage through the theology of Revelation as they did through Genesis. The "man child" referred to here is the Christ, who was male and female.

Another male-inspired aberration is the popular notion that this woman symbolizes only the nation of Israel. Christendom's tragic denominational fracturing lies at the root of Catholic contentions she be accommodated to the Virgin Mary, while Protestants seize it for Israel. The truth is that she belongs to both and to the church, the physical creation and every woman under God's sun, as well. John's references to the number 12 are astoundingly profuse and obviously correspond to organic time, but his uses of the number 12 are symbols of the spiritual realities that lie behind the physical phenomena.For instance, there are 24 elders that bow before the throne of God in heaven; the tree of life at the end of the Revelation has 12 manner of fruits, one for each month; there are 12 tribes of Israel, 12 Apostles, 12 foundation stones in the Holy City, 12 gates to the city and 12 angels that guard them. The dimensions of the city are 12,000 furlongs on each side, which corresponds to, in square feet, the 144,000 Israelites who sing the "new song of the Lamb."

Woman is the symbol of not only the physical creation, she is the cell to the mysteries of birth and death, resurrection and eternal life, which secrets will soon be unlocked to man's understanding and subject to his control, at Christ's return. There are many aspects of this beleaguered woman's depiction that bear careful scrutiny, within the context of our subject. One aspect is the apparent absence of any male to defend her. There is no reference to a husband or a lover so we know this woman is a virgin mother. Who is the father of the child? The same one who was the father of the Christ, the Holy Spirit. Why is she abandoned to the dragon in her delivery? And what is more puzzling is why is she seen by John to be in such a dire predicament within the territorial limits of heaven itself? The split Godhead is being exposed here, for this woman is abandoned to the hatred of the ancient enmity. After the "man child" is swept up to God's throne in safety, the woman "flees" heaven. Why would anyone flee heaven? Because, for beleagured woman, there is no peace in heaven so long as the dragon is permitted to persecute her there. This pathetic, exhausted woman is helped by being given "the wings of the great eagle." By whom? This is her only help and she is enabled to escape. But note—she flees to get away from her heavenly torment, as preposterous as that is. The Virgin-Mother returns to earth for peace!

So that no one can say that this woman has been totally pauperized, she is given a brief respite from the dragon's torment. Heaven's idea of post-natal care for her is a wilderness of homelessness, loneliness and confusion. Her rest and peace are interrupted by the dragon, ready for round two.

> "And when the dragon saw that he was cast unto the earth, he persecuted the woman which brought forth the man-child. And to the woman were given two wings of a great eagle, that she might fly into the wilderness, into her place, where she is nourished for a time, and times, and half a time, from the face of the serpent."
> And the serpent cast out of his mouth water as a flood after the woman, that he might cause her to be carried away of the flood. And the earth helped the woman, and the earth opened her mouth, and swallowed up the flood which the dragon cast out of his mouth. And the Dragon was wroth with the woman, and went to make war with the remnant of her seed, which keep the commandments of God, and have the testimony of Jesus Christ."   Rev. 12:13-17

Who rushes to her aid? The earth comes to her aid. In short, woman helps herself! Our theme of woman as initiator and instigator, acting on her own, is confirmed again. Woman must act on her own for no one else dares to assist her. The virgin mother is on her own, just as Eve was on her own. The cowardly non-involvement of the male principle is reminiscent of Adam's frightened absolution of his own Edenic complicity.

THE GREAT HARLOT

This unfortunate woman is the anti-type to the virgin mother. She is called the harlot because she has sold out to the male establishment. Her fate is death at the hands of her male lovers. Before we introduce this infamous lady, we refer the reader to a series of great religious, political and commercial upheavals upon the earth that John prophesies will come at the end time. There are "beasts" alluded to, which attempt to create a one-world government which will rule the planet with the serpent at the helm, through the instrumentality of a male. This puppet male will, as Scripture says, "Give no consideration to the desires of women." Dan. 11:37. This is the male whose number is 666. He is the companion of the harlot whose name is "MYSTERY;" 666 is the harlot's offspring and the anti-Christ. He will be the ultimate expression of the male principle on the rampage, leading the world, by way of fire or intellect, without the restraining influence of female spirit, into final destruction. In the end, he becomes so swollen with serpentine pride that he actually sets himself up in the temple of God, declaring himself to be God, and demanding worship as God. This is the grand climax of the Edenic issue, in which the male principle finally turns all his theological cards face up, and openly declares that the true God is ALL MALE. He is the personification of Satan, woman's enemy. His number 666 represents solar or intellectual energy (male) taking complete control of the creative dynamic, wherein the female (lunar energy) is prostrated into non-function by force of violence. Its offspring will be world-wide nuclear holocaust. In the person of the male, 666, we see the results of the severed Godhead, flopping to the male side. When the prophesied Armageddon occurs, the earth will shake and tremble as if it too had flopped 20 degrees on its axis.

Under the auspices of the all-male deity, the Edenic issue reaches its final fulfillment, as the unrestrained male principle appropriates more and more of the Godhead to itself. The floods, famines, pestilences, tidal waves and earthquakes envisioned by John are the tortured spasms of the female principle, woman enraged but impotent under the male principle declaring itself God.

This woman, the harlot, who has thrown in with him out of fear, guilt and passivity, had consented to the love affair with a wild passion to please him, as Genesis recorded:

"And your desire will be to your husband and he will rule over you."

But the romance ends when her slavish adoration turns his love to disgust and he murders her. Here is John's introduction of the pathetic harlot, third member of the unholy female trinity:

"So he carried me away in the spirit into the wilderness: and I saw a woman sit upon a scarlet colored beast, full of names of blasphemy, having seven heads and ten horns. And the woman was arrayed in purple and scarlet color, and decked with gold and precious stones and pearls, having a golden cup in her hands full of abominations and filthiness of her fornication..."   Rev. 17:3-4

She is the woman: "...with whom the Kings of the earth have committed fornication."

A deal has been made. In exchange for her body these male ruling powers, represented by the "beasts," cover her with sumptuous adornment, vowing eternal love. She never suspects that she is more their plaything than a real contributor to the work of the world establishment.

Though she inspires through her passion, passivity and mindless devotion to her male "head" great works of art and technology, he invariably uses them as weapons against her and his fellow man. Her adoration leads him into believing he is all she says he is. Consequently, his world system is born and fed upon pride and violence. One day, disenchanted with the lie of her egoless inspiration, he begins to wish to be rid of her:

> "And the ten horns which thou sawest upon the beast, these shall hate the whore, and shall make her desolate and naked, and shall eat her flesh and burn her with fire."
>
> Rev. 17:16

She is called: "MYSTERY, BABYLON THE GREAT, MOTHER OF HARLOTS AND ABOMINATIONS OF THE EARTH."[2]

Rev. 17:5

In her slavish idolatry of the male half of the true Godhead, the whore has contributed to the attempted destruction of the "man child" the terrorized virgin mother has delivered. Here is the description of her murder:

> "And the Kings of the earth, who have committed fornication and lived deliciously with her, shall bewail her, and lament for her, when they shall see the smoke of her burning...saying, Alas, alas, that great city Babylon, that mighty city! for in one hour is thy judgement come."
>
> Rev. 18:9-10

This is Eden all over again and women submit to it willingly! Judgment upon the whore is the old double standard of the male God. Male ruling powers consort willingly with the harlot, and when she outlives her usefulness, she is judged and killed by her male accomplices. This is justice Marduk style; Babylonian style. It is not the justice of the true God who is male and female.

John records the shock of her demise by her male lovers:

---

[2] Author's capitalization.

"And the merchants of the earth shall weep and mourn over her; for no man buyeth their merchandise any more: The merchandise of gold, and silver, and precious stones, and of pearls, and fine linen, and purple, and silk...and all thine wood, and all manner vessels of ivory, and all manner vessels of most precious wood, and of brass, and iron, and marble, And cinnamon and odors...and wine, and oil...and wheat, and beasts, and sheep, and horses, and chariots, and slaves, and souls of men. And the voice of harpers, and musicians, and of pipers...shall be heard no more at all in thee; and no craftsman...and the light of a candle shall shine no more at all in thee...and the voice of the bridegroom and of the bride shall be heard no more at all in thee...for by thy sorceries were all nations deceived. And in her was found the blood of prophets, and of saints, and of all that were slain upon the earth."

Rev. 18: 11-13; 22-24

We won't go into all the implications in this passage of how the severed Godhead and the violent subjection of the female principle to the male is related to this great commercial whore, but only to say she is the culmination of the doctrine of woman's subjection to the power-pride syndrome of the Adamic catastrophe.

The name "MYSTERY," written across her forehead, traces her origins back to Babylonian religion. This pathetic woman is again the female, slain by the male Marduk, whose body is flung half skyward into the heavens of the male intellect, and her other half flung to the ground, below the conscious male mind, where the beasts of his subconscious prowl in animalistic ego aggressions.

So far, we've seen three women doomed to either virginity, and loneliness, motherhood and terror, rejection and wilderness or whoredom, disappointment and death. Adam, Moses, Paul and Augustine and now John, complete the portrait. Woman comes to Revelation trailing the old wounds, the old hatreds, the ancient cosmic insanity. The pattern is diabolically plain;

woman is hated, used, then slain by the male principle, at the command of the all-male God.

By way of minor theme Mary, the Virgin Mother, bears the "man child" and enters her holocaust of sorrow and wilderness, for at the Cross it appeared that Satan had won the victory, devouring the child.

Eve, the harlot, consorts with her male heads and contributes to the violent anti-Christ factor in the world. Her conspiracy does not earn her mercy but murder. The circle is completed.

The Virgin Mother is the archetype of all women who, like Mary, takes no male husband as her head, in legal marriage or otherwise. In refusing male rule, she sets herself outside the approval and support of her society unless she seeks her support within one of its institutions which will succour her.

The Virgin Mother is the woman, who though she finds herself in the body of a woman, does not sell out to her femininity nor to the myths males have created about her femininity for their own ends. This woman steadfastly resists the idolatrous pedestal the self-seeking male wishes to place her upon. By refusing the adulation of her "pure femaleness" (which he equates with non-self, dependency, feeling and emotions devoid of intellect) she divests him of his trump card for seizing control of her, her children and the life of the world. This Virgin Mother suffers for her loyalty to the true God, which in the end, is loyalty to herself and mankind. If we translate the wilderness and persecution of this woman to the any woman of any age who pioneered for God and man, with an immaculate conception, she has always had to do so outside of society's help or approval. She bucks the male establishment and the female as well. The biographies of great women of history will bear this out.

The Virgin Mother conceives within her spiritual as well as physical womb, for heaven is the realm of idea. It is in the realms of idea her heavenly conceptions occur, for woman herself is idea! *The female Pentecost is an awakening of the mind and spirit that challenges the pelvic fantasies of males who have chained her body to babies and her mind to their pride. For* their "immaculate conceptions," these women are tormented and driven from heaven. But their "man children" are being caught up to God's throne before the carnivorous male can devour them. Though they wander an earthly "wilderness," they never lose their vision.

I will audaciously apply to these women Paul's grandiose hymn of praise, in which he catalogued heroic examples of male faith:

> "And others had trial of cruel mockings and scourgings, yea, moreover of bonds and imprisonment: They were stoned, they were sawn asunder, were tempted, were slain with the sword...wandered about in sheepskins and goat-skins; being destitute, afflicted, tormented; (Of whom the world was not worthy:) they wandered in deserts, and in mountains, and in dens and caves of the earth."
>
> Heb. 11:36-38

These have been, and still are, the women who have not sur-rendered to the severed Godhead. They are the new women, the self-women, the intellectual women, the true women, at war in heaven and earth in a wilderness of spiritual famine. They are the new women pitted against the sex-oriented, idolatrous male mystique of woman, chatteled to his pride, devoured by his passions and struck to silence in his church. These will be the women of the new age.

The "other woman," the harlot, is the Virgin Mother's anti-type in every way. She clings to the old order (dispensation), still fascinated by her male god. The harlot loves the male mystique of Paul's headless woman. She counts herself rich for having sold her intellect for the treasures of her body. She lives in a luxury of approval and support from her husband's rule, content in her primitive racial drudgery, replenishing the graves her male ruler systematically fills by way of famine, pestilence, war and poverty. She raises male godkin, boy-children to carry on in her husband's footsteps, and godless female girl-slaves, trained to the glories of wombdom and obeisance shaped to non-identity and almost mindless dependency. The harlot lives for her lovers and through her children in whatever set of principles, whatever world system her lovers dictate. The harlot is silent in the church, the home and the world, in major issues. The harlot is the church's feminine mystique. The old order of the silent whore and the arrogant goat who slips the diamonds on her fingers and the minks on her back remains her security, even though her end is death at his disgusted hands.

The question: will woman be released from this perpetual madness? The Scriptures say she will, but only after her ancient enemy, the serpent, is dropped in his tracks. The serpent is finally chained and John describes the great event:

THE CHAINING OF THE SERPENT

John saw a 1000 year period of peace and justice upon the earth, ruled by Christ, the male and female God, in which the ancient dragon is rendered inoperative. Since it had been dragon inspiration that has empowered male dominance, this "chaining" will bind "the strong man" and signal the liberation of woman.

John sees thrones and upon them sit those who will judge the earth. The Babylonian conspiracy will be exposed and dealt with. The exposure will make possible the cessation of the cycle of enmity between male and female principles which has condemned the creative dynamic to violence and death. His vision sweeps the multitude of bodies and souls of those slain for their refusal to participate in the drama of rape and violence. These, he says, "rule with Christ a thousand years." Here is how John describes the chaining of the serpent:

> "And I saw an angel come down from heaven, having the key of the bottomless pit and a great chain in his hand. And he laid hold on the dragon, that old serpent, which is Devil, and Satan, and bound him a thousand years, And cast him into the bottomless pit, and shut him up, and set a

seal upon him, that he should deceive the nations no more, till the thousand years should be fulfilled: and after that he must be loosed a little season...."   Rev. 20:1-3

The passage that follows repeats the theme of the virgin mother who must help herself. John now introduces the fourth woman in Revelation—the holy city, New Jerusalem, called the "bride" of Christ. This woman, as the passage indicates, makes herself ready for her bridegroom; which points up the theme of woman freeing herself to equality:

> "Let us be glad and rejoice, and give honor to him [the Lamb]: for the marriage of the Lamb is come, and his wife hath made herself ready."   Rev. 19:7

"Hath made herself ready," is probably one of the most potent lines in the whole of the Bible, for it gives to woman the freedom to make herself ready. No man's hand is allowed to participate in this preparation. Woman acts alone, as Eve and Mary acted. There is a deeper meaning to the symbol of the "bride in relation to a male and female God. Woman's present-day rebellion is sanctioned by the Scriptures. In "making herself ready," she has won the victory over the serpent and the angel is able to chain him.

The cycle is broken, and woman comes into her own and the glory that has so long been withheld from her by the jealous male serpent is ready to be revealed. Her new status is presented in the form of a "Holy City, New Jerusalem:"

> "And I saw a new heaven and a new earth: for the first heaven and the first earth were passed away; and there was no more sea. And I John saw the holy city, new Jerusalem, coming down from God out of heaven, prepared as a bride adorned for her husband...the tabernacle of God is with men, and he will dwell with them, and they shall be his people...And God shall wipe away all tears from their eyes;...and there shall be no more death, neither sorrow...

nor the former things are passed away. And he that sat upon the throne said, Behold, I make all things new...."

Rev. 21:1-5

She is called the "bride," "the Lamb's wife." This is quite a change from a dragon to a lamb. This prophesies the humbling of the male pride to new obedience, in a new order of creation which will not include the violent rape of the female principle. The old violence will be replaced with a new equality and a new co-operation between the two sexes. The New Jerusalem is symbol of the new woman and the "bridegroom" is the symbol of the new man. It is the ultimate vindication of woman and restoration of the balance between the two. It is consummated in the "marriage feast of the Lamb." Here is the description of the "New Jerusalem:"

"And there came unto me one of the seven angels which had the seven vials full of the seven last plagues, and talked with me, saying, Come hither, I will show thee the bride, the Lamb's wife. And he carried me away in the spirit to a great and high mountain, and showed me that great city, the holy Jerusalem, descending out of heaven from God, Having the glory of God: and her light was like unto a stone most precious....And I saw no temple therein: for the Lord God Almighty and the Lamb are the temple of it. And the city had no need of the sun, neither of the moon, to shine in it: for the glory of God did lighten it, and the Lamb is the light thereof." Rev. 21:9-11; 22, 23

That there is a totally new order of creation is supported by this description of the "New Woman." Remember, the virgin mother was "clothed with the sun, had a crown of twelve stars upon her head and the moon under her feet." If we accept the sun as representing solar or male procreative energy, and the moon as lunar, female spiritual energy, then we see that the old balance and the old enmity will give way to a new balance and a new peace, for the "lamb" who is the light of the city, is a perfect combination of both solar and lunar energy (male and female). The erroneous concept of Paul's theology of woman, "lorded over by her male head," will be seen in its full light. Woman will be, in a sense, UNMOTHERED from her past child-bearing role as she has known it. Once released from the biological chains of her body, she will be free to enter into a new partnership with males, in the subduing and releasing of the physical creation, her sister, who "groans to be delivered," from the anarchy of rape and abuse through the long centuries of sinful dalliance on the part of mankind.

> "And he showed me a pure river of water of life, clear as crystal, proceeding out of the throne of God and of the Lamb. In the midst of the street of it, and on either side of the river, was there the tree of life, which bare twelve manner of fruits, and yielded her fruit every month...and there shall be no more curse: but the throne of God and of the Lamb shall be in it...."   Rev. 22:1-3

The "curse" referred to was the curse of creation through violence and death. Its removal will mean creation through mutual co-operation and respect. Woman, restored to her direct relationship to God, will find a new disciplined freedom to co-create with males.

What are some of the evils of the old order that must go, before the new is established? This past order had buried deep into the psyche of both males and females some deadly roots that will require radical surgery if the two sexes are to achieve total reconciliation.

Incest is the Name of the Game

Breaking the Babylonian myth in the psyche of mankind is not so simple as it appears. One thing Christendom has failed to learn about our ancient foe is his marvelous ability to take a basic truth and twist it with just enough of a flourish so that it appears false. The opposite is also true. This is what he has done in the doctrine of woman's subjection. While I do not wish to offend my Catholic brethren, I must attack the Mariolatry which has fed the Babylonian monster to the Godzilla it has become. After plodding through sixty-six books to prove that woman has been abused and tortured by males, it may seem an irrational contradiction that I now make ready to attack the worship of Mary, but it is necessary.

The worship of Mary has been the serpent's game, first of all, to hide from woman the fact of her persecution by ornamenting virginity and maternity with ego flattering, diversionary baubles. Mary's marble feet upon a clay pedestal have served to soothe the female ego into what she has believed to be a beautiful passivity. Honest women do not wish to be worshipped, nor do honest males. In raising virginity and motherhood as the highest expression of feminine spirituality, the old dragon has trapped woman in the very cycle from which she agonizes to be released. There is a semblance of truth in his theology. Woman did need to be raised from her enslavement, but dragon liberation is implemented by new chains. Once trapped in the virgin-mother-harlot syndrome, woman is called to a new anguish which has imprisoned her the more, for it is a prison she is loathe to be delivered from. She senses that beyond the prison, she is set free to the old violence once again. Dragon liberation is not liberation at all, it is simply the trade of a cell for an honor system. Cell or honor, woman is still in a male manufactured correctional institution.

Every woman born and raised in the Judeo-Christian ethic has felt the invisible hand that has shaped her in and out of the legal institution of marriage. Some more than others will be able to identify with the three women depicted in the Book of the Revelation of John. Rich or poor, dull or bright, educated or uneducated, all women have felt the impact of intractable tradition in the doctrine of the subjection of woman.

There is a new surge of Pentecostalism rising today, and caught within the currents of this rise has been the modern woman of all persuasions of Christendom, swept back under the old Pauline concepts of the subjection of woman. In the more fundamentalist denominations, women are being exhorted to "return to willing and sweet subjection" according to Paul, while women in the so-called secular church, quietly straddle the discrepancies between a doctrine that is still "on the books" but seemingly abandoned in visible practice. No matter. Psychiatrists' offices and pastors' parsonages are bulging at the seams trying to counsel women caught in the final squeeze of a tradition that is no longer bearable to them.

It is acutely embarrassing to observe the lengths that pastors and ministers will go in counseling Christian women with problems of leadership in the home, to preserve the order, "according to Paul." In most cases where males have been unable or unwilling to take their places as "spiritual heads" of the family, the woman is invariably told she must "lift" him to it. In most cases she is encouraged to employ whatever means at her disposal to keep from him the obvious truths of his inadequacies. The toll in mental and emotional anguish in women who cannot get from their husbands, and the fathers of their children, the emotional and spiritual support they need, is becoming catastrophic. Few women have escaped, for few marriages are insulated from the invisible but ever-present ghost of the Pauline doctrine still worshipped by the male arm of the church. Paul's ideal, based as it has been upon injustice and an ancient violence, is incongruous with the advances women have made in areas other than the traditional role of child-bearing. But most of all, it is in deadly contention with the basic principles of the Christian doctrines of faith, Christ's mediatorship, free will and spiritual equality of all men (male or female), before a sovereign God. Wearied of the struggle to bridge the chasm between what her church has said she should be and what she knows herself to truly be, woman is breaking down under the strain of a lie. She is fast accepting the fact that "the bloom has worn off the rose," as she strains to gasp for air in her attempts to maintain her position "under" her "head." Only so long as she bends lower and lower will he retain his position above her. Yet the church loves this myth of the order of Paul for it is a male myth.

Women have been carrying their males emotionally and spiritually for too long and they are in rebellion at last. The weekend father in a cataleptic trance in front of the TV set has become an American institution. In the privacy of the priest's or parson's office, the woman weeps and does not know what ails her, yet she knows. The desperation is growing every day by Christian counselors to keep failed marriages together, by trying to convince the woman that only by her "sweet submissiveness" will this naturally superior animal take up his latent superiority. No matter how long or low woman bends, the lie will out that headship or superiority lie where they are merited, and are not determined by the genitals!

Modern woman's dilemma is the dilemma of the mother-virgin of Revelation. She is swollen with male-child, a child who does not wish to be born. Content that he is male and for the most part, assured by the world that that alone is sufficient, he lingers in the dark and watery haven of the womb in eternal fetal position, parasitic upon the body of woman for his life. But woman will be delivered of this child because she can stand her agony no longer. We are seeing today in the angry and determined thrust for women's total emancipation from male domination, a rising awareness on her part that she has carried the male child in her spiritual womb from the dawn of consciousness and she would be, at last, done with it. From the day Eve tired of the status quo existence of the uncurious Adam and ate the fruit, he has clung to her in hate and love, despising her for the harshness of the real world she flung him into and loving her for the partnership with God it has made possible, but never has he thanked her. Yet in her worship of him, she has consistently bolstered his ego. It has been his hand which swung the cleaver that split her into three parts, each locked in deadly combat in the beast-ridden caverns of his subconscious mind. The ancient and hysterical fear of castration demanded that in self-protection, woman be castrated also, hence, part one: virgin, part two: mother, and part three: harlot.

Obsessed as he has been to selfishly control and possess her, he set up taboos against her body which demanded that each man have his own wife and that she come to him untouched by another. Yet, no sooner has his selfish possession of her been satiated in the consummation of the marriage bed than he realizes her virginity has flown in carnal pleasure. Thus he has, as Paul put it, not "kept his virgin." Used to having his ecclesiastical cake and eating it too, he ingeniously devises a method whereby she may again lave her body in purity so he invents "mother-love" and builds the fantasy that it is, above all loves, the purest a woman may aspire to, Part Two: mother. He had his pure virgin restored and with fantasy intact, resumes his lordly rule until another contradiction overwhelms him. So perfectly has he cast her in the role of mother and so easily did she accept it that she has become to him also a mother. Mothers, however, do not have sexual relations with their sons. That is the crime of incest. He is torn between self-imposed reverence of her as mother and contempt as incestuous mother and former virgin. Longing for a true bedpartner, he is forced once more to assign her a final role. This he does to wash her clean again.

But who can admit to the shameful travesty openly? He sets about with consummate skill to transform his wife and daughters through their clothing and cosmetics and through advertising in his male-controlled media, motion pictures, etc. to realize his fantasy. The dilemma is solved. After a hard day's work the American male hurries home to his virgin-mother and the shadow of incest.

Chronically sex-agitated, the male may manage to shape his wife so that she will attempt to live up to the trinity of roles he has cast her in. He fantasizes her as a virgin in a bikini. Most are not too successful, for most wives either fail or refuse, not knowing exactly why they refuse, to decorate the bedroom into a "quick change" dressing-room where each slips on the masks necessary for the roles that the triune woman must play in bed. A lot will depend upon how fast and well she can peel and apply the masks of virgin, mother or harlot. If one or the other partner lacks the versatility or the imagination required for these leaps of faith in the dark, one or the other is bound to feel defiled in the marriage bed and it is usually the woman, for it is upon her that the "three faces of Eve" have been painted. Defilement leads to shame and shame, according to Paul, is woman's natural and proper condition. The depiction of the triune woman of Revelation, embodied in modern woman is terrifyingly plain.

What's the solution? Break the myth! Woman, for her part must exert herself and steadfastly refuse to mother their husbands and reserve against all male pressure that mother love for those children to whom it rightfully belongs. Males; fathers must stop competing with their offspring for their mother's breasts. They must surrender or be forced to surrender their obsession that mother-love is the purest of loves. Males must learn and women must teach them that intelligent, sensitive fully human women do not wish to be mothers to their husbands. Lastly, women must conceive of themselves as spiritual virgins, married or mothered. It must be woman who will shatter Paul's erroneous theology of virginity that resides in the body alone, and announce to the world that she is finished with the carnal concepts of males. When she becomes no longer susceptible to the idols males have placed before her, she will find her God, in whose image she is made, male and female. At last "her desire will not be for her husband," but for her God.

The poet William Blake put it expertly:

EPILOGUE

(To Satan who is the accuser of this world)
"Really my Satan thou art but a dunce
and doth not know the garment from the man,
every harlot was a virgin once
nor canst thou ever change Kate into Nan."

Let woman move into this greater female Pentecost which is pouring from the hand of God at this hour, fight to the death, if need be, for the truth that virginity is of the spirit. Release the physical virgin to human love. Teach her that whether a male hand touches her or not, she remains a virgin forever; for virginity is of the spirit which no human hand may touch, for it is of God. Let this female Pentecost serve warning upon the all-male God that woman is through catering to the male god who never learned to love her, being too busy using her to whelp and whine and wander, in a wilderness of shame and degradation of her body, sorrow at her soul because she never found her spirit.

Let woman take possession of her body and cherish and guard it fiercely from the dirt male pride heaps upon it so he may wash his own. Let woman in this Pentecost, find the power of her mind and the might of her spirit. Let her become master, not only of her body, but of her personal identity without which she will perish.

THE CHURCH AND THE TRIBULATION

The greatest message the Book of Revelation has for man concerns the time of great tribulation that will come upon the world, over a period of seven years, in which the wrath of God will fall upon mankind devoted to idolatrous Babylonian worship. While His earthly, political, religious and commercial focus will be upon the nation of Israel, His spiritual sights will be set upon the Church. The "time of Jacob's trouble" has already begun.

What has been happening in the church? For the most part, the church has been engaged in business as usual; squabbling over doctrines, teaching the doctrines of men rather than of God, building lush churches with educational compounds and soliciting funds for Bible schools dedicated to grinding out mediocre teachers of cliché-ridden theology that ignores the real move of God among the nations of the world and outside the institutional structures of corrupted Christendom.

The time of the great tribulation will be a time of judgment upon every institution and tradition of men and the apostate church is among them. Does the orthodox church realize how deeply wrapped within the silver coils of the serpent she is? How could she? What vision has she had to offer the sheep entrusted to her care? She commands to morality rather than to truth, to law rather than love, and to orthodoxy rather than growth. The church is a harlot hopelessly in love with her image, believing she will never sit a "widow." Yet she has loved the created thing instead of the creator, for she clings to the worn-out doctrines of Pauline hypocrisy just as vehemently as the Jews clung to Moses' "bill of divorcement," for the harlot church is madly in love with the all-male God.

Sad to say, every domination upon the face of the earth must be included in this sweeping accusation. The more fundamental sects have arrogantly excluded themselves from the judgment to come by wagging the accusing finger at what they call the "secularized church" or the church of the "social gospel," not realizing that the gospel of Jesus Christ was expressed socially not religiously. Yet, under her auspices, society is in an agony of change from the old to the new, while she hugs to her breast the filth of an entire system which must go down, based as it is on injustice and the principle of creation through hatred and violence against half of the human race: WOMAN.

The church uses the "good book" like a "how-to-do-it manual," "ever learning but never coming to the knowledge of the truth." In her frenzy to maintain the spiritual status quo of a dying age, she teaches her charges to be imitators rather than creators, strapped to morality for its own sake and pious sacramentalism for her own. She has preached from the top of her head, a creator God, but has resisted his creations with all her power, persistently mistaking His move among common men, as Satanic influence.

She continues to define love, as total self-sacrifice for all by all, to all. She shuns what she calls intellectualism for all the wrong reasons. She preaches the forgiveness of sins through blood shed but persistently points her finger at men, probing away every good and lively enthusiasm of their lives to an icy death of resignation and defeat. Humility she preaches for all, but demands it only of women. Her heart lies deep within Babylonian religion for her doctrine of the subjection of woman, which has kept woman bound to maternity, is rooted in the ancient worship of fertility goddesses. Catholics have steeped themselves in this idolatrous worship openly. Because of their ceremonious adoration of Mary, Catholics have had little need to preach Paul's doctrines of subjection. Not furtively, therefore, have they burned their candles and recited their rosaries, nor ornamented the world's nooks and crannies with statues to her honor. Protestant and fundamental denominations, however, have hidden their idolatry from themselves, by lifting Paul's doctrine of subjection above Jesus' doctrine of liberation.

We predict a coming storm wherein women will be persecuted by their own churches for taking any active part in the women's liberation movement, for this is soon to break in a new way and with fierce intensity, and the apostate church will be woman's toughest foe. The ranks of the true church will be thinned in this issue beyond the comprehension of most who call themselves the "true church."

The church has, for the most part, failed to recognize the trinity of time contained within the Book of Revelation. Should she stumble upon it, her heart would fail her for fear. She would see herself as the virgin mother turned harlot. How does a virgin become a harlot? By failing to retain her virgin status with God, as she guides and nurtures the "child" through its 2000-year development with her God as her "head," rather than her husband. The "bride of Christ" became the bride of the all-male God. Now her "desire is for her husband," the male establishment of the male God. By failing to accept the truth that this past dispensation has been a female age in spirit; a female Pentecost, intended by her Creator to dynamite the female principle out of its passivity, into action which would restore the male-female Godhead, she becomes a harlot.

The harlot's idolatrous devotion to Paul's doctrine of the silenced, subjected woman is her male and female mystique which causes her to stub her spiritual toe upon the old "rock of offense," that by allowing Paul to command the subjection of woman, the Creator was commanding us to evil that we might learn the good. The harlot's spiritual vision has been clouded so that she cannot see the steady strides, painful and slow as they have been, of the female principle as it has worked its way towards full liberation from the Babylonian poison that inspired Paul's doctrine. The earth is ready for harvest. The good, which is woman's demand for co-equal regency in the lordship of this planet, recognition of her role as initiator, and a recognition of her metaphysical function as "idea," should be the wheat which the church joyfully separates from the chaff to be gathered into the heavenly storehouse. The evil, woman's passivity, should be the chaff to be burned. But the harlot resists in the name of her golden calf of male domination. The coming tribulation will fall upon her startled head as suddenly and as traumatically as it will fall upon all the whoring institutions of a system built upon a shattered Godhead. The true church? Who are they? Those who Revelation says, will not receive "the mark of the beast." That mark may be hidden now, but the days are coming when the harlot will discover who she is.

Strive as we will, nothing can hold back the "new creation" of God. We have had two of three dispensations that correspond to the trinity of the Godhead. The first Old Testament age was the age of pure ego, a male age in which a male sacrificed every other man to himself if the expression of his faith towards his God demanded it. It was the age of the Father.

The second dispensation was an egoless, female age in which Jesus taught that each man must sacrifice himself to all other men, in his expression of faith towards his God. It was the age of the Son.

The coming third dispensation will be the age of superb creativity ruled by the Holy Spirit of creative truth wherein both of the past ages will be brought together in a divine fusion; a new reconciliation of male and female, principles in a co-equal regency, not only within the collective consciousness of mankind, but within each individual. The coming age will be signaled by a restoration of the male-female Godhead. Intellect and idea will fuse, guided by a quest for truth. We will at last unlock the secrets of our physical creation and enter the cosmic community beyond earth. But we will not be allowed to contaminate the universe with a rampaging male principle dragging behind it a bound and gagged female principle.

Intellect and idea must subject themselves to each other in a new mutuality which will require that the female principle rise from passive acceptance to active participation. Before this is realized, however, there remains one last chain to be removed from the captured female. She must be released from the legal institution of marriage, the oldest and hitherto most impenetrable male stronghold that keeps her prisoner. Will the harlot resist? She will resist with all her might, for the demise of legal marriage will signal the demise of her Babylonian tower of confusion upon whose topmost pinnacle she "sits a queen," worshipping her husband and cloaked in mystery.

INTRODUCTION TO A GOODBYE

Contained within the ethical and moral revolutions underway today is an intense search for new answers to traditional "rights and wrongs" that have as their catalysts a suspicion of the changeless God who has dispensed to man immutable laws from His changeless hand. Man in search of himself can no longer find his peace in the old categories of good and evil that once comforted him. His search springs from a heightening of his consciousness within the framework of his humanity, not as a striving towards Divinity.

In short, man wishes to become more human. Within all of today's moral and ethical experimentation lies a valid intensity of spirit which would re-examine the persistent ambivalence of much of the church's stands on vital issues. One of the immutables of the ambivalent church has been its prohibition of divorce as contrary to the general welfare of man and the individual. Yet, in the prohibition of the taking of life, we have seen a strange ambivalence. Witness the *abolition of*, and *retention* of capital punishment which in one case takes life and in the other spares death for taking life.

The same ambivalence is visible in the sanction and the encouragement of war. Yet in the command against adultery, there has been an attitude of consistent inflexibility and ritual condemnation. The extenuating circumstances of capital punishment and war have not been extended to divorce and adultery. As has been usual in matters relating to human sexuality, there is an unbending puritanical resistance to any alleviation of the moral imperatives that bind men and women in legal marriage. Just as Paul placed marriage back under the law, so too, for the most part, has the modern church made its appeal to law. The church has generally been content to construct unsealable institutional walls of stone mortared by the law to prevent divorce. There are so many answers left unanswered by the Bible as regards human sexuality that the institution of legal marriage emerges more as a refuge from the laborious pursuit of pertinent inquiry than a dynamic expression of relevant persuasions. Male theologians will commit grave error if, in dealing with marriage, they take their impetus from the comfortable and simplistic equations of the past. We have had centuries of male theology: Father, Son and Holy Ghost. We now need, and woman demands, a theology of woman, written by woman. The old theological dictionaries must be discarded. The long night of woman as subject for males has given way to the day of woman. We suppose the study of legal marriage, divorce, adultery and procreation from the biblical frame of reference, or even the subject of the subjection of woman itself, may seem to be modern anachronism to many. Who, after all, truly cares what the Scriptures say about woman, among those who have forged ahead to "promised lands" of new morality or the new radical Christianity? The answer is, more than we have believed for we predict that the push for woman's liberation in the fields of education, politics, equal pay, etc. has not yet touched the solar plexus of the male God. We predict that in the near future it will be all-out war when the battle touches upon the subject of the dissolution of marriage itself as a traditional institution of the church. It will be from the pages of Holy Writ that the arsenals will be filled, for it has been from these pages that the roots of woman's tree have shriveled and stunted. It will, in short, ultimately become a religious battle, for the male God has not yet been dethroned.

One male theological fancy has been the projection of a sexless heaven, based on certain Scriptures. Moses' Ten Commandments and ordinances and Paul's antifeminist, feminist theology, for example. The constant factor in both ages was the imposition of monogamy for women which did not change with dispensations, whereas males went from polygamy to monogamy. Women lost nothing in the dispensational change and in truth gained, for male monogamy certainly put an end to the chatteling and harem life of concubinage. Still, women did undergo a transition of a sorts in that virginity, a new ideal of womanhood, in the concept of physical chastity, was introduced. The Jews had never thought of virginity as the highest expression of the female spirituality. Though it was, unlike the imposition of male monogamy, optional, it was a stirring of what had been motionless monogamous waters for her.

Are we then witnessing a spiraling upwards towards the sexless heavens of religious Christianity? Is physical virginity a training course for the next life? Is the church justified in teaching that the attainment of this ideal is to be sought *here* rather than to expect it to be bestowed upon us as a gift, there? Perhaps the popular wisdom which ignores such concerns, is the best one after all, being born of the intuitive knowledge that such a de-sexed would entail much more than the reordering of the physical. The concept of the sexless heaven stands on shaky ground theologically as well, since it is in contradiction of the doctrine of the Resurrection. Unless we are willing to claim that what died at Calvary was Jesus' divinity rather than his humanity, we cannot toss human sexuality to the scrap heaps of heaven, for the Resurrection must be a resurrection to that which died in its fullness. Yet Jesus taught that there would be no marriage in the Resurrection which seems to contradict a resurrection to full humanity and so it does if we persist in equating human sexuality as metaphysically inseparable from legal marriage: a sort of spiritual biology, unsubject to modification. But the Scriptures have not justified such an absolutist conclusion which is based on traditional rather than scriptural authorities for legal marriage as we know it, is a man-made institution. If we are to uncoil the tentacles legal marriage has wrapped around the nature of human sexuality we must reinspect the Bible definitions of marriage, wife, husband, mother and father, which in the Creator's "immaculate conception" of Genesis, have nothing to do with legal marriage.

The flux we have witnessed in the change from polygamy to monogamy for males indicated that it has been man who has been calling the marital shots, not God. Further evidence is that the static state of woman in monogamy indicates that marriage in its initial founding was instigated as a method of the control and confinement of women. The monogamous woman has been the fixed star around which the dominating male has orbited in experimentation, for all changes have been instituted by him. Marriage has been the private possession and passion of males. Woman did not choose marriage for herself.

What does the Bible really have to say about what we call legal marriage? In fact, nothing at all! Genesis has been offered as unshakeable grounds for marriage as a concession to its primarily procreative purpose. But is this true?

In Genesis, the purpose is indicated as being unitive rather than procreative. The command to "increase and multiply" is prefaced with the highly personal act of bestowing a blessing upon them:

> "And God blessed them, and God said unto them, Be fruitful, and multiply, and replenish the earth, and subdue it." Gen. 1:28. Going into the second Genesis account where the creative process has begun, we see a unitive purpose stressed:
> "...It is not good that the man should be alone." Gen. 2:18

This is uncontestably unitive in purpose. Had He meant as

Christianity has assumed, the male of the species had an inherent superiority over the female, He would have said: "It is not good for man to be alone;" meaning mankind. What is marriage, according to the Bible? Man-made tradition has required vow-taking before a third party such as a priest or minister acting as mediator, yet we find no such command in the Scriptures.

The Scripture which follows is the first of few references to the term "wife," which incidentally, is barren of any implication either directly or indirectly to justify the future doctrine of female subjection:

"...and shall cleave to his wife...."   Gen. 2:24

Still no note of vow-taking or legal binding, for in this context there can be no other meaning except that "wife" refers only to the female of the species. The male shall "cleave to his wife." Webster defines cleave: "to adhere to, cling to." If we try to wring out of the term "cleave" a legal binding, we must do so outside the context of legal marriage as we have instituted it for to "cleave" as stated here is a one-way motion (male towards female) while legal marriage is a two-way binding. As a matter of fact, this line plays havoc with the concept of subjected woman for here we see a one-way direction; that of the male to the female. Males have not subjected themselves. In the Creator's original conception of mankind, the man and woman were to take dominion as co-regents. There is not a single word to imply that Adam was to rule over the female. The enmity towards the female was begun after the expulsion and though prophesied, was not pronounced as a curse but as an order which could not be avoided due to the lack of faith and knowledge of both the male and the female in their new state.

From everything we can glean in the Genesis accounts, the subjection of woman as a reactionary measure was an unplanned but foreknown consequence of the burden of godly knowledge the couple had moved into. This chapter deals with the subject of legal marriage as an institution of the male god. We will investigate it according to divorce, adultery, sexuality and procreation. Having reappraised the biblical definitions of "wife, husband, mother and father," from which male theologians have drawn their matrimonial doctrines, we are better prepared to understand how we have come to the point we are at, at present.

That something was drastically wrong with legal marriage, was confirmed by Jesus Himself when He stated that there would be no marriage in the Resurrection. Men and women today reflect the same disenchantment. Still, we have mixed emotions about relinquishing the only institution males have allowed us in which to exercise our sexuality without the onus of serious sin. The conflict is reaching apocalyptic proportions and threatens the whole fabric of religious, political and commercial world systems, since woman, for the first time, is making verbal and active commentary upon herself and her sexuality; a phenomenon the male Godhead has not previously had to cope with.

It is entirely in keeping with Jesus' ministry to propose shocking new ideas, as in the marriageless resurrection. Few truly realize how revolutionary His teachings were in the time He presented them. He overturned the cherished traditions of moral, ethical and religious beliefs of the men of His time. Jesus threw the bombshell that marriage would be done away with in heaven.

Part Two

As I began to write this chapter an article appeared in a recent edition of the Buffalo (N.Y.) *Evening News*. It told of the fight of an Egyptian female cabinet minister who had managed to stir up a religious and political holocaust by proposing legislation that would end the age-old polygamous marriage laws that permit Moslem males to take as many as four wives.

In reality, this is a revolt against the Moslem Bible, the *Holy Koran*, which like our Bible, has been the wellspring of polygamy for males and monogamy for females. The proposed legislation demands that divorce be transacted before a judge, thereby eliminating the former method which consisted of the male pronouncing three times, "I divorce thee, I divorce thee, I divorce thee." It also presses for the right of a woman to divorce her husband for taking a second wife.

"Marriage has been a risky business for women," the article said, "and the long hot summer is the peak season for divorce."

An Egyptian male may break or reinstate the marriage at will, unless his wife marries another man. Then the relationship is finished for good. The issue has thrown male university students into massive demonstrations in protest. Needless to say, the religious opposition is strong everywhere.

The article continues: "Supporters of the arguments are met by religious arguments quoting the holy Koran which emphasizes male superiority." A weekly political newspaper which supports the amendment of the personal status law, said,

"Married women live in constant fear of divorce." One of the measures Egyptian women have resorted to has been to bear many children to tie their husbands down, resulting in a population boom. The proposal would also restrict the right of conjugal domicile under which, to avoid paying alimony, a man can force his wife to live with him against her will, or refuse to divorce her. Strong masculine objections have won out over the years of struggle by Egyptian women to preserve marriages in Egypt.

Elsewhere in the world another marital battle is raging in Italy by way of the first national referendum that nation has had in almost forty years. It is the referendum to repeal the three-year-old divorce law, the first national referendum since the Italian people voted on the monarchy in 1946. Until three years ago divorce was illegal in Italy. As in Egypt, the issues of divorce and the toppling of old customs and traditions are not entirely rooted in religious convictions founded in Holy Writ. In Italy the political and commercial repercussions will be monumental for the loser. A vote against the repeal would be a serious setback for the Christian Democratic Party. Politicians on both sides of the divorce issue said the vote could affect church-state relationships and the future Italian government alignment. The Vatican is fighting with every weapon at its disposal to repeal the law. The Pope called for prayers to the Virgin Mary asking "for her assistance for the restoration of strong and healthy civil morals, violated in these times and scorned by base permissive forms and scandalous immorality." Politicians and Vatican officials agreed that a defeat of the repeal effort would all but end church influence in Italian politics and signal a new effort towards revision of the 1929 concordat between the Vatican and Italy.

This battle emits an odor tinged with the smoke of Armageddon. Legal marriage, having been the institution within which the Babylonian role playing has been forced upon woman, is in serious danger. When Jesus said that there would be no marriage in the resurrection he lit a torch that would light the way for men and women two thousand years later, trapped in a dying world system dedicated to the enslavement of the human soul and spirit. Legal marriage is one of these systems.

Two Scriptures in the account of Matthew and Mark seem to confirm that Jesus taught the indissolubility of marriage under pain of serious sin, except for adultery or fornication. It appears that in the case of legal marriage, Jesus dropped His penetrating insights into men's hypocrises and heartaches and settled for a hard line attitude with no options for negotiation.

This is not the Jesus who went about healing the broken-hearted or setting captives free. This is a legalistic Jesus who takes no thought for the differences between men or the hallowing of the personality. It would seem, as Christendom has believed, that Jesus, like Moses and Paul, saw sex as a human timebomb whose ticking must be silenced through the dismantling of legal marriage. No one denies the reality of sexual lust in the use of sex for its own sake, yet who, including Jesus, has ever come up with a constructive insight as to how to replace lust with a higher motivation for men? The appeal to love, in the form of Christian forgiveness, may keep bad marriages from the scandal of public schism, but it rarely helps change a bad situation. The morality of sacrifice is a stop-gap measure; a tribute to endurance. Sacrifice endures the wrong without malice but it should not be forced to embrace the wrong itself as worthy of its love.

In short: forgiveness has no power to change another person except in the persuasion of our love. When change ultimately fails to occur sacrifice is a powerless anachronism to injustice. Marriage has been considered to be the controlled laboratory conditions to isolate and treat the germ of lust but it has treated only symptoms while failing to touch the disease. To say that a man or woman who seeks compatibility outside of an incompatible marriage is guilty of lust, is to declare that marriage automatically bestows compatibility with anyone. Marriage has no such magic elixir.

Why did Jesus not address Himself meaningfully to the causes of lust which may exist even within marriage itself? The only answer lies in the possibility that He was engaged in dealing with a much deeper issue than the forbidding of divorce as a thumb in the dike of individual lust. He was dealing with the Edenic issue which was the disease, and legal marriage its symptom. We need a thorough understanding of the biblical definition of the term "wife" and all it implies.

The edifice of legal marriage was erected upon the foundation stones of a mere four lines of Scripture found in the second chapter of Genesis. Our use of the term "wife," in no way resembles the original meaning intended in the context of the source from which it was taken. These are the lines:

> "...This is now bone of my bones, and flesh of my flesh: She shall be called Woman, because she was taken out of Man. Therefore shall a man leave his father and his mother, and shall *cleave unto his wife*: and they shall be one flesh."
>
> Genesis 2:23-24

Religious Christians' understanding of these lines can best be compared to a man who discovers a single maple tree, who has never seen a tree before. He rightly calls the tree a tree, but later he spies a poplar but refuses to believe it is a tree because it is straight and tall with no flung branches to give shade. To him, only a maple tree is a tree.

This is the way we have come to think of the term "wife." A wife is the mate of one single man. She may not become the wife of another man since to her mind and his, there are no other men. In the order of creation, Adam was made after the plant life from the dust of the ground, followed by the animals which were made from the ground alone. Animals are flesh and bone and blood as Adam is, yet Adam was made from the dust and the animals from the ground, implying a difference between dust and ground.

When the animals were brought to him to be named, he divided them into species. Dogs belong to the canine species; lions to the feline; mules to the equine, etc. Yet, there are differences within species called breeds. Within the feline species is male and female of the lion, leopard, puma, tiger, siamese cat, etc. There are dozens of breeds within the canine family. There are genetic barriers between breeds that are not crossed. A lion does not mate with a horse or a collie with a beaver. There are also barriers within breeds. A female lioness will not permit a male leopard to mate with her and vice-versa. These very real genetic and instinctual barriers prevent inter-mingling which would sully the integrity of the breed.

Adam was of the species Man. He existed in the Garden alone for a time, without a female of his species. In naming the animals prior to the arrival of the female of his own species, when the woman was brought to him he exclaimed: "This is now bone of my bone and flesh of my flesh," which means that she was simply the female of his species. Nothing more can be wrung from this line while in this context. At this point she is just the "woman." Eve was yet in the future.

He goes on to say, "For this cause shall a man leave his father and his mother...." For what cause? For the cause of male and fe-male of the species and sexual intercourse, naturally. But when Adam refers to a mother and a father are we to assume that he had a human mother and father? We can take our choice. Either he did, in which case, nothing is implied as to legal marriage or vow-taking between them. If he didn't, then we assume he literally put two and two together in observing the animals mating and came up with three; mother, father and offspring. Whichever the case, what can we wring out of these lines to indicate marriage between mother and father, other than sexual intercourse? Where, we repeat, is the mention or even the hint of legal binding, vows or even a third party via minister or priest to perform the marriage? There is none. Now, what did he mean to "cleave to his wife?" That means every male will "cleave" to every female of the species. This is a mandate to the male principle to adhere to the female principle, and scuttles the theory of the subjection of the female. To whom does the female "cleave?" The Bible doesn't say! Man, however, has said that she is to "cleave to her husband in headship;" an out and out contradiction of the one-directional cleaving spoken of here.

To sum it up; the term "wife" denotes only the female of the species; and mother and father, male and female mates who produce offspring. Eve was therefore Adam's wife even before she received her personal name, from which we may deduce that, as Jesus said, "from the beginning God made them male and female" as universal men and wives, without the preacher to officiate or without the exchange of legal vows.

In the mandate to legal marriage, we see the application of universalism in the prohibition against divorce, plus a little of personalism in its philosophy of one wife to one male and vice-versa. If, after receiving her personal name through sin, Eve moved out of universalism into personalism and therefore legal marriage, one Eve to one Adam in an indissoluble fashion, then can she not by way of sin move from Adam to Adam and vice-versa? Or, to put it even better, can Eve not now move back into complete universalism; free love between the male and female of the species through the atoning blood of Christ which removes sin? In short, haven't we got a bit of a confused mess in legal marriage?

In the universal relationship between male and female before the fall, Adam was the male, and the woman the female of the species. They were not married legally by way of vows or mediation, but by way of their procreational function of producing offspring. We can assume that Adam and Eve were either one historical man and one historical woman or a race of males and females. Whichever we choose, we still have the necessary factors for computing the facts of our origins. In view of this universalism, if there was sexual activity between the male and female, it was free love; that is, in a term we will coin, "illegal or unlegal married love;" "married" meaning sexually mating. Since the woman did not move into personal identity until she sinned, after which she knew good and evil, we can assume that the innocent universal free love between all males and all females which existed before the fall into knowledge was guiltless. After the fall, universalism also fell into personalism as typified by the woman's personal name: Eve.

Freedom fell into law and law to sin and sin to guilt and guilt to shame and we're back home, all the way. But, here's the catch to watch for: If Adam had intercourse with Eve only after the fall, then it means he did so with knowledge of her; her sin lifting the veil from her personality, character, mind, soul and spirit. We can therefore deduce that before this, in the universal innocence, Adam did not "know" Eve, in the time they spent together before the fall. Whatever the relationship between them, prior to the fall, it was not based on knowledge, at least not full knowledge. Does this mean that males and females coupled in the garden (assuming they did, since they were allowed to eat from every tree in the paradise) at random like animals, without discrimination based on preference, based again, on knowledge? What else can it mean?

Now we conclude that the fall from innocent universalism into personal guilt was accompanied by a fall from ignorance and rise to knowledge about each other's personality. Was it, at the same time, a move from free love to legal love on a one to one basis, as we know it in legal marriage? No. It fell to legalized polygamy which indicates that the male made a poorer adjustment to the transition from free love in ignorance to restricted legal love in knowledge. The reason the female made a better adjustment was, perhaps, due to the fact that she had desired a change from the old order proven by her instigation of a new one.

The woman desired sex based on love due to knowledge, while the male preferred love based on sex due to ignorance. Polygamy is the proof of the male penchant for sex for its own sake. In the fall from ignorance and innocence and total sexual freedom, sex rose to the possibility of love, for after the fall, personal knowledge entered between the male and female and is based on knowledge. If sin plunged us to knowledge and the possibility of love, then it is upon knowledge which we will base love. The question is, do we always love what we come to know? Free will decides for each man what he will love. Legal marriage is an attempt to force men and women to love each other for better or for worse. In taking such vows, we bind ourselves to good and evil in an indissoluble manner. How does this speak to free-will in choosing between good and evil? It doesn't. It narrows free-will to one single choice at the time of marriage; not based on anything comparable to full knowledge about the other person or even the self, after which we are no longer free to choose but ordered by law to accept both the good and the evil in a mate.

To accept good and evil by force of law is not the same as to choose between them. This invalidates the accountability of knowledge, for to remain passive to evil when we know it is evil is not good. To define legal marriage as a vow to accept the evil as well as the good in one's mate is, in essence, pledging to wed one's self to evil as indissolubly as good. It is the surrender of the faculty of volition to neutrality. The price of knowledge and love was offset by the paralyzing power of the law. Free will would have to find a new dynamic—faith. Faith alone could resolve the terrible tensions between love and law, for while knowledge made love possible, it also made hate possible. Legal marriage is either heaven or hell, depending on what knowledge reveals to us about the mate we are bonded to indissolubly for life. Common sense tells us that knowledge becomes a curse when it is subjected to legal chains, as in marriage. We have two choices to end the dilemma: get rid of knowledge, the root of love, or get rid of the legal bonds, the root of an enslaved will. If we opt for knowledge and love, we have to justify other ways of attaining to the knowledge of good and evil in persons in a situation where the free-will is left intact to choose between the good and the evil. This can only be done by replacing all forms of legal binding with a return to universal freedom, for inherent in the concept of universal freedom is the factor of innocence; knowing neither good nor evil until it manifests, after which, if not bound legally, we are free to accept or reject.

Equipped with the proper definition of the term "wife" and, more important, armed with insights into the universal issue of cosmic divorce as the alienation of the male principle from the female principle, let us explore Jesus' stand on legal marriage and divorce.

JESUS AND THE PHARISEES

"And the Pharisees came to Him, and asked Him, Is it lawful for a man to put away his wife? tempting Him. And He answered and said unto them, What did Moses command you? And they said, Moses suffered to write a bill of divorcement, and to put her away. And Jesus answered and said unto them, For the hardness of your heart he wrote you this precept. But from the beginning of the creation God made them male and female. For this cause shall a man leave his father and mother, and cleave to his wife; And they twain shall be one flesh: so then they are no more twain, but one flesh. What therefore God hath joined together, let not man put asunder.
And in the house His disciples asked Him again of the same matter. And he saith unto them, Whosoever shall put away his wife, and marry another, committeth adultery against her. And if a woman shall put away her husband, and be married to another, she committeth adultery."

Mark 10:2-12

Jesus ignores their opener, "Is it lawful?" He knew they knew it was lawful, for Moses had made it so. These were Pharisees who, after all, were sticklers for the law. Instead of haggling Moses' law with them He simply apologizes for Moses' bad judgment in giving in to their hard hearts by allowing a bill of divorcement.

Aside from challenging Moses, Jesus indirectly set Himself up as a questioner of the Most High, since Moses was His anointed servant. Could an anointed servant of the Most High make a mistake in matters of faith or morals? Jesus said he could. We must keep in mind that Jesus was addressing Himself to a polygamous society.

According to Jewish law, a male could take many wives if he so chose. David had many wives and Solomon, hundreds. Moses had two. The polygamous laws were still on the Jewish books at the time of this encounter. What aspect of polygamy was Jesus addressing Himself to? Was He, in attacking Moses' bill of divorcement, attempting to lead the polygamous male to monogamy for the sake of enforcing chastity in a new monogamous marital state? How could He have been? What is contributed towards chastity by a man who refrains from putting away one wife out of nine? On the other hand, the reverse is also true. Would a polygamous male be any more chaste by putting away one in nine? Jesus wasn't grappling with the issue of physical chastity within and without marriage. Was He addressing Himself directly to love? Again, the same rebuttal. Can a man love nine women at the same time? Does he love better if he has only eight rather than nine or vice-versa? Was He accusing the injustice of the situation for her who was put away? How could He? Unless He pleaded the case of all nine wives He could not have been primarily striving for justice for the many concubines of one male. A Jewish male, under these laws, could get rid of all his wives and replace them with others if he wanted to. It is obvious that He was not directing His rebuttal at the individual injustice, unchastity or unloving aspect of the polygamous situation. It was something much more universal. It was cosmic divorce. Proof lies in the fact that He refers them to the Genesis passages that we have just reviewed, which deal with man and woman only on a species level by quoting to them:

"In the beginning God made them male and female. For this cause shall a man leave his father and his mother...."

The cause of being female and male not only refers to a primal species relationship, but also to the male and female Godhead the Pharisaical male god had "put asunder." Jesus always geared His teachings to the idiosyncrasies of the person or group with whom He was dealing. The Pharisees were "letter of the law," men. They were at odds with the Saducees, another priestly caste, disagreeing on such issues as the immortality of the soul and the punishment of the wicked. They generally despised Jesus for His teachings about women, who occupied the lowest rung of the religious as well as social ladder. It is interesting to note that, like the Saducees, the Pharisees tempted Jesus with theological questions using the issue of woman and legal marriage as their spearhead. Most of Jesus' encounters with the Pharisees directly involved women. He dealt with them legally, through the Scriptures, which contained the laws they lived by. Woman at that time was not permitted the option of divorce under Moses' laws. He took a hard legal line on the issue, closing the door males had left ajar for themselves via law; slamming it by the power of the law. Woman would have to willingly endure until such time of her total liberation.

When inspecting the other Scriptures on divorce, we see Jesus fighting fire with fire. First He ignores the challenge to legal battle by taking care of first things first in directing the Pharisees to the primary issue of cosmic divorce; then He attacks them with their own weapons on a legal basis by snapping the male legalists within the trap they had manufactured for the woman. Here is where we are most struck with the legalistic Jesus who appears to be allowing for no divorce, except for adultery or fornication. What He is really doing is sealing off all routes of escape for the unwilling male. One of the most startling thrusts He makes is the suggestion that woman as well as males may divorce:

> "...Whosoever shall put away his wife, and marry another, committeth adultery against her. And if a woman shall put away her husband, and be married to another, she committeth adultery."   Mark 10:11-12

This was a Jesus no longer on the defensive. He took the offensive by introducing an unthinkable possibility to the male Jewish mind: that woman could take the initiative and divorce her husband, something unheard of until that time. Imagine how the hearts of women must have leapt with shock then joy at this sudden equalizing of the sexes and what a thunderbolt it must have been to the Pharisees! How easy it was for women to love this Jesus and for males to hate Him! He further makes a differentiation between males and females in divorce by saying that when a woman divorces she only commits adultery, but when a male divorces his wife he commits adultery "against her." What does He mean by the term "against her?" What else could He mean but that woman was slapped, with no consent of her own will, into an institution designed for her by males which doubles their culpability in that they not only sin against the universal order, but against her whom they have forced into the adulterous situation.

Why would Jesus encourage women to commit sin in seeking divorce if she so desired? For the same reasons God permitted Moses to receive the Ten Commandments and then give a bill of divorcement which abrogated the Sixth Commandment. Jesus was treating the disease, not the symptom. It would have to run its course before the cure was affected. There would be a stretch of 2000 years in which males and females would grope their way out of the legal tangle that males had instigated and women submitted to. To do this, women had to be granted the equal privilege of divorce. The ultimate plan was the final equalization of the sexes and the resultant restoration of the balance of power in the Godhead.

It is obvious that Jesus could not be addressing Himself to the individual male and female, per se. With woman as subject, adultery is committed against her: divorce by the male causes her to commit adultery. Woman, in divorcing, does not commit adultery against her husband. The last possible route of escape is sealed off. Not even in the privacy of his own thoughts can he find sanctuary for escape:

> "...Whosoever looketh on a woman to lust after her hath committed adultery with her already in his heart."
>
> Matt. 5:28

Jesus stalks the male relentlessly. Why, for instance, does He not exhort woman to refrain from looking at a male to lust after him? Is Jesus saying that lust is the sole province of males? This can only be taken as further proof that Jesus is addressing Himself to a much deeper issue: dealing not with the victims but with her oppressors.

In this struggle, which has lasted so long, we see perhaps more clearly than in any other issue what the Virgin Mary really gave her consent to when she allowed her body to be used for the incarnation. Jesus was using woman in the issues of marriage, divorce and adultery, as Moses had used her, but this time, with her consent. In Moses' use of her, she had been taken by force of rape but in Jesus' use of her she made herself a willing pawn to checkmate the male godling.

In the issue of marriage, divorce and adultery Jesus style, we see Jesus forcing the male to "cleave" to his "wife." The ancient battle rages today with increasing intensity and will become more ferocious as time goes on. The last club poised over the hated body of woman is the male concept of the sexless heaven in which he makes his last desperate effort to escape woman by way of a heaven that has been de-sexed, de-loved, and de-humanized.

Happily, Scripture says differently.

MARRIAGE VERSUS THE LAW

As we get deeper into the deceptions of the Edenic issue we have been simultaneously uncovering the life blood of Babylonian religion. Clues crop up and fall into place and all point in one direction, legal marriage. The mystery of Babylon is not, as we have been taught by our churches, the emblem of lawlessness in our world, but of lovelessness. Though the harlot has been described as a woman, actually her function has not been to challenge the male principle of law, but to uphold the letter of the law for the sake of her male god. In this perverted loyalty she has betrayed woman and rendered love to a passive state under the law. In short, Babylon's Queen lies passive to love in her worship of law.

Everything in Babylonian religion conspires against love.

Before Jesus came to redeem us from the curse of the law, mankind was bound by the Ten Commandments, which consised of myriads of other laws that sprouted as offshoots of it through ordinances, traditions and rituals. One of the most hotly contested issues in Christendom has been the debate of how to apply the new freedom from the law that Jesus Christ claimed to give us. Where, after Jesus, did the law leave off and "grace" begin?

Some have believed that to be free of the law in Christ has meant to be free to do as one pleased, and for males this has in one way been true. Paul extended to males the right to claim their freedom from the law but blocked the channels through which this freedom should apply to woman. Paul placed woman, in legal marriage, under males by binding her to the law of her husband. Actually, this was a repetition of Old Testament theology which cut woman off from direct access to God. Woman's bound condition in the church actually gagged her, preventing any spiritual participation in the developing theology of the infant church. We are still bound by a theology developed solely by males. The things "bound or loosed in heaven and earth" have been decided upon only by males.

Still the controversy raged. What did the new freedom really comprise? Jesus has said:

> "Think not I am come to destroy the law, or the prophets: I am not come to destroy, but to fulfill. For verily I say unto you, Till heaven and earth pass, one jot or one tittle shall in no wise pass from the law, till all be fulfilled."
>
> Matt. 5:17, 18

Jesus was saying that His main mission was to satisfy the demands of the law. Would we not have expected that the Messiah would take the sting out of the letter of the law—the "eye for an eye and tooth for a tooth" stringencies of the Patriarchal profession? He said He came to satisfy the law, yet He came preaching love. Could oil and water mix? 2 Corinthians had said: "...the letter [of the law] killeth, but the spirit giveth life."

II Cor. 3:6

Male Christendom, beginning with the young male-dominated church under the auspices of the Apostle Paul, had never really fathomed the whole truth Jesus had come to teach them. It wasn't long before the Edenic poison took hold in the bloodstream of the infant church and nearly killed it.

As the old Edenic poison took hold down through the centuries, the virgin church slipped back into the grip of the ancient hatred of woman and the arrogance of male autonomy. Creation through violence continued and the Babylonian male god was back upon his throne, with his fertility goddess at his feet.

The gravity of this backsliding into the spirit of the law is demonstrated in the ambivalent posture of the church which pressures the sheep to strive towards moral perfections of the law while relegating love to the position of stop-gap expediency, to be used only in crisis dilemmas, until such time as we achieve legal perfection. With love relegated to this "tokenistic position" as a reluctant concession to defeat, woman is shackled again to secondary importance, doomed to a semi-salvation within an all-male Godhead.

This is clearly demonstrated in the question of legal marriage. No matter what the cost in human misery the church has galvanized all her forces against divorce. This she does in the name of the law masquerading as love.

The Christian marriage vow is Babylon's craftiest device of human exploitation for it appeals directly to his basic weakness: selfishness. Prone to acquisitiveness as he is, the dangling of the legal carrot by which he may, in the first passion of new love, be assured that he may take life-long possession of his beloved is more than he can resist. Man most always can be counted upon to succumb to lust of legal possession of a love object. Yet, with persons as with gold, the temptation can lead to self-immolation. You are thinking that Paul was right after all? But Paul's lust he took to be the lust of sexual intercourse. The "lust" we speak of is the lust to possess another human being legally, which makes Paul right but for the wrong reasons. Like Moses, Paul received a revelation of the Christ. Within it was a truth: that legal marriage was a concession to lust. That's as far as God went with him. The rest He left up to Paul.

Perhaps the most tragic aspect of legal marriage has been in the absolute indissolubility of the vow except for fornication or adultery. We have come to accept divorce for but a few reasons other than these two; but only in the case of strong anti-social behavior stretched out over long periods of time, such as chronic alcoholism, philandering or addictive gambling, have we allowed relief without the stigma of serious sin. It is still religiously stigmatic and socially unacceptable to seek to divorce the chronically lazy, the infantile, the hopeless dull, the apathetic, the shallow, the crude, the willfully ignorant, the religious fanatic, the lecherous, lewd or incestuous, the over-sexed, the under-sexed, the grossly insensitive, the mentally and emotionally slothful, the liar, the cheat, the tightwad and the thief, the murderer, the insane, the hypocritical, the wife beater, the child beater, the foul-mouthed, the homosexual, the traitorous, etc.

Doesn't it seem strange that Jesus was willing to die for us to save us even from death itself, but drew the line at marital happiness?

If we can accept the mandate to personal growth as the law of godly life, then we can better understand the dynamic that is frustrated when the church pronounces incompatible marriages indissoluble.

Legal marriage has been the great "shakedown cruise" for personal growth. "For better or for worse" is to be taken literally. When a couple finds they have outgrown each other it simply means they are not the same breed. When Christendom forces incompatibles to remain together it is like asking a tiger to occupy the same cage with a zebra. Tigers eat zebras. Lions don't mate with panthers and they are smart enough not to try. Only man thinks he can throw a cat into a cage with a dog and manufacture a honeymoon.

The wisdom of the animal creation is the wisdom of our Creator for He Himself exercised great selectivity among His creatures to reserve for His intimate fellowship. Some He chose for great intimacy. Scriptures are clear that God divided mankind into classes or groups. He fellowships with each according to His own preference. While it is true that God loves all men who will accept His love, it is not true that He has divested Himself of the freedom to discriminate among them when selecting intimate companions.

Love Versus Law

Now we will search out legal marriage inspecting its fruits, taking as our authority the words of John, the "disciple that Jesus loved:"

"Beloved, let us love one another: for love is of God; and everyone that loveth is born of God, and knoweth God... for God is love....If we love one another, God dwelleth in us, and his love is perfected in us...God is love; and he that dwelleth in love dwelleth in God, and God in him...."

I John 4:7-16

No sooner do our spirits find rest in these words than we are thrust headlong into church ambivalence towards law and love when we recall the church's theology of resurrected man, in which we again see Jesus teaching one thing and the church teaching another. The numbering of the Ten Commandments vary according to how they are broken down within the original decalogue. Some number the Commandment against adultery as the seventh. Others number it as the eighth. The Commandment against coveting one's neighbor's wife is likewise numbered differently. For our own use here we will number them as the seventh and ninth.

The church has insisted upon importing all of the Ten Commandments into the heavenly rule. Yet, when we inspect its equally unanimous agreement that there will be no sex or marriage in the same heavenly rule we ask why. If there will be no sex or legal marriage in heaven, why drag in the Ten Commandments? Who has ever heard a sermon preached on the sexless, marriageless heaven?

If the sexual instincts of man can be removed by divine

surgery then why not his proclivity to kill his fellow man? Couldn't heaven be made a better place than just a sexless, marriageless society where liars, cheats, murderers and profane persons roam as they do in this world? The attempt to delete the seventh and ninth Commandments from the ten is not so much a final onslaught against legal marriage as it is against the possibility that woman might retain her sexuality outside of legal marriage!

Why do we wonder that the world has never been truly evangelized by the gospel when Christendom attempts to pawn off such drivel? Either the entire Ten Commandments enter heaven or none of them do. The divine surgery that desexes the heavenly populace is contrary to the doctrine of free will. Not only is it against free will, it is a mutilation of the human body. Just as we refuse to accept a mutilated body as constituting a redeemed body so do we challenge a mutilated Ten Commandments.

The only synthesis possible is that legal marriage without love is not a marriage. Love must temper law and cannot be legislated. In this way we can retain the Ten Commandments and keep our bodies unmutilated for what it amounts to is "free love." Paul's insistence that marriage was a concession to sexual lust was bound up in his typical male racial hysteria. The law, being intellectual, could recognize only the collective good. But when we reinspect Paul's morality of sex, we see a sick morality born of his legalistic Jewish mind.

> "The wife hath not power of her own body, but the husband: and likewise also the husband hath not power of his own body, but the wife. DEFRAUD YE NOT[1] one the other...that Satan tempt ye not for your incontinency."
>
> I Cor. 7:4-6

The terminology is legalistic placing marital sex within the context of fraud and extramarital sex as evil.

---

[1] Author's capitalization.

Paul's definition of the mutual ownership of each other's bodies in marriage but woman's added subjection to the law of her husband as spiritual "head" has stacked the cards against woman. Most Christian denominations have ritually taught wives that to "deny" their husbands is a very serious mistake. According to the letter of Paul they have preached "wifely duty" to be sexually generous with their husbands. With woman, on the other hand, all conditioning has been towards victorian "modesty" wherein a "good woman" would never wish for sexual intercourse nor dream of actually soliciting her husband for it. In which case, guess whose body was defrauded and whose was not? Who ever heard of a male being admonished to provide for his wife's sexual demands until the last few decades or so? With woman craftily oriented into sexual non-aggression the male has been left to pursue woman's body freely, crying "fraud" if need be, with few encroachments upon his sexual duties, by women.

Paul now does an about face:

> "...It is good for a man *not* to touch a woman. Nevertheless, to avoid fornication, let every man have his own wife, and let every woman have her own husband."   I Cor. 7:1, 2

Why is it good for a man not to touch a woman? Paul says, in essence, that if a man wishes to avoid fornication (fornication in this passage referring to unmarried sexual intercourse) he had better marry. To Paul a wife is a sexual outlet. What about a woman touching the male? Is it good or bad, or doesn't it matter? The answer is obvious, for woman can automatically be sexually controlled if males will exercise their will-power against her.

Paul's whole theology of human sexuality, legal marriage, and the subjection of woman was negativistic. One's attentions were to be riveted upon the threat of "fraud" and avoidance of fornication. There was positive theology because Paul was legislating human love between the sexes by the spirit of the law which placed love under law. Paul negated the Lord he believed he served when he did this. He began a long train of males in the church who have never been able to equate human expression of profound love and admiration between the sexes with anything but law, just as they have never been able to equate a human Jesus with a divine one, or a human body with a sanctified human spirit. Paul severed again man's body from his soul and Satan made a grab for it.

Love cannot be legislated. Past, present and future attempts to do so will fail. Even the barren love-deserts of the Old Testament, where the law flourished, could not alleviate the hunger of the pathetic Leah, Jacob's "hated wife." Leah hoped to win his love through her fecundity but though she bore him many sons, she failed, for his heart belonged to Rachel. How does this story address itself to the ambitions of the Babylonian fertility goddess, who keeps her war lord's adulation through fecundity? How does it address itself to today's loveless marriages, hanging by a legal thread for "the sake of the children?" Offspring couldn't make Jacob love Leah and his heart resisted legislation against his love for Rachel. Poor Leah was doomed. Though she may have born a nation, the weight of that entire nation could not have lain any heavier upon Leah's heart than the unutterable loneliness of her unloved personal existence.

To insure that woman did not escape to sexual freedom outside of marriage, Paul instituted virginity on both males and females as the only other alternative to sexual lust and its concession in legal marriage. This was new for women as well as males, for Jews had never considered virginity to be more acceptable than the married state. Just as in today's male-dominated society, woman had nowhere to go for a meaningful existence, since motherhood was her only excuse for breathing. For woman, this was an excruciating sacrifice. Where could the virgin woman go? Where does she go today? She is a displaced person, a second-class citizen, alternately pitied and envied by both women and men. That is exactly the tragedy of it all. The punitive attitudes towards those who do not wish to enter marriage is a violation of the law of love for all men. It is also a prohibition against the singular identity of selfhood. This herd instinct against the single person's right to intimate human companionship is the hard-hearted child of the law, Babylon's weapon for whipping to their knees all who will not conform to her safety first morality of racial survival.

Legal marriage is not the only responsible way to a full humanity. It is not preordained of God. To insist that it is, is to regress to the barbarism of former ages. To withhold a full humanity from the unfettered among us is to legislate against the greatest potential of those who are truly free to work and love without the relentless restricting coils of legal marriage. The old wives' tale that a truly dedicated man or woman cannot work and love at the same time is absurd. Some of our finest minds have active love lives, and many outside of legal marriage.

We vigorously challenge the priestly rebuttal that the rigors of legal marriage makes it the best schoolhouse for human development. How could it be, when it has held half the human race virtually captives from society—when the totality of talents and potential of woman has been detoured within its restrictive coils into uncreative "tending."

How many centuries have the crippled of mind and afflicted of spirit been dictating to the majority of humans that the only eternal option for responsible human sexual love is in legal marriage? How many more countless millions of lives must be herded into this Babylonian institutionalized racial drudgery?

What is Christian Love?

If true Christian love is anything, it is love motivated by the knowledge that first of all we learn through suffering, because suffering is inescapable because of innocence. The true gut level meaning of the death of Christ is to be understood as the death of the old systems that serve man in every age, conceived in innocence, fraught with error and subject to demise.

Legal marriage is an outmoded, archaic and primitive concept of man which insists that man can live on "bread alone." In proposing a marriageless society in which human sexuality is retained and births subject to full human control we prepare ourselves for the death of a system. Just as the dynamic of all living organisms is the universal life principle of growth, so too, is the universal death principle of the passing of that which no longer serves life. Man must surrender to growth, for growth is life and eternal growth is eternal life. In every collision of an old order with a new, some adjust readily and with joy, some flounder in indecision, some are lost, and some do not wish to be found. Today's orthodoxies are some men's heavens, choosing as they do to live among the relics of the past for they fear change as nothing else. The truly saved are those who both welcome and assist the change.

Excesses and abuses are to be expected in the birth of any new order. Yet what would we have to fear in making the transition from a marrying society to a marriageless society that could be worse than the excesses and abuses we already have in this system?

Those who mourn the loss of legislated pressures to provide them with added security in male-female relationships will have to live with that insecurity until the lust of possession and being possessed is defeated by a singular identity. Human love is not in conflict with self-actualization. A revolution is under way as more and more men and women strive to attain a new reality, born of honesty and fed by desperation to surrender all legal claims upon each other. They will exchange the old myths of Babylonianish human impotence for a new dynamic. Some are already marching to the rhythms of a not so distant drummer costumed in ideas of a new way of living and loving which will evolve into new relationships between the sexes that have hitherto not been conceived. Perhaps in the advent of the concept of wholeness, divinely fused within, males and females would for the first time cease taking each other for granted. Woman will be the first to panic at the withdrawal of approval from such dependency relationships that thrive in the soil of legal halfhood. Perhaps women more than men suffer from the peculiar love disease which may appear as compassion but in reality is a clandestine superiority obsession.

Where there is weakness there is always law. We suppose that most men and women are still too selfish, too power prone, too jealousy ridden, to be willing to relinquish the legal hold that marriage gives them upon love objects, including children, for most are enslaved to the lust of possession. However, that is no reason to surrender the vision of a marriageless society to hopelessness. We are beginning to awaken to the knowledge that man cannot alive by the bread of tired moral law alone.

AGAPE OR EROS?

We have spoken of the easy love for the weak and the difficult love of the strong. Another Babylonian tower of love confusion has been in Christendom's definition of spiritual love which refuses to recognize human sexuality except in the context of monogamous marriage, thereby contributing to its dehumanization. In our society, sex has become as mechanized as our industry.

Christ's love has been characterized by the church as "agape love," which is pure spirit. This "spiritual" love is touted as the highest expression of love that one may aspire to. Agape is a Greek word meaning "wide, openmouthed." Yet, if you want a curious experience of total confusion, try securing a definition of what constitutes agape love from your nearest clergyman. The church has achieved its long sought after unity in one area alone. That area is in the definition of agape love in which everyone agrees unanimously as to what *it is not*. Nowhere have I been satisfied with a definition of what *it is*. Agape love is not sexual, says the church, nor is it merely fraternal nor paternal per se, nor maternal alone, nor is it platonic. It can be most closely compared to brotherly love, but that's not the whole story either.

There is another love referred to in the Bible. Again it is a Greek word "eros," meaning erotic or sensual love. The church has dictionaries of definitions of what constitutes erotic love, detailed and authoritative. Eros is selfish love. It is typified by the love of man for woman and vice-versa. It is sensual. It is romantic. It is unreal and given to delusion and always beneath the divine image. In short, erotic love is beneath the divine dignity of man because it is, in essence, born and inspired of woman.

Eros is that hated necessary evil, as woman has been that hated necessary evil, that coerced the Babylonian warrior godling to the distasteful obligation to impound men and women within legal marriage.

Agape is spiritual, selfless. For example, selfless agape may never become so selfless as to give sexual love outside of marriage, or deep mental companionship outside of one's legal mate, no matter what the need. Selfless agape may never cover up for the criminal, no matter what the extenuating circumstances. Selfless agape may never lie or cheat or whatever, no matter how selfless the motivation.

When we subtract from selfless agape all other forms of love mankind is capable of, what we have left is bound to be the ghost of agape.

Theologian Paul Tillich came up with true definition of agape love but he had to use eros to do it. He saw that the two are inseparable, making them impossible to place in conflict with one another. Tillich defines agape love as the willing surrender of the lover for the sake of the beloved. This is done with the recognition by the lover that the beloved is an independent self, capable of loving and being loved, but also with a potential to autonomous selfhood. In other words, agape love salutes the selfhood of the beloved and makes no moves towards possession of him.

However, unless erotic love which seeks self fulfillment in the beloved is equally active, love is open to every type of self-sacrifice possible. Babylonian male-female mystiques are obvious in a tyrannical agape. Agape being defined as spirit and equated with the male principle. It is the male warrior god's concept of how woman must wander egoless through the world, loving him selflessly in an orgy of eternal obeisance and self-giving. When agape is distorted in this manner, it becomes the iron fist of the law disguised in a velvet glove, and an agent of moral repression that borders on the demonic. Agape love enthroned as king leads ultimately to self-annihilation.

When agape love is placed in conflict with erotic love, it inescapably annihilates both as a creative dynamic. Two people coming together in agape create a standoff. How can selfless giving authentically exist if there is no one to receive the gift? It all amounts to an infantile and uncreative concept that the church itself would define as carnal, for all that is uncreative is carnal. One reason this travesty has taken hold has been due to the abolition of the concept of selfhood. True to the preceding Mosaic age, where ego reigned, Christians overcompensated for ego by obeying Christ's command to selflessness in a new "letter of the law." Self was to be denied. Eros was self.

Since ego, self had had its free ride in the patriarchal age as the special privilege of males, Christ's command to selfless agape was seized by male Christendom as their "thing." To stake out a claim upon it while not suffering too badly from its astringent effect upon the male ego, ambivalence was sure to solve the dilemma. It imputed to woman a natural proclivity to agape. Paul bound her to eros, as symbol of all that is "flesh," but denied her the selfhood that was its spirit. To "sell" agape love to males, it was necessary to insure them that woman's prior selflessness, her patriarchal previous agape, had been taken from her by silencing her in the church.

With woman dethroned from agape, yet silenced, the old necessity for duplicity was met by contradictions that have served man for the last 2000 years. For instance, the surrender of the selfhood under Christ was mandatory. It was to be voluntary, of course. Yet the exhortations to praise and worship remained the same. How a self which was non-existent could praise or worship at the feet of a God was never subject for serious theological debate. A self that does not exist cannot receive, nor can it give. A self that does not exist can never be forgiven for with what could forgiveness be received?

The contradictions in Christian theology regarding total self-lessness and agape love, unbalanced by eros (woman) was another lie of the deceiver. Males have been his instrument. The lie has survived so long because men have always found it easier to believe the lie than to impute logic and rationality to the divine personality.

Within the context of agape love between a man and woman, how can we surrender a self we do not possess, to our beloved? Agape is impossible without equality between the sexes, without a restored Godhead. When we say eros must be restored to the love dynamic, we are again saying woman must be liberated to ego and selfhood. Once the self is restored, then both male and female are liberated to approach love with both agape, (selflessness) and eros, (selfishness).

Eros is selfish. It wishes to seek fulfillment in the beloved. It is the material of Genesis, chaotic and formless if left unordered by agape. Yet agape has no existence without eros to order. If eros is severed from agape, it becomes idolatrous and demonic.

When we move from a concept of halfhood to wholeness we will experience the self love vital for survival and growth (in eros) and the willingness to accord the same to all other men in agape.

The conflict of agape in league with the law leaves love devoid of eros; cold, moralistic, sterile, without warmth, without longing or reunion; attempting by way of legalized eros the subjection of the female principle to the male principle by force.

Today's world is ruled by fear. Every nation under the sun fears every other nation. "Men's hearts failing them for fear...." Where God is a puzzle, life is a puzzle, and where life is a puzzle only materialism makes sense. Men today are strangling upon the uninspired works of agape love for we are choking on an edifice of law that is so complex one needs a battery of legal technicians to undertake the simplest moves.

Human love is strangling on the same legal inedibles— strangling on the uninspired works of agape technicians who have dabbed the theological paint to the canvasses of our lives according to the letter of the law. Without erotic love, without the arts co-equal with our heads, without beauty as well as truth, without woman to move us coequally with males and arouse us to artistry, we will continue to observe each other upon life's stage as accomplished craftsmen of agape. But to be moved to the divine touch of artistry, we must arrive at the moment of self-love again, in a new way. We must restore to the Godhead a balance of love. To do that we must rescue the scandalized eros from the marriage bed of legal agape.

> "...in the Resurrection they neither marry, nor are given in marriage, but are as the angels of God in heaven."
>
> Matt. 22:30

Like Noah, we must save the male and the female within the ark of the new age. We are called again to divine poetry. Will we make it this time? The world is being polarized again, as it was before the flood, and after Jesus died. We need to review our theologies with renewed minds. We must cast away the fantasy of the sexless heaven and the sexless man, and seize our personal identities before God and man, appropriating selfhood with the same zeal we discarded it in the past. Eros must be restored to agape in a creative reconciliation. Legal marriage must be replaced with a new relationship in which men and women will come together and stay together for one reason alone— creative love.

Intimate love between the sexes will be lifted to a new sanctity and made holy, without the law to ravage justice and mercy. It will be privy to man's judgment so long as couples acknowledge the selfhood of all others as well as their own with respect and honor. To the pure all things will be pure, and to the defiled all things defiled.

The body will be glorified in a free poetry of flesh and spirit. Like the burning bush of Moses, burning but not consumed, the longing for reunion with our bodies, loosed from the ancient shame, will signal our redemption as completed, for only when these bodies have been reunited, co-equal with our soul and spirits, washed from the shame and humiliation they have borne these long millenia, will we be able to say:

> "O, death, where is thy sting? O grave, where is they victory?"
>
> I Cor. 15:55

Chapter 10
GOODBYE MARRIAGE

Another group of religious leaders called the Saducees haggled with Jesus over the question of marriage, but this time having to do with woman after her death. It was customary, after a death, for someone to claim the body, but these Saducees asked Jesus which of seven men could claim the body of a deceased woman.

The Saducees, unlike the Pharisees, did not believe in the spirit world, or the immortality of the soul. They denounced both Jesus and John the Baptist, accepting the law but rejecting the oral traditions the Pharisees held so dear. Cocky and clever, they came up with the subject of woman and legal marriage.

They used a peculiar type of marriage called the Leverite marriage. It was a self-seeking, male-instituted, marital democracy for males and a communistic labor camp for females. Brothers lived in a communal style. If one brother died his living brother could impregnate his widow to raise up "issue" to his name. There was an economic motive involved as well, for this arrangement prevented a widow from siphoning the inheritance to her own family. In the Leverite marriage woman was totally disenfranchised, physically, economically and spiritually.

While it was natural that the Saducees should question Jesus about the Resurrection, it was not natural that they should use the subject of woman and marriage to do so. Their first question as to whose wife she would be in the Resurrection bared their concept of woman as a soulless pawn. Jesus' answer is blunt: "In the Resurrection they neither marry nor are given in marriage, but are as angels before God in heaven."

Just as He equalized the sexes, in granting women the right to divorce, He equalizes them again by liberating the woman to full standing before God. Jesus swings into the question of the Resurrection but places it in the context of the woman's redemption:

> "And, as touching the dead, that they rise: have ye not read in the book of Moses, how in the bush God spake unto him, saying, I am the God of Abraham, and the God of Isaac, and the God of Jacob? He is not the God of the dead, but the God of the living...."   Mark 12:26, 27

Such a statement was severely shocking, for it placed woman in the possibility of covenant relationship with Jehovah in the manner of Abraham, Isaac and Jacob. The Saducees knew the importance and significance attached to a personal name. Had not woman been denied mention in the geneological records and had not the word of God come through males whose names, with but few exceptions, had been preserved and revered? The nugget was, that in spite of sin, faith qualified the sinner for remembrance before God. As in the case of Eve, so too would all women stand living before her God, in possession of an immortal name.

ARE ANGELS SEXLESS?

A walk into any Christian bookstore will reveal a veritable plethora of male-penned literature about the nature of angels. It is, to be sure, a fascinating study. Angels are mentioned some 300 times in the Bible and surprisingly, more in the New Testament than in the Old, where the ministry of angels was more dramatic than in the New.

In the Scripture account of Jesus' encounter with the Saducees, there is another interesting point about angels: they have personal identity as the hypothetical woman was promised identity. Everyone is familiar with the angel Gabriel and Michael the Archangel, not to mention the astoundingly beautiful Lucifer. Though the Bible has taken the trouble to name these powerful agents there are numerous accounts of anonymous angels. But names were not reserved for the mighty alone, for Jacob was involved with an angel in a most unusual way, which reveals still more about the likeness we might share with these heavenly beings. Jacob had gone off alone one night and as he was about to fall to sleep:

> "...there wrestled a man with him until the breaking of the day. And when he saw that he prevailed not against him, he touched the hollow of his thigh.... And he said, [the angel], Let me go, for the day breaketh. And he said, I will not let thee go except thou bless me. And he said unto him, what is thy name? And he said, Jacob. And he said, Thy name shall be called no more Jacob, but Israel: for as a prince thou hast power with God and with men, and hast prevailed. And Jacob asked him, and said, Tell me, I pray thee, thy name....And he blessed him there. And Jacob called the name of the place Piniel: for I have seen God face to face, and my life is preserved.   Gen. 32:24-30

The angel is called "a man." The significance in the night-long wrestling match is to dramatize Jacob's self-willed determination to have his way. Who else but Jacob could maneuver an angel into the position of having to beg for release? In true Jacob style, he bargains with the "man" for a blessing he does not receive until he couples his stubbornness with insolence in asking the angel his name.

This episode illustrates the faith and courage required to attain to the eternal identity of a personal name with God. So impressed was the angel with Jacob's tenacity that he names him the way Adam named the animals in the Garden. The name "Israel" is a signal of covenant relationship with God. When the angel leaves him, Jacob proceeds to imitate the angel by renaming the place "Piniel," which, like his new name, takes on a special significance. This angel had a name he did not care to tell Jacob. The point of the encounter was not so much to record that the angel would not disclose his personal name but to reveal Jacob's understanding of deity by the very fact that he inquired after it.

Peter Pan in Heaven

Jesus, when asked how we should pray, said we should pray in the manner of His own prayer, which we all know as the Lord's Prayer. Contained within the first two lines is a petition that God's will in heaven be done on earth. The author of the Bible has fulfilled every one of hundreds of prophecies literally. Within a twenty-four hour period in Christ's life, there were some twenty-five prophecies of thousands of years' standing, and all were fulfilled literally, by way of cataclysmic events. With this record we can expect that Jesus' petition, which He said should be ours also, will be fulfilled by a literal translation of the Father's will in heaven to earth by way of a marriageless heaven, for Jesus said there would be no marriage in the Resurrection. Has this not been one of man's unconscious prayers admitted to only in moments of high humor or deep despair?

Orthodox Christianity, in ignoring this portion of the prayer when formulating their theologies of the sexless heaven, betrays a considerable lack of sincere and unbiased scholarship in the interpretation of the Scriptures. It has, quite readily, accepted the assumption that heaven will be a place where murder, theft, etc. will be banished forever, yet no sooner does Jesus banish marriage from the same heaven, than a way is found to banish sex as well. From this eagerness to exclude human sexuality from the marriageless heaven, a whole theology of celibacy, pseudo-spirituality and aesthetic mysticism has sprung up around the sexless heaven and the temperament and aspirations of the populace of the heavenly community. This body of theological super-sanctity is the piety we all remember.

Should the theologians be correct in their antiseptic appraisals of the next world, we had better begin to say our farewells to existence as we have known it and all that is human nature, as we have loved it.

According to its appraisal, sex is repulsive to God and at best tolerated by Him as means of replenishing the earth. Being an all-male God He, like Jesus, Who was not married, is the epitome of the perfect spiritual male; untouchable by the "flesh" of woman's craven desires and men's weakness. Imperturbable to her beauty, warmth, inspiration, Jesus recognized only one love emanating from woman, untainted by the scum of human sexuality: mother love. Yet, His moral code demanded that all mothers should be as His had been; a virgin mother.

Ever cognizant of human frailty, Jesus knew that to reach the great spiritual heights His mother had reached, human woman could, through the cultivation and practice of all the superior virtues of humility, submission, self-sacrifice, absolute obedience crowned by physical chastity, attain to that sweet subjection wherein she might free herself of the depravity of nature which is hers, to that sublime approval of God as His own earthly mother. That the practice of superior virtues by an inherently inferior creature was a contradiction in terms would never occur to any except a rebellious woman whose intellect is darkened by her sinful nature. However, if she conformed to this perfect female archetype, she might aspire to that virgin mother love Mary had achieved for all women. True, this presents a dilemma for them, since if one remains a physical virgin, one can never qualify for this love, which is alone, most pure.

In His tolerance for the tainted soul of woman, He opened a tolerance of all mankind. Woman, who had given Him His body, could now be democratically endured in the same manner that body had to be endured.

Still how could heaven be defiled with the scum of human

sexuality? Since it was promised to us that we would be like the angels, our certificate to the heavenly entrance will be the deposit of our sexual baggage outside the pearly gates. Awaiting us with a joyful welcome will be all those who received their celestial promotions before us by the rigorous practice of celibacy while on earth, for did not the Scriptures teach:

"...there are some eunuchs, which were made eunuchs of men: and there be eunuchs, which have made themselves eunuchs for the kingdom of heaven's sake...."? Matt. 19:12

Woe to those who could not receive this teaching for they will not be allowed to carry the lusts of their bodies into that heavenly clime. However, we should not despair if we have failed. No matter! So long as we wrestle with every weapon we have to cut out the cancer of human sexuality, Jesus will mark it on his heavenly charts that we tried. What a joy to know that though we fail, this side of the veil we may be assured that Jesus will somehow de-sex us.

When we have been swallowed up in agape love, then and then alone will love be unselfish, having accomplished that grand demise; the total death of the self which Jesus commanded us to. Whatever our bodies will be like, they will have been rendered free of human refuse. Every thought will soar on eagle's wings of purity. Every touch will be as white as snow, if touch will be allowed. Every appetite celestial only. Never again will lust dim the eye of male or female, since lust and love cannot abide in the same place.

Hello! Heaven

We have exhaustively explored woman's physical Babylonian captivity, now we will touch upon her spiritual exploitation as well, for only in the realm of the occult has the male God granted woman an authentic spiritual power and authority.

Freud, a man who did more to elaborate upon woman's subconscious promptings as correlated with her ovaries, at one point agreed with Carl Jung that the real problem with woman was her natural involvement with the "mud of occultism." They both agreed that it would serve the male establishment better to focus upon the sexual myths instead of the real source of woman's contamination, as a diversionary tactic to control her. Woman, said Freud, Jung, Moses and Paul, and the black arts were one.

When Moses bound and gagged her and Paul silenced her, beheaded her and placed her under the "two-headed" rule of her husband's law, they spiritually castrated woman. Paul's assessment of woman carried forward the ancient theme of Eden. It pronounced woman again as a danger and a threat to man unless her spiritual emanations are monitored by the male God. Woman they say, can never discern, if left to her own devices, whose voice it is that comes to her. Only males could decide if woman's supernatural agents were the dulcet tones of the shimmering Lucifer or the gorgeous Gabriel.

Paul left Mary out of the picture entirely, never even mentioning her in all his writings. Despite her advent, the male godling embarked on his pompous way making great pronouncements that the historical virgin was only one woman, as the historical Jesus was one man, and we couldn't and shouldn't expect that others would follow in their footsteps.

Since woman was literally forced into silent submission, it was truly necessary to keep her in body chains. A mindless body is a dangerous thing. But what is more dangerous is a male bodiless mind. Male fantasy assured that the subjected woman was the way of safety once her chaotic spiritual wells were suppressed under the weight of his ordering powers. If woman was the "temple built over the sewer," male irrationality was the hand that flushed the temple toilets.

The reasons for woman's occultic displacement in the Babylonian religion of corrupted Christendom are found in the doctrines of sin and redemption. The church's present theologies of basic doctrines is so subtly twisted by the deceiver that one needs a powerful microscope to see the hairline cracks at their base. Woman no longer believes that her ideas are spiritual sewerage, for she no longer needs to depend upon male ordering alone. She has found her own intellect, and it is telling her that the male god is not the intellectual giant he had deceived her into thinking he was. She will no longer believe the lie that only human males, no matter what their abilities, qualifications, aptitudes of spiritual disposition, may order ideas. Hiroshima and Dachau tell her so. Munich and Nuremberg tell her so. Lee Harvey Oswald and Watergate tell her so. Gethsemane and Calvary tell her so, for these were all male orderings of male inspiration.

The world system as it stands today is a system poured into the mold of male made golden calfs. It is his world shaped by his church, his politics and his commercial systems. Woman had neither ideational nor implementational participation in it.

In consigning woman to occultic knowledge by way of her spiritual perceptions, the male God pronounced mystery preferable to knowledge. That is why we still suffer and die.

Once woman flings her final ladder of the mind by which to climb out of her male-imposed nether world (the dungeon of the sub-conscious) into the sunlight of full consciousness, the male God is finished. She will know that her hunger to know was a blessing and not a curse, a glory and not a dishonor, a victory not a defeat. The male God, like Lucifer, longs for his sinless, "immaculate" standing before God.

Once woman is liberated from her captors, heaven is within our grasp. Not the heaven of Edenic innocence, for that is gone forever, but the heaven commonly referred to as the "Golden Age" or millenial reign of Christ. When Christ reigns, "the mystery of God should be finished" (Rev. 10:7); and "there should be time no longer" (Rev. 10:6); and "the earth shall be full of the knowledge of the Lord...."   Isa. 11:9

What does the Bible have to say about immortality and a promised heaven? Jesus promised to return and set up a kingdom generally referred to as the Golden Age. The prophet Isaiah gave us many insights into the biblical description of that age. It does not promise physical immortality. It promises only a greatly extended life span, and an order of peace, unprecedented prosperity, and justice for all. He even intimates that the psychological heavens and earth will undergo radical change.

As interesting and as hopeful as the promise of extended life is, the reference to a "new heaven and new earth" is startlingly exciting. Radical and sweeping changes will be made in the ideational life of the world. We see in this prophecy the promised liberation of males and females to a new psychic awareness. These projections of the Golden Age promise a bright future for man. However, a very dark night will precede his dawn. The night will be so dark that he will be convinced that all is lost. We are in that time now, and it has much to do with the coming sun. These are forces which would prevent the new day. The battle of the occult is one of them.

Babylonian Christendom believes in the waving of supernatural wands designed to move mountains and raise the dead with a word. We contest the idea that man, in his present state of consciousness, is able to do more than crawl, much less sprint. If the Scriptures teach us anything, it is that our Creator allows for growth at the rate of the organism's development. Man is not going to inherit a fiat wand. We cannot explain Jesus' miracles. Man, barely emerging from his supernatural caves of superstition, cannot yet handle such power on the collective level. He is just now emerging to the consciousness so he can know the laws of his universe.

The road of ignorance and mystery is the left road to Babylon revisited. At the right, the road of knowledge leads to freedom, plotted in the direction of truth. This spirit contends that the truly moral man is the man who knows—that is the highest morality, consciousness in the supreme.

Who can say at this point what the relationship between men and women will be in the future, when woman has won her freedom? Probably the old enmities will die out and new ones arise, but at this time in time the mandate is towards the future in which God intends to do a "new thing." In other words, we have finally understood what Jesus came to teach us. Now, 2000 years later, we prepare to step into a new age. Woman will enter it freed from male domination, but at the same time both males and females step into an unknown, just as they did at the beginning of this age, as we grow from "grace to grace."

Who can say what the future ordering of the concept of a marriageless society will be? How will woman exercise her freedom from racial drudgery? In what way will she emerge from the semi-isolation of her former condition to fully participate in the shaping of the new world? One thing is certain, woman must remain true to her call so that the new quantity she will add to the all-male equation will be the right one to do this. Woman must help formulate the equation.

There has been a lot of feminist literature written which traces woman's psychological and physical subjection. There has been excellent research into woman's emotional conditioning via the theology of literature, explorations into ancient and modern mythology that has defined her, and even some philosophical works that have attempted to organize the plethora of material that is flowing from the pens of articulate women and men.

While all this is encouraging, we have come to the place where it is not enough to awaken to the knowledge that we are chained and that we must throw off the chains. We must begin to know where we wish our freedom to take us. Woman needs a *world vision* from the female point of view. Any world vision of necessity includes the vision of woman herself. Woman's imperative now is to project upon the squalling infant of the new age her own vision.

At this point, woman's first priority is to find her mind. Mythology and mystery have no place in the universal community except as an evil to be fought. A man who knows nothing about the potentialities of fire cannot make judgments on its possible utilization. Woman, unless she finds her mind, will know only that fire burns, cooks meat and should always be used with caution. Will woman, through lack of knowledge, remain a fire-tender, guarding the home planet from conflagration once more, while males are busily engaged in inventing cosmic gunpowder to stupidly store next to the open fireplace?

Unless woman exerts her mental capacities to their fullest,

and males their heart capacities to *their* fullest and come together as equals, Satan will divide and conquer again. Males must temper ambition with meekness and woman must temper meekness with ambition. For each this means becoming whole persons. The powers that lie within man's grasp at present forbid a passive, unconscious woman.

WHAT DOES WOMAN WANT?

Woman's present thrust for liberation, her pluck and determination to beat down the doors of the male establishment are more than a natural outgrowth of her long history of oppression. They are God-inspired. Today's women are experiencing a modern day "Annunciation," as portentous as that of Mary's 2000 years ago.

They are the vessels of the Female Pentecost of the new age. As in Mary's day, so in ours, God has selected women whose humility has taught them honesty and whose honesty has given them strength, for the strong need not fear the proud.

After woman bursts into the spiritual and material "board rooms" of the male world, where has she truly arrived? She has arrived inside the front offices of her prison. That is all. Woman must understand the roots of her enslavement or she will abort her mission. She must be made to see that her chains are ancient and deeply rooted in man's psyche. They are the insidious tentacles of Babylonian mystery religion. Though they are visible and clank when she walks, males wear neck collars which are invisible but are, nevertheless, there.

We see in the movement today a falling back into the old deception, that her decisive battles will be fought and won within the male establishment. Like the American negro, she is pounding upon the highly polished doors that can only open upon established, discovered and developed male creations. "Equal opportunity" is not a battle-cry for a man or woman made in the divine image! Opportunity is only a step toward a higher goal.

The genius of Babylonian religion lies in its ability to masquerade opportunity to mankind as authentic possibility. With the confusing towers of Babylon, possibility is an impossibility unless we are willing to submit to the relentless lashes of creation through violence, which devours as rapidly as it creates. Woman must resist male machinations that would reduce her guilt and fear again. In short, she must seize her possibility and believe, as Mary believed.

How does the Babylonian dynamic affect woman today? How can she escape it? Woman can break loose to Godliness or she can break loose to demonic forces that neither liberate her nor prevent the coming storm. The egoless female must surrender maternity as her glory. She must acquaint herself with her own history.

What does woman want?

She demands that she be physically UNMOTHERED! She demands her equal share of possibility. She claims her body and her mind, and demands that her spirit be returned to her.

Woman intends to put an end to the universal plagiarism of the male godling. She wants full credit for her achievements past, present and future. Woman reclaims her ego. She aspires to the highest positions of power and authority based on merit alone. She is ready to demonstrate her ability to achieve the sustained performance positions of high responsibility demand. She insists that the dull of mind and imagination, the intellectually slothful and willfully uncreative male (as well as woman) be sent packing from positions of importance to positions of "tending" and not allowed to clutter up the payrolls via male nepotism.

Woman demands that her virginity, whether physical or spiritual, be her own business for it is of the spirit, not the body. She wants to get out of the legal marriage trap. Woman intends to enter the life of the mind in *full* participation. Woman wants males who can feel as well as think, so that *she* may be free to think as well as feel. She is finished with her former enforced preoccupation with the fragility of the male ego. Male spiritual homosexuality must end. Future theologies will be conceived, received and recorded *by* both males and females, *for* males and females.

Woman intends to strive towards conscious creation as freely as males have in the past and she will not compromise with the token blandishments of opportunity disguised as possibility. If doors continue to close to her she will embark on a new chastity. New life will have to come via rape, if it is to come at all.

She has outgrown the eagerness to please papa's incessant, egocentric demands. Her former pleasure in ministering to the errands of his life's inconsequentials is gone. She has things of her own to do.

The Babylonian cosmic Bluebeard must lay away his knife for good. If Father insists that he must slay Mother, to raise up a Son in his own image then Mother may submit in fear but she will never love him.

Babylon has one last mystery tower in which woman has been imprisoned. It is in the realm of the occult. The shaking down of this tower will signal her final deliverance and the death of the Babylonian godhead. It will be the bloodiest battle of all.

Chapter 11

THE CONCEPT OF HALF PERSONS

The human race has displayed a great fascination with the anonymity which is acquired in the role playing that society foists upon the individual as a type of sanction for the abdication of the selfhood the system demands. Like an actor playing a part, the individual escapes into a fictionalized scenario of his life which serves to protect him from the reality that lies beyond the blinding footlights of his staged existence. Woman's triune roles of virgin mother and harlot have been scripted by the power structure, produced by organized religion and backed by the political and commercial systems of the world.

Man has always searched for the complete love; the love that makes whole and satisfies the soul. He fails to recognize that in a system built on the concept of half-persons, only half-loves are possible.

Since the fall, man has lived like a Cyclops in a one-eyed existence.

In his frenzy to keep the law, he collapsed in an apathy to love. In seeking the spirit he lost the body.

We said that legal marriage was the institution of half love. Our arithmetic has been as follows: One-half and one-half equals one. That is, one half man (male), plus one-half woman (female), equals one whole member of mankind. Why does it take two halves, one each of maleness and femaleness to make one whole person? Does this mean we can never hope to achieve to a totality of personality except by way of marriage? Doesn't this mean that men and women are indeed only half persons until completed by one of the opposite sex? If such is the case, then how did Jesus get whole? And aren't persons who live the celibate life improperly classed as single when they are truly half persons?

The arithmetic of Genesis starts with wholes, not fractions, saying: "And the two shall become one flesh." One and one make two. One-half and one-half do not make two, but one. The Bible is explicit enough to have stated it otherwise if it was intended to be otherwise. Adam and Eve could never have been created as halves of each other except as to the biological functions of procreation for, by his very nature, man is a conscious, potentially rational being which, in view of our doctrines of free will, accountability and the gifts of intellect, could not be limited to halfhood in any way except procreatively. If total accountability is accepted, persons are not only commanded to wholeness but were conceived as such.

Let's explore the concept of half-persons in legal marriage as it stands in opposition to true holiness. The law says: two halves equal one. This offers a sublime security of semi-responsibility for one's personal happiness, life goals and actions. Single persons have no built-in scapegoat or legal clubs to hold over the heads of loved ones such as married persons do. And can half a person love wholly? Since love is based on knowledge and spiritual discernment, which is the highest knowledge, we, as half-persons, can only know other half-persons, and that only in ideal, half conditions.

The trouble in legal marriage usually begins when it dawns on one or the other or both, that the darkness that lurks within himself is the shade of that half of himself he can never get to know because of his surrender to legal halfdom. The darkness increases as he gropes in the half dark of his partner's half-light. When marriages begin to break up it is a signal that one or the other is moving towards wholeness of selfhood. Sadly, the forms of this discontent are many times destructive, taking expression in forms of anti-social behavior and ultimately falling due to social and religious pressure and a failure to realize that the schism is within the personality.

The twilight exile to semi-personhood has been far more torturous for women who have been disenfranchised to a greater degree. The greatest threat to the ancient Edenic conspiracy of the subjection of woman and the command to halfhood, would be for men to find their selfhood and liberate themselves to wholeness of body and spirit.

The command to singular identity before God is revealed nowhere more clearly than in the reality of death. Eve's first bite of that apple earned her a personal name and a potential to selfhood. Death was its price but eternal life was also its reward. Death entered Eden first through the selfhood of sin. Knowledge scampered in after it but so did eternal life which is eternal identity before God; inviolate and singular whether male or female.

Death is the most forceful argument against the demonic elements in legal marriage for it alone may break the bonds of halfhood. Death is God's final statement addressed to the holiness of inviolate selfhood before him. Death takes the dearly beloved or the nearly hated.

A new world vision shapes up like a risen Lazarus, emerging from the tomb; bound until the word is spoken and the command is given to "loose him!" Our world is in the death throes of a worn out system of religious mystery. That great harlot of Revelation across whose forehead is written, "MYSTERY, BABYLON THE GREAT, THE MOTHER OF HARLOTS AND ABOMINATIONS OF THE EARTH," is giving way in fear and confusion to a mankind on the verge of discovering his mind.

In view of the catastrophic events that roll upon us like ceaseless waves from an unending sea of troubles, the issues of the unjust subjection of woman and the concepts of a marriageless yet sexual heaven may at the outset seem shallow and somewhat incidental to world-wide famine, war, treachery and nuclear overkill; but these two subjects are directly related to each other, for the subjection of woman has lain at the heart of the harvest we are reaping and will continue to reap. We have loved mystery and ignorance more than we have loved truth. We are faced with two alternatives: to ignore the gift of conscious thought, thereby acquiescing to a God and an eternity of mystery, or we can become men and take up the tools of our intellects and subdue this creation.

We have never yet lived the good life. We have been content to survive. We are still spawning in mental and spiritual caves, surviving between the sperm and the grave. It will never be enough to grovel at the feet of an irrational God upon whom we heap the blame for all our own stupidities and hardnesses of heart. It is time we demanded to KNOW, as Eve demanded to know, for only in the knowledge of God will our salvation be found.

The marriage game, as we have played it, has been the deadly pantomime of a stark spiritual reality; a motion to music in the imaginations of our delusions unbelieving that "the truth shall set us free." The tool of the intellect, when coupled with creative imagination guided by a Holy Spirit of love, is powerful enough to shatter any secret of this cosmos. We must develop new taste buds and eliminate from our diets that appetite for messes of mysterious pottage for which we have sold our birthright. The humility we imitate, in amateurish incompetence, is the humility of a darkened mind determined to bear the whips and lashes of the unknown, until we have had enough and seek to find our relief in the light of one more discovered law of the universe.

But where do we find men and women honest enough for such truth? The majority hover over the altars of sacrificial love, weeping and wringing their sanctified hands, pleading in prayers that the God they malign should aid and abet them in their escape from Him, who is a God of law and order. In the context of our subject of the subjected woman and the marriageless sexual heaven, we alluded to universal divorce as the putting away of the female by the male principle. The purpose for the enforcement of legal marriage upon mankind was that it should be a training ground in the flesh for what was to be later embraced in the spirit; not primarily in two's, but singly. Legal, earthly marriage was a parody of two halves as they should function in one person, for in the man and woman the male and female energies or principles will fuse in an invisible matrimony of the mind.

In the earthly or carnal marriage, the male was to "cleave" to his "wife" as female of the species. So too, in the world of spirit, must the male principle, intellect, cleave to his female principle, idea or imagination. In this divine union the "two shall become one flesh." Metaphysically speaking: *sexual intercourse is the probing of an idea by an ordering power.*

What is idea or imagination? Idea is female in principle. It is that faculty of the imagination which is rooted in the subconscious. Things which emit from it come as things as they appear or seem to be, or even as they ought to be. Neither intellect nor imagination may function creatively without the other. Most people are in various stages of expertise in one and badly wanting in the other but few find their way to that fusion of genius which still requires unbelievable drudgery to produce new works.

In the battle of the sexes, we have been witness to the cosmic enmity towards the female principle by the male and the resultant rupture of the creative Godhead. Unless the intellect (male), is fertilized by imagination (female), we can only hope, at best, to order that which already is. Still, to engage in an act of creation requires that an idea give to the intellect a vision of that which ought to be. Reproduction is not creation. It is imitation; an ordering only of what is. We see that in legal marriage, the racial priorities we have assigned to reproduction in no way qualify us for the title of creators. We are, in this, only ordering that which is. A woman knows that the baby forming in her womb does so without her conscious efforts. The male knows, also, that his seed is also working, in an ordering that he is, in no way, conscious of controlling. The making of babies is an unconscious affair for both male and female and explains woman's refusal to accept, any longer, that the boundaries of her consciousness be set at unconscious creation. We are called to full consciousness.

We are called, once again, of God to become poets. At first glance, it would seem that persons who have fused would lose their sexuality but then, why should they? Would a woman be any less a woman for having developed her intellect to its highest potential? Our male-dominated society has moved heaven and earth to prevent her from doing so as a necessity in perpetuating role playing so indispensible to racial survival. But that antique notion is making a rapid exit as woman demands equal freedom to think as well as to feel.

Likewise, would a male be any less a male if he allowed his latent subconscious promptings (intuition) to ascend freely, as women do? This has been discouraged by males, for males, for the same reasons females have been discouraged from applying themselves to the intellectual disciplines: out of a fear of defilement, due to age old traditions. It would not defile but enhance each, as it lifts them to a heightened consciousness, which in no way could be said to detract from the beauty of their sexual gender, except in the minds of those still bound in the traditional male advantages of freedom and domination and the ease of female passivity.

Would there not be changes and would we not find ourselves in deeper estrangement, losing contact in a semi-platonic state of semi-sexuality? Would we lose interest in love? We believe that whole or completed persons would approach sex in a different way, to be sure, but could not human love only be enhanced by one-half of the race attaining to that full freedom without which human dignity goes abegging?

Let's take another look at the unsatisfactory sexual experience which has been our common lot in this system of half-hood. With woman in the position of subjection and inferiority to the male, we have had a relationship akin to that of a ruler and his subject. When the male ruler penetrates the body of the female, by the very nature of their enforced inequality, we have, in essence, an act of violence performed by a stronger against a weaker, or by a superior over a lesser. He who enjoys such a taking by force, no matter what the conscious convictions of love or tenderness, and she who permits and perhaps enjoys such violence as a willing victim, are hopelessly manacled to a psychology of shame. Now we may see more clearly Paul's proper assessment of shame as being woman's birthright in legal marriage based upon the doctrine of the woman's subjection. Such a psychology is bound to terminate in defilement. What we need therefore, and would get in the completed man and woman, would be a "new heaven and a new earth." New heaven, being a new consciousness, and new earth, meaning a freed subconscious from which the demon has been exorcised.

The new man and the new woman will come together sexually unashamed, because they come together as equals, as Genesis states:

> "And they were both naked, the man and his wife, and were not ashamed."
>
> Gen. 2:25

Freed of the urge for completion, in or through the other, man and woman could come together sexually for love alone.

Men have been attempting to define human love in all its complex forms for millenia. The new definition would be that the spirit which underlies all love is the stupendous drive instilled within man by his Creator, to create. Are we not made in the image and likeness of our God? Is His prime attribute not that of creator? John said that God is love and since God is the Creator love is rooted in the urge to create. The metaphysics of creation are ordered to the reconciling of two opposites by the spirit of love and truth. This is the dynamic of creation and the dynamic of love.

How does this apply to the divine marriage within the single person? Intellect is inspired by an idea or an idea goes in search of an orderer. In human physical love, both the lover and the beloved wish to probe the idea of the other (male), and be probed (female). When this idea grips the imagination and emotions profoundly, we have passion. In this old order probing has been the exclusive domain of the male. Being probed by order has been the domain of the female. The confusion has been in the act that each is confined to one aspect or the other. Such is the condition of halfhood. Wholeness would replace sexual utilitarianism with sexual delight. This can only be achieved where there is equality and freedom between the participants.

Whence do we draw our license to total sexual freedom outside the bonds of legal marriage? If we compare the marriage of intellect and idea to the marriage of a man and a woman in legal marriage, we must also be prepared to apply to legal marriage the same rules that govern the heavenly marriage and in both we are prone to error. No one thinks it strange that we may probe and reject ideas freely in the world of *thought*. We develop some and after sometimes preliminary ordering, reject others. Yet in its counterpart, legal marriage, we forbid the dissolution of incompatible fusions. Just as some ideas work and others don't, so too, some couples make it together and some can't. What are the factors that decide the success or failure of a legal marriage? To begin with, many ideas: "wives," are beyond the ordering skills of their husbands. After the initial probing or conceptualization of an idea or ideas, we are forced to abandon them if they are clearly beyond our conceptual or ordering skills. To persist in a faulty conception on through the ordering, which is bound to come to a point of contradiction, is sheer folly. What is true in the world of spirit is likewise truth in the world of flesh. Incompatible marriages are not sins, as such, but only legitimate failures. The culpability lies not in their dissolution but in the denial of failure. To persist in an abortion rectifies nothing, but serves to stunt growth in areas where it is possible to succeed. Artists and thinkers have attempted works or ideas that defy their powers. Failed ideas are sometimes improperly conceived while others are beyond their ordering skills. If I cease all efforts to begin new ones, choosing to remain legally married to those aborted, I sacrifice upon the altar all chance of future success and growth. Still, that is not the worst sin, for to persist in a known failure with an idea clearly beyond my powers constitutes spiritual adultery.

This dynamic addresses itself to legal marriage which demands indissolubility as the price of even one single necessary probe of an idea. What justification can there be to demand indissolubility? One of the best definitions of hell is that it is a state in which persons repeat their mistakes, bound to them with chains of repetition. Hell is being bound to an idea that won't work. The same applies to a bad marriage or a good one. If it's bad, it will never become good by way of legal binding and if it is good, legal bonds won't make it better.

Freedom is essential for the creative spirit. So should freedom be essential in the exercise of human sexuality as a creative celebration of the act of love.

The old must give way to the new if the universal life principle is not to be thwarted. The mandate of every man, and the race as a whole, is to growth and greater self-realization. What we see in the epidemic of middle-aged marital breakups which the pious attribute to irresponsible selfishness, is the decisive action of those who know that in their case, the idea has died. Most men and women who terminate a marriage do so with sorrow and reluctance, but with honesty and courage born of an understanding of the creative potential of the universal life principle. To insist that incompatible couples remain together at any cost is really to deny to some the right to live creatively within their ordering powers. If we were to fling open the doors of most legal marriages we might be shocked to find how many are living graveyard sanctuaries; havens of the legally vanquished in almost total withdrawal from a full humanity. True creative integrity contains within it the courage to reject, after diligent effort, that which has been improperly conceived. The sanctity of the personality, like the instinctual genetic barriers between breeds, is hallowed ground and not to be tampered with by legal technicians. The vow "till death us do part" should be taken to mean the spiritual death of the "idea" of the other. All legitimate striving in a true, mature and productive relationship should be for one primary purpose: the creation of our own selfhood. We may contribute to another's growth, certainly, but on their terms not our own. To insist that all couples may reconcile their differences creatively is a theologian's pipedream.

There is yet one other validity to the need for whole persons to come together in love, and that is the need to cross pollinate; feed off of one another for inspiration. Who can self-conceive entirely on one's own? Even genius of the highest order must build upon the edifices of men and women who have gone before them. With men liberated to wholeness, a new concept of selfhood, divinely married within yet retaining their original genders, love would be free. The idea of the subjection of woman has come to its time to die, and upon the death of the host, its parasite, legal marriage, will perish with it.

There remains one more theological dragon to be slain before men and women make their final break to full freedom. It is the most formidable dragon of all: the beast of procreative slavery; the beast from the bottomless pit. Until this final foe is put in everlasting chains, all hopes of drinking freely from the fountains of life's waters are only lush mirages.

In the great female Pentecost sweeping the planet, woman is fulfilling her office of instigator of a new age. In her final motherhood, she stands eye to eye with the beast, and she will not be moved.

The question of children and where they would fit into any new order that shakes the foundations of legal marriage is understandably the gravest concern of all members of the human race, for even nudging the cornerstone of legal marriage causes the world-system skyscraper to sway in the wind and the common man to run for cover. Most are convinced that the moralities they practice, the laws they observe, the God they worship, are all of their own conscious volition. Such faith is not so much born of true conviction sprung of choices made from among real options, but more out of the resignation of the vanquished who have long ago lost hope that there were any valid available alternatives. It would seem a heroic exploit were it not so poignant in deception and violence against the willfully innocent and unthinking masses.

When one surveys the human predicament in the stark reality of its deception, one is struck by its unspeakable tragedy. The great racial drudgery has demanded that everything in our lives be laid upon the altars of species survival. We are shackled with a body, driven by a subconscious programmed by instinct to perpetuate our kind; a drive so powerful that it overrides even the instinct for self-survival. Our whole existence is commanded to orbit the racial instinct like a satellite, held captive by the gravitational pull of its primal power. Yet we think we are free. We are, each of us, born of the tyranny, spend a few short innocent, carefree years in which we are secretly inculcated with all the racial propaganda to make certain that we conform, then are ceremoniously dipped from impersonal cold to impersonal hot by sudden permission to surrender to sexual urgings by way of marriage. No sooner have we sired our first than we become aware the trap has sprung, and we must content ourselves, "for better or for worse," that we are duty bound to the grave to serve, first, the offspring we have spawned and after they are launched safely into the same duty, bound to our mate.

All this while we are sworn in monogamous marriage, to battle for marital chastity, censuring every thought and word to keep the lid on the conscious mind which might shock us to the thought that we are being ruled by a tyrant we can control if we wish to.

Yet to believe we are free; heirs of the tyranny, damned if we do not control the instincts and damned most when we do; bound by laws, taboos, threats of hell, exhortations to love; appeals to nobility, pleas for self-sacrifice so that all things in heaven and earth may bow down before the fertility gods and goddesses of racial drudgery. We are captives in Babylon; slaves; hopeless Hebrews building the pyramids of the racial Pharaohs whose scepter is a baby and whose throne is the family. We accept marriage; that severe black widow's garb of obedience and resignation in which to clothe our nakedness, basting a little lace or tatting to the neckline to ornament our desolation by calling it fidelity.

We embroider it with our finest sentiments, our noblest motives, to cover from our conscious minds the positive rage that lies just below the surface of our spirits that we should be so duped by what we suspect is a cosmic tragedy. Below the great deception lies the silliest pathos of all. We wish to make love but are doomed to make babies. The truth that chills the bones is the obvious fact of our own impotence and transiency and the inevitable transiency of our offspring and theirs after them. We believe we have invested love with an ennobling morality by what we call the sanctity of marriage, when we know that the highest morality is racial survival.

We think we refrain from siring offspring out of wedlock for reasons of immutable laws of mutual love and sacred trust, but these are necessary sublimities the tyranny finds expedient to insure the stable family unit in which to perpetuate itself. Unmarried mothers and fathers are poor risks as junior executives in the procreational corporation. The only profound and eternal verity against the chaos of adultery is the everlasting threat of offspring from it, or lack of offspring. Behind every beauty lies the shadow: behind every broken dream and every sundered hope; every quest for freedom failed, stands the taskmaster for whom we obediently hoist upon our collective and individual backs the endless Genesis of procreational chaos.

But we can separate the fact from the fiction. It does not have to be so. We can become conscious; thinking beings able to control our use of this drive. If we desire that it be used as an expression of love and admiration, let it be so but remove from it the retaliatory aftershocks of unwanted births. In short, let's put the beast under our subjection. Once out from under the biological nuclear bomb we can dismantle it and use it to serve us.

While writing this book, I undertook a private poll among married women in the 35 to 50 age bracket of all educational, religious and professional backgrounds, including housewives. All had had children. I limited my questions to three:

1. Would you marry and raise children again, if at this moment you could go back to the age you married?
2. Would you find the same fulfillment in the role of wife and mother, in your present state of growth, that you did then?
3. How would the prospects of a marriageless society strike you?

Their answers amazed me for most were of the 45 to 50 bracket, some of whom had been and still are the typical housewife with perhaps a small part-time job or outside work. All said they would *not* do it again if they had it to do over. They hastened to add that they loved their children and certainly would not wish they did not have them but they felt the whole role of women in marriage and motherhood was too conflicting with personal growth, and all mourned the loss of personal careers in which they could have made contributions to the work of the world in a more direct manner. All were disenchanted with marriage as an institution and the position of extreme isolation it had placed them in.

Most were turned off on sex, yet held a hope of a more satisfying sexual experience. Most agreed that their husbands desired mothers more than wives or companions and admitted to a confusion of roles imposed upon them in the virgin-mother-harlot trinity. Most admitted to the evocation of only maternal instincts by their husbands which made sexual relations difficult. All looked forward to a new way of life, free of the traditional legal bonds of marriage. Among younger women there was a consistent openness to more honesty in areas of human love and sexuality and a rejection of motherhood as woman's primary role. While most professed love for children and desired to have perhaps one child in any new order, most felt they would never wish several or many again, in any new order. The prospects of a marriageless society seem possible in spite of what seems to present moral resistances to the average person, but the question of how the young will be raised, once the traditional mainstay of the home and family is dissolved, understandably evokes fear.

Yet there are ominous signs presenting themselves to the planet that the family as we have previously conceived it through the instrumentality of legal marriage, is already undergoing radical change. Coupled with woman's insistence that she be freed of her biological chains is the ogre of over-population whose head and shoulders loom above our horizons. With famine at the door and disease at the window, we are forced to face the unpleasant truth that the birth rate must be controlled. Yet birth control on a world-wide scale is still meeting with the resistances that have plagued it in the past. This resistance has always arisen from religious scruples. We believe in the sanctity of life but we believe in the sanctity of all life. Rationality must be employed in every area of our existence. The same ambivalence which has characterized us in other areas of our Christian faith afflicts us in the province of the control of our environment. We fight nature to the death in our emergencies and fraternize with her in the lulls between battles. We say we may fight disease, tooth and nail; resist aging, prevent accidents, warn of impending natural catastrophe. We manipulate the energies and materials of the physical creation to produce and distribute the goods and conveniences which have contributed to the better life we have won, without a qualm, yet in birth control, we have for the most part rejected it. Once again we witness the holy ground of the ancient issue. The Scriptures are not ambivalent about man's lordship of the planet. Does this passage sound like mandate to control everything but births?:

> "For he must reign, til he hath put all enemies under his feet."   I Cor. 15:25

or this:
> "...according to the working whereby he is able even to subdue all things unto himself."   Phil. 3:21
> "Thou hast put all things...in subjection under him...."
>   Heb. 2:8

Even death itself will come under his final subjection:
> "The last enemy that shall be destroyed is death."
>   I Cor. 15:26

"All things" is all things, not *some* things or *almost* all things. Though we have begun to find ways to control births physically in manners that provide more security than in the past, our true challenge is not that of physical prevention as it is mental. We must banish the "sacred cows" we allow to wander the Indias of our minds in total autonomy of freedom and reverence while we starve for life worthy of a man. Unwanted and unplanned births will continue in the face of our hunger until we arrive at a wisdom which has the courage to believe that the abundant life must be for all, and in equality of quality. We must arrive at the wisdom which refuses to ordain that those who have reached the age of procreative power be whipped to unwilling or willing surrender of their consciousness to forfeit the remainder of their lives to birthing and nurturing the next generation, relinquishing all hopes of personal fulfillment for the sake of the perpetuation of the race. The cycle of self-annihilation by one generation at the puberty of life for the one to follow is classically vicious and a well-designed plot against us by the Satanic forces that hate and work to destroy us. There are options we can think about. Perhaps an order could be devised where only those who wish to engage in the business of procreation and nurturing of children should be allowed to do so. Orwellian? This world has long since surpassed Orwell's world for horrors and wastes.

The trauma of the "broken home" is the inevitable consequence of the concept of the unbroken home. The trauma is self-inflicted by way of the system we have chosen. Could we not envision a new system where couples would willingly come together to procreate, and stay together for an allotted time and teach the children the order? But the isolation of the procreative privileges of the race and the private family unit is a selfish institution that does not contribute to a heightened social or collective consciousness but to the anarchal and rampant disunity of the planet today.

What is so immoral in a concept where all children are held precious to all men and each becomes his own, regardless of who sired and who conceived? Is this antipathic to Christian love and would not the reasons for opposition be reasons of selfishness born of the lust to possession which has been the old lust of legal marriage? If the present generation of youth is to be taken as testimony to our system of legal marriage and parental autonomy, we will be forced to check our premises. I believe in this generation of youths, and admire their courage and honesty and the accusing finger they point towards our institutional hypocrises.

There is a passage in Scripture that is sublime in its praise of love as opposed to duty, which seems like an anachronism in light of the compulsive acceptance of our procreational sacrifices:

> "Though I speak with the tongues of men and of angels, and have not charity, I am become as sounding brass, or a tinkling cymbal....And though I...understand all knowledge and though I have all faith, so that I could remove mountains, and have not charity, I am nothing. And though I bestow all my goods to feed the poor, and though I give my body to be burned, and have not charity, it profiteth me nothing."   I Cor. 13:1-3

We may suffer, in quietness and resignation, the agonies of incompatible marriages, work our fingers to the bone and die a thousand daily deaths of self-sacrifice for the race, the system, the material and spiritual well-being of our children. But what love is it that does so only that they may, sooner than they realize, be called upon to do the same?

Never believe that they do not see through our delusions for they do and have been acting upon that vision. They seek to change the system; right the wrong and we resist them: dead men who have long ago ceased remembering the possibilities of life other than of defeat against what seems impersonal forces of the great tyranny. In our obeisance to the prime directive of collectivist survival, we are duped into thinking that the absolute monarchal powers bestowed upon us as rulers of our children, in kingly autonomy, surpass the reign of all kingdoms in history for, after all, what does a potential potentate require to seize a kingdom but a marriage certificate? With this as the only decree to absolute power, we ascend our throne above the innocent populace.

Take a look at the laws on our law books and see how little legislation there is to protect children, then compare it to the libraries of corporate law where our hearts really lie. A glance at the laws designed to protect the young and innocent, the un-shaped and helpless, shows our subjects to be usually beyond the help of individuals and society at large, except in extremities. Parents have the power of life and death over their children, mentally, emotionally, spiritually and physically. We "strain at the gnat and swallow the camel," coping with the blackened eyes and swollen mouths of child abuse of body, but fail to notice the fractured limbs of innocent consciences cracked over the knee of a God who bullies and whines, threatens and smites the disobedient and ignorant: this anthropomorphic God of our own paranoia. We have succumbed to semi-consciousness in the lie of legal marriage legislated to compulsive reproduction; imitators driven by prehensile fears for racial survival. We must refuse compulsion for consciousness in full.

The concept of the universal parenthood of our young would demand a universal unity of mind and spirit. We would have to become one as Jesus said we were to become "one." It is the unity of mind and spirit that drives man to arrive at the unanimous surrender of war as an institution of negotiation; the unity towards which the church strives to surrender the anthropomorphic God, as an incarnation of the "word made flesh." Such unity will place at our disposal the freedom to move into the truths that will sever the Edenic artery which has pumped the poisoned blood of inherited error into the bloodstreams of our newborn who, in turn, have passed it down to theirs in a succession of hells.

We are rapidly approaching an Armageddon of planetwide proportions.

The knowledge explosion that threatens to sweep us all away as in the flood of old is ours. Unless we find a way to properly correlate what we know with wise decisions as to how to use what we know, the world will end in fire, riding the crest of a flood. Man is on the threshold of Godlike powers. Biomedicine has already acquired the techniques to isolate and the technology to gravely alter man genetically. Artificial insemination and gestation via the laboratory are only the tip of the iceberg. The new Godlike powers foresee an ability to select genetic makeup at will; inserting, removing or altering genes to achieve or delete certain desirable human traits. Upon what priorities will we base these alternatives and who will make them? With such power man could drastically reduce or eliminate genetic malformities and inherited diseases, prolong the life-span immensely and ultimately indefinitely in light of the biblical promise of immortality. But man could also lose it all, in the demonic use of such power in an utter destruction of his humanity, to synthetic extravagance, devoid of spiritual values.

In our context of the subjection of woman in regards to legal marriage, and her great racial drudgery, woman will joyfully accept her new emancipation from the whelping box to a full humanity, but with every freedom comes a responsibility. Will she grab her biological liberty and, at the same time, evade her summons to totally surrender her abject passivity and take the grave responsibilities of sharing equally with males the awesome decisions *which* must be made? If she forfeits her responsibility by lapsing into her former idolatry; semi-conscious in ardent worship at the feet of the all-male God, then she will discover that the agonies of her past will be as minor skirmishes in a backyard brawl compared to the catastrophes which will await the human race without her full and dedicated participation in the age of great decisions.

Once again we are commanded to be poets; to pluck from the tree in the middle of the garden neither from the right or left alone. We can run the procreational beast off our property and keep him off if we don't panic to either hemisphere. We need the beast to replenish the race and we further need it to enhance our lives as an expression of love and admiration. The solution is not to choose sides, but to make a reconciliation between the two by means of taking conscious control of the power and subduing it to our own ends.

But first we need the courage of honesty to decide what we really want, then we must move heaven and earth to bring it about. Do we desire to retain the strong beast that prowls the subconscious, uncontrolled as tyrant and king, or will we opt to turn it into a docile lamb to serve us? How long will we submit to a tyranny that demands that though we wish to make love, we end up making babies? The abdication to the sexless heaven is a gesture of fear and a sub-humanity conceived as victims rather than masters.

If we choose the great "cop-out" then we will continue to equate the marriageless heaven with the sexless heaven, then we will continue to bind on earth within the institution of legal marriage a chatteled race, bound to the Pharaoh's tombs of racial slavery; and in heaven a humanity collapsed into a new species about which we know nothing, nor can we, until we cross the genetic barriers and the heavenly mutation occurs.

But if this be true, then the sufferings endured here in this state will have contributed nothing valid to a heightening of our human consciousness in terms commensurate with a full human integrity. Then we will know that God did not truly share a full humanity with us in the person of Jesus Christ; fully man and fully God, but came as the old heavenly patroon, not with one divine card up His sleeve but a full deck, making a mockery of the Cross designed to put an end to sacrifice. Then we must resign ourselves to a translation from an incompleted humanity to a new agony of incompletion; like an incompleted melody. We will know that we were created with these bodies and souls, hungry as they are for love and sharing, only for the impersonal procreation of the race until such time as our Creator deemed it expedient for Him to discard them. Finally it foretells that we are strapped to a great impersonal cosmic wheel works of an infinite crucifixion of the human body and spirit; rolling on gigantic conveyor belts, looped between an earth and a life we never lived, and a heaven we can never achieve.

But, if we hold to our faith in a benevolent and truthful creator we can see our agony as a thing he would deliver us from if it is our will to be delivered from it. If we hold to our faith we can, perhaps, see that the command to increase and multiply and replenish the earth came as a necessary evil from an all-wise Creator, who, in view of the catastrophe of events that preceded us saw the repopulation of the earth as a first priority. This would help to salve the wound of woman's prolonged agony as breeder on a planetary farm and males as food and shelter drones among the thorns and thistles of an unyielding earth of ignorance. We believe that it is God's spirit that speaks to us which says it is time to discard this concept of ourselves and move towards the more abundant life we hunger for.

Before leaving the subjects of legal marriage, divorce, adultery and sexuality, let me say that it has not been my intention to offend the innocent or insult the pious. Yet we are aware that this is bound to occur among men who have not yet grasped the concept of a God, in process; *within* our humanity not *outside* of it; a God who has imposed upon man morals and ethics in an immutable manner that takes no thought for spiritual, emotional or mental evolution of individuals or the race.

My moral is love and my ethic is growth. My moral is a loyalty to my humanity and my ethic is a free humanity. I do not have to choose between my God or my fellow man except when I stand in opposition to the Satanic forces that oppress him within and tyrannize him from without, and all the while blame it on our God. I do not envision man so much commanded to climb celestial ladders to become divine as of the divine condescending to become human. It is not so much that we should believe in God but that we should know that he believes in us. Patience, after all, is only passion with a plan. It has been our patience to suffer unimaginable forces of evil against our humanity, but it has also been our passion that in the end our humanity would win the victory. My vision is a vision of a divine humanity; a humanity in which each man knows himself to be the "word incarnate" rather than its opposite of the "flesh" absorbed in a divine annihilation. I am smitten with the heroism of man: his courage, patience, his compassion and in spite of what the worst among us would say, I am smitten by his love, from which neither angels nor devils with thunderbolts or rainbows, can ever separate him.

I see the "living Christ" among us, in every man, as Paul put it, "face to face" who would release the captives, heal the broken-hearted and set at liberty those bruised to a new self-love, self-respect, self-realization through understanding based on knowledge. We must take our prime directive from Jesus who commanded us to love "one another intensely," as He had loved us, and we can never do it unless we embrace our humanity with an intense loyalty, refusing to relinquish it to the death and against all the forces of heaven or hell that says we must.

The repressive, anguished, deceptive, legal chains that marriage has soldered to our human bodies and spirits rank in the forefront of my war upon the forces that hate our humanity. If the reader wishes to take issue with me he must first take issue with Jesus, who said there would be no marriage in the resurrection, and which gave me the vision of a new humanity, freed from the coils of legal marriage: the root of the Edenic issue. Your choice will be the same as mine if you choose to wrestle with angels over the marriageless, sexless heaven, for the final decision to be made will be between a redeemed mankind or a scrapped humanity.

I choose a redeemed humanity.